GRAMMAR
AND BEYOND
ESSENTIALS

1

Randi Reppen

CAMBRIDGE
UNIVERSITY PRESS

CAMBRIDGE
UNIVERSITY PRESS

University Printing House, Cambridge CB2 8BS, United Kingdom

One Liberty Plaza, 20th Floor, New York, NY 10006, USA

477 Williamstown Road, Port Melbourne, VIC 3207, Australia

314–321, 3rd Floor, Plot 3, Splendor Forum, Jasola District Centre, New Delhi – 110025, India

79 Anson Road, #06–04/06, Singapore 079906

Cambridge University Press is part of the University of Cambridge.

It furthers the University's mission by disseminating knowledge in the pursuit of education, learning and research at the highest international levels of excellence.

www.cambridge.org
Information on this title: www.cambridge.org/9781108697231

© Cambridge University Press 2019

20 19 18 17 16 15 14 13 12 11 10 9 8 7 6 5 4 3 2 1

Printed in Mexico by Editorial Impresora Apolo, S.A. de C.V.

A catalogue record for this publication is available from the British Library

ISBN Student's Book with Online Workbook 978-1-108-69723-1

Additional resources for this publication at www.cambridge.org/essentials

Scope and Sequence

Unit	Theme	Grammar	Topics	Avoid Common Mistakes
PART 4 Simple Present				
UNIT 8 page 80	Lifestyles	Simple Present	Simple Present: Affirmative and Negative Statements (p. 82) Statements with Adverbs of Frequency (p. 88)	Avoiding *do/does* in negative statements with *be*; avoiding *be* with simple present verbs
UNIT 9 page 92	Daily Habits	Simple Present Yes/No Questions and Short Answers	Simple Present *Yes / No* Questions and Short Answers (p. 94)	Remembering *Do/Does* in simple present questions with *have*; avoiding *Do/Does* in questions with *be*
UNIT 10 page 98	Cultural Holidays	Simple Present Information Questions	Simple Present Information Questions (p. 100) Questions with *How Often* (p. 106)	Remembering *do/does*; avoiding *-s* with *he/she/it*
PART 5 Conjunctions				
UNIT 11 page 108	Time Management	Conjunctions: *And, But, Or*; *Because*	*And, But, Or* (p. 110) *Because* (p. 113)	Remembering a comma with conjunctions; using conjunctions
PART 6 Simple Past				
UNIT 12 page 118	Success Stories	Simple Past Statements	Simple Past Statements: Regular Verbs (p. 120) Simple Past Statements: Irregular Verbs (p. 125)	Remembering simple past verbs to talk about the past; remembering the base form of the verb after *did not / didn't*
UNIT 13 page 130	Business Ideas	Simple Past Questions	Simple Past *Yes / No* Questions (p. 132) Simple Past Information Questions (p. 135)	Remembering *did* + subject + base form of the verb; avoiding the past form in information questions
UNIT 14 page 138	Life Stories	Simple Past of *Be*	Simple Past of *Be*: Affirmative and Negative Statements (p. 140) Simple Past of *Be*: Questions and Answers (p. 142)	Using *was/were*; Remembering the correct form with *born*
UNIT 15 page 148	Luck and Loss	Past Time Clauses with *When, Before,* and *After*	Past Time Clauses with *When, Before,* and *After* (p. 150)	Remembering the correct spelling of *when, before,* and *after*; remembering the subject in the main clause and the time clause

Unit	Theme	Grammar	Topics	Avoid Common Mistakes
PART 7 More About Nouns, Determiners, and Pronouns				
UNIT 16 page 156	Eating Habits	Count and Noncount Nouns	Count and Noncount Nouns (p. 158) Units of Measure; *How Many . . . ?* and *How Much . . . ?* (p. 164)	Avoiding *a / an* with noncount nouns; avoiding the plural with noncount nouns
UNIT 17 page 170	Languages	Quantifiers: *Some, Any, A Lot Of, A Little, A Few, Much, Many*	Quantifiers: *Some* and *Any* (p. 172) Quantifiers: *A Lot Of, A Little, A Few, Much, Many* (p. 177)	Remembering *many* with plural nouns; remembering *any* with negative statements and *some* with affirmative statements
UNIT 18 page 184	Changes and Risks	Articles: *A / An* and *The*	Articles: *A / An* and *The* (p. 186) Article or No Article? (p. 191)	Avoiding *a/an* with noncount nouns; avoiding *the* when talking about things or people in general
UNIT 19 page 196	Meals Around the World	Possessive Pronouns and Indefinite Pronouns	Possessive Pronouns (p. 198) Indefinite Pronouns (p. 203)	Avoiding the plural with possessive pronouns; remembering *any* + in negative statements
PART 8 Imperatives and Modals				
UNIT 20 page 208	Social Customs	Imperatives	Imperatives (p. 210)	Avoiding *no* in negative imperatives; remembering an apostrophe in *don't*
UNIT 21 page 218	Making Connections	Ability and Possibility	*Can* and *Could* for Ability and Possibility (p. 220) *Be Able To* and *Know How To* for Ability (p. 225)	Avoiding *-s* with *can* and *could*; remembering the base form with *can* and *could*
UNIT 22 page 230	College Life	Requests and Permission	*Can, Could,* and *Would* for Requests (p. 232) *Can, Could,* and *May* for Permission (p. 236)	Remembering the correct word order for making requests; remembering the base form of the verb after *can, could, may,* or *would*

Appendices

Introduction to
Grammar and Beyond Essentials

Grammar and Beyond Essentials is a research-based and content-rich grammar series for beginning to advanced-level students. The series focuses on the most commonly used English grammar structures and practices all four skills in a variety of authentic and communicative contexts. The series practices all four skills in a variety of authentic and communicative contexts. It is designed for use both in the classroom and as a self-study learning tool.

Grammar and Beyond Essentials is Research-Based

The grammar presented in this series is informed by years of research on the grammar of written and spoken English as it is used in college lectures, textbooks, academic essays, high school classrooms, and conversations between instructors and students. This research, and the analysis of over one billion words of authentic written and spoken language data known as the *Cambridge International Corpus*, has enabled the authors to:

- Present grammar rules that accurately represent how English is actually spoken and written

- Identify and teach differences between the grammar of written and spoken English

- Focus more attention on the structures that are commonly used, and less on those that are rarely used, in writing and speaking

- Help students avoid the most common mistakes that English language learners make

- Choose reading topics that will naturally elicit examples of the target grammar structure

- Introduce important vocabulary from the Academic Word List

Special Features of *Grammar and Beyond Essentials*

Realistic Grammar Presentations

Grammar is presented in clear and simple charts. The grammar points presented in these charts have been tested against real-world data from the *Cambridge International Corpus* to ensure that they are authentic representations of actual use of English.

Data from the Real World

Many of the grammar presentations and application sections include a feature called Data from the Real World. Concrete and useful points discovered through analysis of corpus data are presented and practiced in exercises that follow.

Avoid Common Mistakes

Each unit features an Avoid Common Mistakes section that develops students' awareness of the most common mistakes made by English language learners and gives them an opportunity to practice detecting and correcting these errors. This section helps students avoid these mistakes in their own work. The mistakes highlighted in this section are drawn from a body of authentic data on learner English known as the *Cambridge Learner Corpus*, a database of over 35 million words from student essays written by non-native speakers of English and information from experienced classroom teachers.

Academic Vocabulary

Every unit in *Grammar and Beyond Essentials* includes words from the Academic Word List (AWL), a research-based list of words and word families that appear with high frequency in English-language academic texts. These words are introduced in the opening text of the unit, recycled in the charts and exercises, and used to support the theme throughout the unit. By the time students finish each level, they will have been exposed several times to a carefully selected set of level-appropriate AWL words, as well as content words from a variety of academic disciplines.

Series Levels

The following table provides a general idea of the difficulty of the material at each level of *Grammar and Beyond Essentials*. These are not meant to be interpreted as precise correlations.

	Description	TOEFL IBT	CEFR Levels
Level 1	Beginning	20 – 34	A1 – A2
Level 2	Low Intermediate to Intermediate	35 – 54	A2 – B1
Level 3	High Intermediate	55 – 74	B1 – B2
Level 4	Advanced	75 – 95	B2 – C1

Student Components

Student's Book with Online Workbook

Levels 1 through 3 teach all of the grammar points appropriate at each level in short, manageable cycles of presentation and practice organized around a high-interest unit theme. Level 4 focuses on the structure of the academic essay in addition to the grammar rules, conventions, and structures that students need to master in order to be successful college writers. Please see the Tour of a Unit on pages xvi–xix for a more detailed view of the contents and structure of the units.

Online Workbook

The Online Workbook provides extra practice to help you master each grammar point. Automatically-graded exercises give immediate feedback. Each unit offers practice correcting the errors highlighted in the Avoid Common Mistakes section in the Student's Book. Self-Assessment sections at the end of each unit allow students to test their mastery of what they learned. Look for ⌨ in the Student's Book to see where additional online practice is available.

Quiz Your English app

Quiz Your English is a fun new way to practice, improve, and test your English by competing against learners from all around the world. Learn English grammar with friends, discover new English words, and test yourself in a truly global environment.

- Learn to avoid common mistakes with a special section just for *Grammar and Beyond Essentials* users
- Challenge your friends and players wherever they are
- Watch where you are on the leaderboards

Teacher Resources

Grammar and Beyond Essentials offers a variety of downloadable resources for instructors on eSource: esource.cambridge.org. Contact your Cambridge ESL Specialist (www.cambridge.org/cambridgeenglish/contact) to find out how to access the site.

Teacher's Manual

- Suggestions for applying the target grammar to all four major skill areas, helping instructors facilitate dynamic and comprehensive grammar classes
- An answer key and audio script for the Student's Book
- Teaching tips, to help instructors plan their lessons
- Downloadable communicative activities to add more in-class speaking practice

Assessment

- Placement Test
- Ready-made, easy-to-score Unit Tests, Midterm, and Final in .pdf and .doc formats
- Answer Key

Presentation Plus

Presentation Plus allows teachers to digitally project the contents of the Student's Books in front of the class for a livelier, interactive classroom. It is a complete solution for teachers because it includes the answer keys and audio.

Lesson Mapping Guides

Grammar and Beyond Essentials is designed to be used easily alongside academic English titles from Cambridge University Press. These include: *Academic Encounters, Final Draft, Making Connections, Prism,* and *Prism Reading.* Visit www.cambridge.org/essentials/LessonMaps to download a Lesson Mapping Guide for each title.

Academic Encounters   FINAL DRAFT   Making CONNECTIONS   PRISM   PRISM READING

About the Author

Randi Reppen is Professor of Applied Linguistics and TESL at Northern Arizona University (NAU) in Flagstaff, Arizona. She has over 20 years' experience teaching ESL students and training ESL teachers, including 11 years as the Director of NAU's Program in Intensive English. Randi's research interests focus on the use of corpora for language teaching and materials development. In addition to numerous academic articles and books, she is the author of *Using Corpora in the Language Classroom* and a co-author of *Basic Vocabulary in Use*, 2nd edition, both published by Cambridge University Press.

Corpus Consultants

Michael McCarthy is Emeritus Professor of Applied Linguistics at the University of Nottingham, UK, and Adjunct Professor of Applied Linguistics at Pennsylvania State University. He is a co-author of the corpus-informed *Touchstone* series and the award-winning *Cambridge Grammar of English*, both published by Cambridge University Press, among many other titles, and is known throughout the world as an expert on grammar, vocabulary, and corpus linguistics.

Jeanne McCarten has over 30 years of experience in ELT/ESL as a teacher, publisher, and author. She has been closely involved in the development of the spoken English sections of the *Cambridge International Corpus*. Now a freelance writer, she is co-author of the corpus-informed *Touchstone* series and *Grammar for Business*, both published by Cambridge University Press.

Advisory Panel

The ESL advisory panel has helped to guide the development of this series and provided invaluable information about the needs of ESL students and teachers in high schools, colleges, universities, and private language schools throughout North America.

Neta Simpkins Cahill, Skagit Valley College, Mount Vernon, WA

Shelly Hedstrom, Palm Beach State College, Lake Worth, FL

Richard Morasci, Foothill College, Los Altos Hills, CA

Stacey Russo, East Hampton High School, East Hampton, NY

Alice Savage, North Harris College, Houston, TX

Acknowledgements

The publisher and authors would like to thank these reviewers and consultants for their insights and participation:

Marty Attiyeh, The College of DuPage, Glen Ellyn, IL

Shannon Bailey, Austin Community College, Austin, TX

Jamila Barton, North Seattle Community College, Seattle, WA

Kim Bayer, Hunter College IELI, New York, NY

Linda Berendsen, Oakton Community College, Skokie, IL

Anita Biber, Tarrant County College Northwest, Fort Worth, TX

Jane Breaux, Community College of Aurora, Aurora, CO

Anna Budzinski, San Antonio College, San Antonio, TX

Britta Burton, Mission College, Santa Clara, CA

Jean Carroll, Fresno City College, Fresno, CA

Chris Cashman, Oak Park High School and Elmwood Park High School, Chicago, IL

Annette M. Charron, Bakersfield College, Bakersfield, CA

Patrick Colabucci, ALI at San Diego State University, San Diego, CA

Lin Cui, Harper College, Palatine, IL

Jennifer Duclos, Boston University CELOP, Boston, MA

Joy Durighello, San Francisco City College, San Francisco, CA

Kathleen Flynn, Glendale Community College, Glendale, CA

Raquel Fundora, Miami Dade College, Miami, FL

Patricia Gillie, New Trier Township High School District, Winnetka, IL

Laurie Gluck, LaGuardia Community College, Long Island City, NY

Kathleen Golata, Galileo Academy of Science & Technology, San Francisco, CA

Ellen Goldman, Mission College, Santa Clara, CA

Ekaterina Goussakova, Seminole Community College, Sanford, FL

Marianne Grayston, Prince George's Community College, Largo, MD

Mary Greiss Shipley, Georgia Gwinnett College, Lawrenceville, GA

Sudeepa Gulati, Long Beach City College, Long Beach, CA

Nicole Hammond Carrasquel, University of Central Florida, Orlando, FL

Vicki Hendricks, Broward College, Fort Lauderdale, FL

Kelly Hernandez, Miami Dade College, Miami, FL

Ann Johnston, Tidewater Community College, Virginia Beach, VA

Julia Karet, Chaffey College, Claremont, CA

Jeanne Lachowski, English Language Institute, University of Utah, Salt Lake City, UT

Noga Laor, Rennert, New York, NY

Min Lu, Central Florida Community College, Ocala, FL

Michael Luchuk, Kaplan International Centers, New York, NY

Craig Machado, Norwalk Community College, Norwalk, CT

Denise Maduli-Williams, City College of San Francisco, San Francisco, CA

Diane Mahin, University of Miami, Coral Gables, FL

Melanie Majeski, Naugatuck Valley Community College, Waterbury, CT

Jeanne Malcolm, University of North Carolina at Charlotte, Charlotte, NC

Lourdes Marx, Palm Beach State College, Boca Raton, FL

Susan G. McFalls, Maryville College, Maryville, TN

Nancy McKay, Cuyahoga Community College, Cleveland, OH

Dominika McPartland, Long Island Business Institute, Flushing, NY

Amy Metcalf, UNR/Intensive English Language Center, University of Nevada, Reno, NV

Robert Miller, EF International Language School San Francisco – Mills, San Francisco, CA

Marcie Pachino, Jordan High School, Durham, NC

Myshie Pagel, El Paso Community College, El Paso, TX

Bernadette Pedagno, University of San Francisco, San Francisco, CA

Tam Q Pham, Dallas Theological Seminary, Fort Smith, AR

Mary Beth Pickett, Global LT, Rochester, MI

Maria Reamore, Baltimore City Public Schools, Baltimore, MD

Alison M. Rice, Hunter College IELI, New York, NY

Sydney Rice, Imperial Valley College, Imperial, CA

Kathleen Romstedt, Ohio State University, Columbus, OH

Alexandra Rowe, University of South Carolina, Columbia, SC

Irma Sanders, Baldwin Park Adult and Community Education, Baldwin Park, CA

Caren Shoup, Lone Star College – CyFair, Cypress, TX

Karen Sid, Mission College, Foothill College, De Anza College, Santa Clara, CA

Michelle Thomas, Miami Dade College, Miami, FL

Sharon Van Houte, Lorain County Community College, Elyria, OH

Margi Wald, UC Berkeley, Berkeley, CA

Walli Weitz, Riverside County Office of Ed., Indio, CA

Bart Weyand, University of Southern Maine, Portland, ME

Donna Weyrich, Columbus State Community College, Columbus, OH

Marilyn Whitehorse, Santa Barbara City College, Ojai, CA

Jessica Wilson, Rutgers University – Newark, Newark, NJ

Sue Wilson, San Jose City College, San Jose, CA

Margaret Wilster, Mid-Florida Tech, Orlando, FL

Anne York-Herjeczki, Santa Monica College, Santa Monica, CA

Hoda Zaki, Camden County College, Camden, NJ

We would also like to thank these teachers and programs for allowing us to visit:

Richard Appelbaum, Broward College, Fort Lauderdale, FL

Carmela Arnoldt, Glendale Community College, Glendale, AZ

JaNae Barrow, Desert Vista High School, Phoenix, AZ

Ted Christensen, Mesa Community College, Mesa, AZ

Richard Ciriello, Lower East Side Preparatory High School, New York, NY

Virginia Edwards, Chandler-Gilbert Community College, Chandler, AZ

Nusia Frankel, Miami Dade College, Miami, FL

Raquel Fundora, Miami Dade College, Miami, FL

Vicki Hendricks, Broward College, Fort Lauderdale, FL

Kelly Hernandez, Miami Dade College, Miami, FL

Stephen Johnson, Miami Dade College, Miami, FL

Barbara Jordan, Mesa Community College, Mesa, AZ

Nancy Kersten, GateWay Community College, Phoenix, AZ

Lewis Levine, Hostos Community College, Bronx, NY

John Liffiton, Scottsdale Community College, Scottsdale, AZ

Cheryl Lira-Layne, Gilbert Public School District, Gilbert, AZ

Mary Livingston, Arizona State University, Tempe, AZ

Elizabeth Macdonald, Thunderbird School of Global Management, Glendale, AZ

Terri Martinez, Mesa Community College, Mesa, AZ

Lourdes Marx, Palm Beach State College, Boca Raton, FL

Paul Kei Matsuda, Arizona State University, Tempe, AZ

David Miller, Glendale Community College, Glendale, AZ

Martha Polin, Lower East Side Preparatory High School, New York, NY

Patricia Pullenza, Mesa Community College, Mesa, AZ

Victoria Rasinskaya, Lower East Side Preparatory High School, New York, NY

Vanda Salls, Tempe Union High School District, Tempe, AZ

Kim Sanabria, Hostos Community College, Bronx, NY

Cynthia Schuemann, Miami Dade College, Miami, FL

Michelle Thomas, Miami Dade College, Miami, FL

Dongmei Zeng, Borough of Manhattan Community College, New York, NY

Tour of a Unit

UNIT

10 Simple Present Information Questions
Cultural Holidays

1 Grammar in the Real World

A What is your favorite holiday or celebration? Read the interview about a Mexican holiday. What is the Day of the Dead?

B Comprehension Check Choose the correct answers.

1 On the Day of the Dead, people remember _____ .
   a their parents   b their dead relatives   c their children

2 People put pictures of the dead _____ .
   a on altars   b on sweets   c on skulls

3 The Day of the Dead takes place _____ .
   a every month   b one day a year   c on November 1 and 2

4 People _____ their ancestors' graves.
   a decorate   b paint   c celebrate

C Notice Answer the questions with the correct question word. Use the interview to help you.

1 Which word asks a question about **time**?   What   When   Where

2 Which word asks a question about **places**?   What   When   Where

3 Which word asks a question about **things**?   What   When   Where

What word comes after *when, where,* and *what*?

Simple Present Information Questions

Coffee Time

Today's Topic:
MEXICO'S DAY of the DEAD

[1]**ancestor**: any member of your family from long ago

[2]**altar**: a type of table that people use in religious ceremonies

[3]**grave**: a place where you bury a dead person or people, usually under the ground

[4]**skull**: the bones of the head around the brain

[5]**symbolize**: use a sign or mark to represent something

[6]**rebirth**: a new period of growth of something

Michelle Hello, everyone! This is *Coffee Time.* Our topic today is celebrations around the world. Today our guest is Elena Lopez, from a university in Mexico. She's here to tell us about the Day of the Dead. Welcome, Dr. Lopez!

5 **Dr. Lopez** Thank you. It's nice to be here.

Michelle First of all, **where do people celebrate the Day of the Dead?**

Dr. Lopez They celebrate it in many parts of the world, such as in Mexico.

10 **Michelle** **When do people celebrate it, and how do they celebrate it?**

Dr. Lopez Well, the Day of the Dead takes place on two days: November 1 and 2. We remember our dead relatives – our ancestors[1] – and friends. People build little altars[2]
15 in the home and in public schools. They also clean and decorate the graves.[3]

Michelle **What do they put on these altars and graves?**

Dr. Lopez They put candles, food, drinks, flowers, and pictures of
20 the dead. There are sweets in the shape of skulls,[4] too. The traditions are a little different in every region of Mexico.

Michelle **What do the different things mean?**

Dr. Lopez Well, for example, the candles are a guide for our ancestors. They guide them home. There are bells, too.
25 They call the dead.

Michelle **What do the skulls symbolize?**[5] Do they symbolize death?

Dr. Lopez Well, yes. But they also symbolize rebirth,[6] according to the first Day of the Dead thousands of years ago.

98

Cultural Holidays **99**

2 Simple Present Information Questions

Grammar Presentation

Information questions begin with a Wh-word (Who, What, When, Where, Why, or How). They ask for information and cannot be answered with a simple yes or no.	Where do people celebrate the Day of the Dead? When do Americans celebrate Independence Day?

2.1 Information Questions

Wh- word	Do / Does	Subject	Base Form of Verb	
Who			see	at school?
What		I	eat	at parties?
When	do	you we they	celebrate	that holiday?
What time			begin	the celebration?
Where		he	study	for school?
Why	does	she	live	at home?
How		it	meet	new people?

2.2 Using Simple Present Information Questions

A Use a Wh- word with do before I, you, we, they, and plural nouns.	When do you celebrate the holiday?
Use a Wh- word with does before he, she, it, and singular nouns.	Why does she study Spanish?
B Use simple present information questions to ask for specific information.	"Where do you live?" "I live in Mexico City." "What time do you start work?" "8:30."
C Use simple present information questions to ask about habits, facts, traditions, and regular activities.	"When do they celebrate the Day of the Dead?" "In November." "Why does she travel to Mexico every year?" "Because she has family there."
D You can answer information questions with a short or long answer.	"What do you eat on Thanksgiving?" Short answer: "Turkey and pie." Long answer: "I eat turkey and pie."

2.3 Using Wh- Words

A Use Who to ask about people.	"Who do you remember on the Day of the Dead?" "I remember my grandmother."
B Use What to ask about things.	"What do you study?" "Spanish and history."
C Use When to ask about time (days, months, years, seasons, parts of the day).	"When do you celebrate Chinese New Year?" "In January or February."
D Use What time to ask about clock time.	"What time does your class finish?" "4:30. / Five o'clock."
E Use Where to ask about places.	"Where does she work?" "At the University of Mexico."
F Use Why to ask about reasons.	"Why do you like celebrations?" "Because they're always fun."
G Use How to ask about manner – the way people do something.	"How do you celebrate your birthday?" "We eat at my favorite restaurant."

Grammar Application

Exercise 2.1 Questions with Who, What, When, Where, How

A Complete the questions with Who, What, When, Where, or How and do or does.

1 A _Where_ _do_ people celebrate the Day of the Dead?
  B In Mexico.
2 A _____ they celebrate the Day of the Dead?
  B On November 1 and 2.
3 A _____ they remember?
  B Their dead relatives and friends.
4 A _____ they decorate?
  B Graves and altars.
5 A _____ they put pictures of the dead?
  B On altars.
6 A _____ they decorate the graves?
  B With flowers, candles, food, and drinks.

DATA FROM THE REAL WORLD

takes students beyond traditional information and teaches them how the unit's grammar is used in authentic situations, including differences between spoken and written use.

QR CODES

give easy access to audio at point of use.

Exercise 2.5 Information Questions in Titles

Data from the Real World

We often use information questions in the titles of academic articles and books. The article or book answers the question.	Why Do We Laugh?
	How Does a Computer Work?
	When Do People Watch TV?

Titles with *How? What?* and *Why?* are very frequent.

How do/does?
What do/does?
Why do/does?

A Listen to the questions and answers. Mark the questions with ↗ for rising intonation and ↘ for falling intonation.

1 A Excuse me. Are you from Japan? ↗
   B Yes, I am. I'm from Tokyo.
2 A Can I ask you some questions? ____
   B Sure!
3 A What's your favorite holiday in Japan? ____
   B New Year's Day.
4 A Why is it your favorite? ____
   B Because we have special food for the holiday, and we relax all day.
5 A Do you help your mother with the cooking? ____
   B Yes, I do. We also see all our relatives on New Year's Day.
6 A Do you play any special games? ____
   B No, not really. But we watch some special TV programs.
7 A What else do you do on New Year's Day? ____
   B Well, we read all our holiday cards then.
8 A Do you really save all the cards to open on the same day? ____
   B Yes, it's a special custom.

B Listen and repeat the questions.

104 Unit 10 Simple Present Information Questions

HOW TO USE A QR CODE

1 Open the camera on your smartphone.

2 Point it at the QR code.

3 The camera will automatically scan the code. If not, press the button to take a picture.

* Not all cameras automatically scan QR codes. You may need to download a QR code reader. Search "QR free" and download an app.

Exercise 2.2 Questions with *When* and *What Time*

A Complete the questions with *When* or *What time* and *do* or *does*.

1 A <u>When   do</u> you graduate?   B On June 15.
2 A _____ _____ you have the ceremony?   B At 3:30.
3 A _____ _____ Sandi turn 21?   B Next Saturday.
4 A _____ _____ her birthday party start?   B At 7:00.
5 A _____ _____ you celebrate Thanksgiving in the   B At the end of November.
   United States?
6 A _____ _____ your family usually have the meal?   B In the late afternoon.
7 A _____ _____ you usually start cooking on that day?   B At about 8:00 a.m.

B Pair Work Ask and answer the questions in A with a partner.

Exercise 2.3 Asking Information Questions

A Read the paragraph about a holiday celebration in Massachusetts. Write information questions using the words in parentheses. Find the verbs in the paragraph, and use the information to write your questions. Remember to use *do* and *does* in your questions.

One of my favorite holidays is Patriots' Day in the Boston, Massachusetts, area. Every year, Boston residents celebrate Patriots' Day on the third Monday of April. On this day, people remember the beginning of the American Revolutionary War. Many towns have parades and speeches.[1] The second important event is the Boston Marathon.[2] The marathon happens every year on Patriots' Day. The race starts around 10:00 a.m. in Hopkinton and ends in Boston. Thousands of people watch runners from all over the world. The third event is the special Patriots' Day baseball game. The Boston Red Sox play a team from another town. The game starts around 11:00 a.m. in Boston.

[1]**speech:** a formal talk | [2]**marathon:** a race in which people run 26 miles and 385 yards (42.195 kilometers)

1 (what / people / celebrate) <u>What do people celebrate on the third Monday of April?</u>
2 (what / people / remember) _____
3 (what / towns / have) _____
4 (when / marathon / happen) _____
5 (what time / marathon / start) _____
6 (where / marathon / start) _____
7 (who / people / watch) _____

---

4 your family / go out to a nice restaurant
   Question: _____
   Answer: _____
5 your friends / eat at a fast-food restaurant
   Question: _____
   Answer: _____
6 your relatives / visit your home
   Question: _____
   Answer: _____

B Over to You Use *How often* to write your own questions on a separate piece of paper. Use words from the box and your own ideas. Then ask your partner the questions.

| board game | hiking | movie | swimming | TV |
| gym | library | music concert | text message | |

How often do you watch TV past midnight?

4 Avoid Common Mistakes ⚠

1 **In simple present information questions, use *do* or *does* before the subject.**
   Where ~~you~~ *do* work?   Why ~~he~~ *does* drink so much coffee?

2 **Use *do* or *does*, not *is* or *are*, with the verb.**
   What time ~~is~~ *does* the concert begin?

3 **Do not use -s on the verb with *he / she / it* or a singular noun.**
   Where does Tom ~~goes~~ *go* to school?

Editing Task

Find and correct seven more mistakes in these questions about Thanksgiving.

                do
1 How~~you~~ celebrate Thanksgiving?
2 Where do you celebrates Thanksgiving?
3 What are you does during Thanksgiving Day?
4 What you watch on TV?
5 What time are you usually have your meal?
6 What you do on the Friday after Thanksgiving?
7 Why people celebrate Thanksgiving?

THEME-RELATED EXERCISES

boost fluency by providing grammar practice in a variety of different contexts.

EDITING TASK

gives learners an opportunity to identify and correct commonly made errors and develop self-editing skills needed in their university studies.

Statements with Present of *Be*

Tell Me About Yourself

1 Grammar in the Real World

A How do you introduce yourself to your instructors? What information do you give? Read the conversation between an adviser and a student. What are two interesting facts about Tomasz?

B Comprehension Check Circle the correct words.

1 Ms. Kim is **a student / an adviser**.

2 Tomasz is from **Poland / the United States**.

3 Tomasz is a salesclerk in his uncle's **store / restaurant**.

C Notice   Complete the sentences. Use the conversation to help you.

1 I _____ Tomasz. Sorry I _____ late.

2 My major _____ computer science.

3 My brother and I _____ salesclerks. We _____ really interested in his business.

FIRST MEETING
WITH AN ADVISER

Tomasz	Hello, Ms. Kim. I'**m** Tomasz. Sorry I'**m** late for our meeting.
Ms. Kim	That's OK. Nice to meet you, Tomasz. Please have a seat.
Tomasz	Thanks.
Ms. Kim	First, I'**m** glad that you'**re** here. As your adviser, I'**m** here to help you. I can help you
5	choose your classes, and I can help you with any problems.
Tomasz	Thanks, I need your help. I have a lot of questions about courses, instructors, and
	my program.
Ms. Kim	Good! But first I'd like to know more about you. Tell me about yourself.
Tomasz	Sure. I'**m** 19, and I'**m** a graduate of Central High School. I'**m** from Poland originally.
10 Ms. Kim	I see. What **are** some of your interests?
Tomasz	Well, I'**m** interested in cars and music. And I really like computers. My major **is**
	computer science.
Ms. Kim	Great. You know, the college has a lot of clubs. It'**s** a good way to meet people and
	practice English.
15 Tomasz	Well, I'**m** pretty busy most of the time. My brother and I **are** salesclerks in my uncle's store.
	We'**re** really interested in his business. I don't have much free time.
Ms. Kim	OK. I understand. Now, let's talk about your academic plans . . .

2 Present of *Be*: Affirmative Statements

Grammar Presentation

Be links ideas.

I 'm a student.

2.1 Full Forms (with Subject Pronouns)

SINGULAR			
Subject	*Be*		
I	**am**		late.
You	**are**		
He She It	**is**		difficult.

PLURAL		
Subject	*Be*	
We You They	**are**	from Seoul.

▸▸ Capitalization and Punctuation Rules: See page A1.

2.2 Contractions (with Nouns and Subject Pronouns)

SINGULAR	PLURAL
I am → I'**m**	We are → We'**re**
You are → You'**re**	You are → You'**re**
He is → He'**s**	They are → They'**re**
Tomasz is → Tomasz'**s**	
She is → She'**s**	
His mother is → His mother'**s**	
It is → It'**s**	
My name is → My name'**s**	

2.3 Using Present of *Be*

A The verb *be* "links" ideas. You can use *be* to link nouns or pronouns with words that give information about them.	*Tomasz is a student.* *They are from California.*
B Use the full forms of *be* in academic writing.	*I am a computer science major.* *I am in your grammar class.*

2.3 Using Present of *Be* (continued)

C Use contractions of *be* in conversation and informal writing.	*I'm* Ms. Kim. *They're* sick today.
D You can use *be* + noun • to talk about occupations.	*He's* a teacher. *They're* students.
• to identify things.	*It's* an English class. *My hobbies are* baseball and music. *My major is* math.
E You can use *be* + number to talk about ages.	*My sister is* 18. *His parents are* 49 years old.
F You can use *be* + adjective • to talk about nationalities.	*I'm* Canadian. *His parents are* South Korean.
• to describe people and things.	*Jun-Ho is* tall. *My sister is* sick. *Our reading class is* interesting.
G You can use *be* + preposition • to talk about hometowns and places.	*My parents are* from Seoul. *I'm* from California.
• to talk about where people and things are.	*She is* at home. *We are* in Los Angeles.
• to talk about the groups, such as teams or clubs, that people are in.	*My friends and I are* in a band. *He is* on the basketball team.

Grammar Application

Exercise 2.1 Present of *Be*: Full Forms

A Complete the sentences about a student, using *am*, *is*, and *are*.

1 My name is Ling. I ___*am*___ a student at the University of Florida.

2 My friend Ana and I _____ in Science 101.

3 Mr. Johnson _____ a good instructor.

4 The class _____ interesting.

5 My classmates _____ crazy about science.

6 Ana _____ smart.

7 Ana and I _____ seniors this year.

B Look at the underlined word(s). Circle the subject pronoun that replaces the underlined words.

1 <u>My college</u> is in Detroit, Michigan. **It / She** is a good school.

2 <u>Jorge and Lisa</u> are in Grammar 110. **They / We** are in a fun class.

3 <u>Mrs. Chapple</u> is a great teacher. **It / She** is also very nice.

4 <u>Marcos</u> is crazy about grammar. **He / They** is never late for class.

5 <u>My brother</u> is smart. **He / It** is an excellent student.

6 <u>My mother</u> is a nurse. **She / It** is always very busy.

7 <u>My sister</u> and I are sick. **She / We** are at home today.

C Complete the student's online profile. Use the full forms of *be* (am, is, are).

My name __*is*__ Cindy Wang. I _____ from
(1)   (2)
Jackson, Illinois. My parents _____ from China
(3)
originally. I _____ 20 years old. I _____ now
(4)   (5)
a student at the University of Texas. My major _____
(6)
public health. My favorite subjects _____ math and
(7)
biology. I _____ interested in sports and drawing.
(8)
My friend Bev and I _____ servers in a restaurant on
(9)
weekends. My sister _____ still a high school student
(10)
in Illinois.

D Over to You Complete the sentences with the correct full form of *be* and the information about you. Then read your sentences to your partner. How many of your sentences are the same?

1 My name _____ _____ .
         (be)   (name)

2 I _____ from _____ .
   (be)   (country)

3 I _____ _____ .
   (be)   (age)

4 My major _____ _____ .
           (be)   (subject)

5 My favorite class _____ _____ .
                   (be)   (name of class)

6 I _____ interested in _____ .
   (be)   (name of things)

7 I _____ .
   (Tell one more thing about yourself. Remember to use *be*.)

Exercise 2.2 Present of *Be*: Contractions

A Complete the sentences with *'m*, *'s*, or *'re*.

1 Ana   Hi, I ___'m___ Ana.
            (1)

  Ron   Hi, Ana. My name _____ Ron. Nice to meet you.
                                (2)

  Ana   It _____ nice to meet you, too.
            (3)

  Ron   I _____ in Ms. Cook's class.
           (4)

  Ana   She _____ my teacher, too.
             (5)
         You _____ in my class.
             (6)

  Ron   Great. I think we _____ in Room 9.
                           (7)

2 Sara   Excuse me. I'm lost. My teacher _____ Mr. Martinez.
                                          (8)

  Ron   Mr. Martinez? He _____ in Room 10.
                         (9)

  Ana   Room 10 _____ over there. On the right.
                  (10)

  Sara   Oh, thanks.

  Ana   You _____ welcome.
             (11)

3 Ana   Ron, this is my friend Cathy. We _____ friends
                                            (12)
         from high school.

  Ron   Hi, Cathy.

  Cathy Hi, Ron!

  Ana   Cathy _____ on the basketball team.
               (13)
         She _____ a great player.
             (14)

  Ron   Really? I _____ a big basketball fan.
                   (15)

  Ana   Well, come to our next game. It _____ on Friday.
                                        (16)

B Pair Work Introduce yourself to your partner. Use contractions. Then introduce your partner to a classmate.

Hi, I'm Alex. This is Hong-yin. He's from Texas. He's on the soccer team.

3 Present of *Be*: Negative Statements

Grammar Presentation

3.1 Full Forms

SINGULAR		
Subject	*Be + Not*	
I	**am not**	
You	**are not**	in class.
He She It	**is not**	

PLURAL		
Subject	*Be + Not*	
We You They	**are not**	students.

3.2 Negative Contractions

SINGULAR

I am not → I**'m not**
You are not → You**'re not** / You **aren't**
He is not → He**'s not** / He **isn't**
She is not → She**'s not** / She **isn't**
It is not → It**'s not** / It **isn't**

PLURAL

We are not → We**'re not** / We **aren't**
You are not → You**'re not** / You **aren't**
They are not → They**'re not** / They **aren't**

📊 **Data from the Real World**

In conversation, people usually use **'s not** and **'re not** after pronouns.	He**'s not** 21. *She***'s not** *in class.* *They***'re not** *here.*
They usually use **isn't** and **aren't** after names and nouns.	*Carlos* **isn't** *21.* *Louise* **isn't** *in class.* *The boys* **aren't** *here.*

🖱 Grammar Application

Exercise 3.1 Present of *Be*: Negative Statements with Full Forms

A Complete the sentences. Use *am not*, *is not*, or *are not*.

1 My roommate and I _____*are not*_____ math majors.

2 My friends _____ in my business class.

3 My cousin _____ married.

4 You _____ late.

5 My friend _____ in the library.

6 I _____ interested in chemistry.

7 Our instructor _____ from the United States.

8 The students _____ interested in history.

B Over to You **Write six negative sentences about yourself. Use the full form of *be*.**

1 I *am not* a teacher.

2 I _____ from _____ .

3 I _____ interested in _____ .

4 I _____ a/an _____ major.

5 I _____ a/an _____ .

6 I _____ in _____ .

C Pair Work **Read your sentences to a partner. Are any of your sentences the same?**

Exercise 3.2 Affirmative or Negative?

A Read the online profiles. Complete the sentences with the correct affirmative or negative form of *be*. Use contractions when possible.

	Yoko Akeda	Luiz da Costa
Age	21	35
Hometown	Los Angeles, California	New York, New York
Occupation or job; location	student at Glen College	instructor at Glen College
Interested in . . .	music, art museums	music, biking
Not interested in . . .	cooking, computer games	movies, cooking

1 Yoko *is* 21. She *'s not* 35.

2 Yoko and Luiz _____ the same age.

3 Luiz _____ an instructor.
He _____ a student.

4 Yoko _____ from New York. She _____ from Los Angeles.

5 Luiz _____ from New York. He _____ from Los Angeles.

6 They _____ interested in music.
They _____ interested in cooking.

7 Luiz _____ interested in movies.

B Listen. Where are these people? Complete the sentences with the correct pronouns and forms of *be*. Use contractions when possible.

at home

at work

in class

at the movies

at the doctor's office

at the stadium

1 Carlos is sick. ___*He's*___ at the doctor's office. ___*He's not*___ at work.

2 Ana and her boss _____ in class. _____ in the office.

3 Juan and his children _____ at the doctor's office. _____ at home.

4 Karen is with her classmates and her teacher. _____ in class. _____ at the stadium.

5 David is a big baseball fan. _____ at the stadium. _____ at home.

6 Ling and John are interested in movies. _____ at Drew's apartment. _____ at the movies.

C Pair Work Tell a partner about four people you know. Where are they today?

My brother is at work. He's a salesclerk in a store . . .

Exercise 3.3 Negative of *Be*

Complete the conversations. Use *'s not* and *'re not* after pronouns and *isn't* and *aren't* after names and nouns.

1 **Sara** Hello. Accounting Department.

Ben Louise?

Sara No, it's Sara. Louise __*isn't*__ here.
(1)
She _____ at work today.
(2)

2 `Sam` Oh, no! My wallet _____ in my bag! It's on
         (3)
the bus!

`Man` No, it _____ on the bus. Look, here it is.
              (4)

3 `Lara` Where are your brothers? The game's on TV, and
they _____ here.
     (5)

`Joe` They _____ interested in baseball. They _____
           (6)   (7)
interested in sports.

4 Avoid Common Mistakes ⚠

1 **Use *be* to link ideas.**
            is
He ⌄ an engineering student.

2 **Use *be* + *not* to form negative statements with *be*. Do not use *be* + *no*.**
            not
Ana is ~~no~~ a science teacher.

3 **A statement has a subject. Do not begin a statement with *be*.**
She is
~~Is~~ my sister's best friend.

Editing Task

Correct nine more mistakes. Rewrite the sentences.

1 This my friend. *This is my friend.* _____

2 Her name Amy. _____

3 Amy and I roommates. _____

4 She 27. _____

5 She is no a student. _____

6 Is a science teacher. _____

7 Is very nice and very smart. _____

8 Amy is no in school today. _____

9 She sick. _____

10 Is at home. _____

Yes/No Questions and Information Questions with *Be*

Schedules and School

1 Grammar in the Real World

I Have class from 6 pm to 10 pm

A What is your class schedule? Read and listen to the conversations. Are Yuko's and Juan's classes the same?

B Comprehension Check **Read the sentences. Circle *True* or *False*.**

Conversation A

1 Yuko and Juan are in Building H now.   True   ⟨False⟩

2 They are late for class.   True   ⟨False⟩

Conversation B

3 Mr. Walters is Yuko's grammar teacher.   ⟨True⟩   False

4 Computer lab is over at 4:15.   ⟨True⟩   False

C Notice **Find the questions in the conversations. Complete the questions.**

1 ___Are___ you in my class?

2 ___Is___ your class in Building H?

3 ___Is___ that unusual?

4 ___Are___ you sure?

Which words are at the beginning of the questions?

YUKO AND JUAN

CONVERSATION A (MONDAY)

 So, **is your next class writing?**

No, it's reading.

 Really? My next class is reading, too. **Are you in my class?** It's at 1:30.

5

Maybe. **Is your class in Building H?**

 Yes, it's in Building H, Room 308.

10

Then I'm in your class, too!

 Hmm. **Where's Building H?**

It's on the hill, over there.

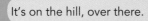 Oh, OK. **What time is it?**

It's 1:20. Uh-oh. We're late!

15 No, we aren't.

Are you sure?

 Yes. Class is at 1:30.

Oh, you're right. That's good. Let's go.

CONVERSATION B (THURSDAY)

20 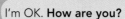 Hey, Juan. **How are you?**

I'm OK. **How are you?**

 I'm fine, thanks.

How are your classes?

 They're fine, but
25 they're all really big.

Really? **How many students are in your classes?**

About 25 to 30. **Is that unusual?**

No, it isn't. **Who's your
30 grammar teacher?**

 Mr. Walters. He's funny, but his class is difficult.

So, **when's your next class?**

35

 Let me see. Today's Thursday. Computer lab is at 3:00.

When is it over?

40 At 4:15. Let's meet after that.

2 Yes/No Questions and Short Answers with *Be*

Grammar Presentation

A *Yes/No* question is a question you can answer with *Yes* or *No*.	*"Is Yuko's class in Building H?"* *"Yes, it is." / "No, it isn't."*

2.1 Singular *Yes/No* Questions

Be	Subject	
Am	I	
Are	you	in class?
Is	he/she/it	

2.2 Singular Short Answers

AFFIRMATIVE

	Subject	*Be*
	I	**am.**
Yes,	you	**are.**
	he/she/it	**is.**

NEGATIVE

	Subject	*Be + Not*
	I	**am not.**
No,	you	**are not.**
	he/she/it	**is not.**

2.3 Plural *Yes/No* Questions

Be	Subject	
Are	we you they	late?

2.4 Plural Short Answers

AFFIRMATIVE

	Subject	*Be*
Yes,	we you they	**are.**

NEGATIVE

	Subject	*Be + Not*
No,	we you they	**are not.**

2.5 Negative Short Answers: Contractions

SINGULAR

No, I am not.	➔	No, I**'m not**.
No, you are not.	➔	No, you**'re not**. No, you **aren't**.
No, he is not.	➔	No, he**'s not**. No, he **isn't**.
No, she is not.	➔	No, she**'s not**. No, she **isn't**.
No, it is not.	➔	No, it**'s not**. No, it **isn't**.

PLURAL

No, we are not.	➔	No, we**'re not**. No, we **aren't**.
No, you are not.	➔	No, you**'re not**. No, you **aren't**.
No, they are not.	➔	No, they**'re not**. No, they **aren't**.

2.6 Using *Yes / No* Questions and Short Answers with *Be*

A Use a question mark (?) at the end of questions.	*Is reading class hard?*
B Put the verb *be* before the subject in *Yes / No* questions.	SUBJECT VERB STATEMENT *Reading class is at 1:30.* YES / NO QUESTION *Is reading class at 1:30?*
C Use pronouns in short answers.	*"Is reading class hard?"* *"Yes, it is."*
D Do not use contractions in short answers with *yes*.	*"Is class at 1:30?"* *"Yes, it is."* NOT *"Yes, it's."*
E Use contractions in short answers with *no*.	*"Is Yuko late?"* *"No, she's not."* OR *"No, she isn't."*
F Say *I don't know*, *I think so*, or *I don't think so* when you don't know or are not sure of the answer. Say *I don't know* when you don't know the answer. *I think so* means "maybe yes." *I don't think so* means "maybe no."	*"Is the library closed?"* *"I don't know."* OR *"I think so."* OR *"I don't think so."*

Exercise 2.1 Singular *Yes/No* Questions and Answers

A Circle the correct verbs to make questions. Then complete the answers with the correct pronoun and form of *be*. Use contractions when possible.

1 **Is**/ **Are** your writing class in the morning? Yes, ___*it is*___ .

2 **Am**/**Are** you free on Fridays after lunch? No, *I'm not*

3 **Are**/ **Is** you always on time? Yes, *I am* .

4 **Is**/ **Are** your teacher busy today? Yes, *She is*

5 **Is**/ **Are** you interested in sports? No, *I'm not*

6 **Are**/ **Is** your roommate in your class? No, *she/He isn't*

7 **Is**/ **Am** this an English class? Yes, *it is* .

8 **Is**/ **Are** your next class in this building? No, *it's not*

B Write two questions and two answers about each picture. Use the words in parentheses.

1 a (late) ___*Is she late?*___ ___*Yes, she is.*___

 b (at home) *Is she at home?* *No, she isn't*

2 a (hungry) *Is he hungry?* *Yes, he is*

 b (at the store) *Is he at the store?* *No, he not*

3 a (open) *Is the library open?* *No, it's not*

 b (a white building) *Is the library white building?*

 No, it's not

Exercise 2.2 Plural *Yes / No* Questions and Answers   Is, Are, Am

Complete the conversation between two students, John and Eric. Then practice their conversation with a partner.

1 **John** (your teachers / friendly) *Are your teachers friendly?*

2 **Eric** (yes) *Yes, they are.*

3 **John** (you and your classmates / happy) Are you and your classmate happy?

4 **Eric** (yes) Yes, they are.

5 **John** (the homework assignments / easy) Are the homework assigments /easy?

6 **Eric** (no) No, they're

7 **John** (your classmates / on time) Are your classmates on time?

8 **Eric** (no) No, they're not

9 **John** (you and your friends / busy) Are you and your friends / busy?

10 **Eric** (yes) Yes, we are

11 **John** (the exams / difficult) Are the exams / difficult?

12 **Eric** (yes) Yes, they are

Exercise 2.3 Singular and Plural *Yes / No* Questions and Answers

Read the paragraph from Julio's essay. Then write questions and answers about it. Use full forms of *be*.

Julio and Paulo

My roommate and I are in the English program at our college. Paulo is from Brazil, and I am from Venezuela. Paulo is a very good student, and he is very smart. I am a good student, but I am a little lazy. My classes are on Mondays, Wednesdays, and Fridays. Paulo's classes are every day from Monday to Friday. We are always busy, but on the weekend we relax.

1 Paulo and Julio / college students
  Are Paulo and Julio college students? Yes, they are.

2 they / from the same country
  Are they from the same country? No, they aren't

3 they / good students
  Are they good students? Yes, they are

4 Paulo / smart
  Is paulo smart? Yes, he is

5 Paulo / lazy
  Is paulo lazy? No, he is not

6 Julio's classes / every day from Monday to Friday
  Are julio's classes every day from monday to friday? No, they're not

3 Information Questions with *Be*

Grammar Presentation

Use the question words *who, what, when, where,* and *how* to ask for information.	*What's your name?* *Who is the teacher?* *Where are the classrooms?*

3.1 Information Questions

SINGULAR SUBJECTS

Wh- Word	Be	Subject
Who		your teacher?
What		your major?
When	is	our exam?
Where		the building?
How		your class?

PLURAL SUBJECTS

Wh- Word	Be	Subject
Who		your teachers?
What		your plans?
When	are	your exams?
Where		your books?
How		your classes?

3.2 Contractions with Singular Subjects

Who is	→	**Who's**
What is	→	**What's**
When is	→	**When's**
Where is	→	**Where's**
How is	→	**How's**

3.3 Using Information Questions with *Be*

A Put a question mark (?) at the end of information questions.	*Who are those students?*
B Put the question word first in an information question.	*What is your name?*
C Answer information questions with information. Don't answer with *Yes* or *No*.	*"When is grammar class?"* *"At 10:00."*
D In conversations, most answers are not complete sentences. They are short answers.	*"Who's your teacher?"* *"Mr. Jones."*
E Note that with singular subjects it is common to use the contracted form of *is* with the question word.	*What's your name?* *Where's your class?*

3.4 Using *Wh-* Words with *Be*

A Use *who* to ask about people.	*Who's our teacher?* *Who are your friends?*	Ms. Williams. Marie and Elsa.
B Use *what* to ask about things.	*What are your favorite classes?* *What's your phone number?*	Grammar and writing. It's 368-555-9823.
C Use *where* to ask about places.	*Where's your class?* *Where are you from?* *Where are your friends?*	It's in Building H. Brazil. They're in the computer lab.
D Use *when* to ask about days or times.	*When's your exam?* *When is lunch?* *When are our exams?*	It's February 14. At noon. Next week.
E Use *how* to ask about health or opinions.	*How's your mother?* *How's school?*	She's well. Great!
F Use *how much* to ask about cost and amount. Use *how many* to ask about numbers. Use *how old* to ask about age.	*How much is the movie?* *How many students are here?* *How old are your brothers?*	Twenty dollars. Twelve. They're 17 and 15.

Grammar Application

Exercise 3.1 Information Questions with *Be*

A Complete the conversation between Joe and his mother. Use the correct *Wh-* word. Use contractions of *be*.

Mother	_What's_ your roommate's name? (1)
Joe	Mike.
Mother	Where is he from? (2)
Joe	Chicago.
Mother	What is his major? (3)
Joe	I don't know. Mom, my history class is in five minutes.
Mother	Who is your instructor? (4)
Joe	I don't know his name. It's the first class.
Mother	What time is your class over? (5)
Joe	At 4:30. Please don't call before that.

B Complete the questions with *How, How much, How many,* or *How old.* Use the correct form of *be.*

1 _How are_ you?   I'm fine, thanks.

2 How old are you?   I'm 23.

3 How much the textbook?   It's $86.

4 How many students _are_ in your English class?   Thirty.

5 How much are the sandwiches?   They're $12.95.

Exercise 3.2 Information Questions and Answers

Write questions about the tuition bill. Then write answers in complete sentences.

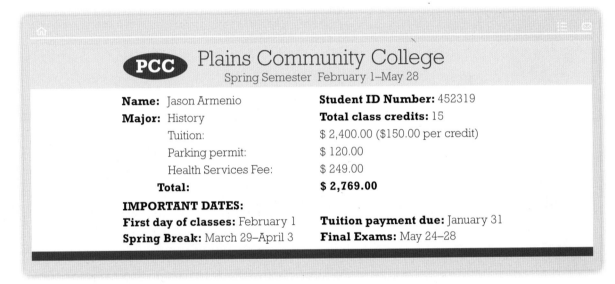

PCC Plains Community College
Spring Semester February 1–May 28

Name: Jason Armenio   **Student ID Number:** 452319

Major: History   **Total class credits:** 15

Tuition: $ 2,400.00 ($150.00 per credit)

Parking permit: $ 120.00

Health Services Fee: $ 249.00

Total: **$ 2,769.00**

IMPORTANT DATES:

First day of classes: February 1   **Tuition payment due:** January 31

Spring Break: March 29–April 3   **Final Exams:** May 24–28

1 (What/the college's name) _What is the college's name? It's Plains Community College._

2 (What/the student's name) What is the student's name? It's jason

3 (When/the spring semester) When is the spring semester?

4 (What/his major) What is his major? His major is history

5 (How much/the tuition) How much is the tuition? It's $2,400

6 (How much/the parking permit) How much is the parking permit?

7 (What/the total) What is the total? the total is $2,769.00

8 (When/final exams) When are final exams? they are may 24~28

3 – It's Feb 1 to may 28

6 – It's $120.00

Exercise 3.3 More Information Questions and Answers

Pair Work With a partner, write five questions to ask your classmates. Ask questions about their classes, schedules, and school. Then interview your classmates. Write their answers in the chart.

Interview Questions	Your Classmates' Answers
1 When are your classes?	My classes are on Monday and Wednesday. ~M T W TH F~
2 What time are your classes?	My classes are from 6-10
3 Where are you classes?	They are online.
4 What is you school's name?	It's Interactive College of technology
5 Who is your favorite teacher?	It's Ms.
6 Who are your classmates?	They're Gloria, Musa, etc.

4 Avoid Common Mistakes ⚠

1 Begin a question with a capital letter. End with a question mark.

W   ?
~where~ is Karla~.~

2 Remember that a question has a subject and a verb.

is
Where ~∧~ Room 203?

3 Don't use contractions with short *Yes* answers to *Yes / No* questions.

I am
"Are you tired?" "Yes, ~I'm~."

4 Make sure the subject and verb agree.

Are
~Is~ John and Pedro here?

5 Put the verb after the question word in information questions.

When is the writing class?
~When the writing class is?~

Editing Task

Find and correct the mistakes in these questions and answers about your school.

W
1 ~where~ is your school?

2 What is the school's name~.~?

is
3 How much ~∧~ the tuition ~is~?

Is
4 ~∧~ "your school expensive." "Yes, it's."
It is

is
5 What ~∧~ your major?

Are
6 ~Is~ you a good student?

is
7 When ~∧~ summer break ~is~?

Are
8 ~Is~ all your classes difficult?

Count Nouns; *A / An*; *Have* and *Be*

Gadgets

1 Grammar in the Real World

A Do you have a smartphone? If so, is your smartphone like these phones? Read the article. Which phone is best for you?

B Comprehension Check Answer the questions. Circle *Yes* or *No*. Use the web page to help you.

1 Are the two phones new models?   Yes   No

2 Is the MAX 3i $129?   Yes   No

3 Is the SmartX 2030's camera good?   Yes   No

C Notice Circle the correct words. Use the web page to help you.

1 The MAX 3i is **a / an** old model.

2 Jen is **a / an** busy person.

3 The battery life is 10 **hour / hours**.

4 This is a great **phone / phones** for me.

www.i-buy.net/electronics/smartphones/compare_products_max3i-smartX2030

GREAT PRICES ON
USED SMARTPHONES

 VS

MAX 3i

It's **an** old model, but it **has** all the basic features[1].

SmartX 2030

It's **a** new model and **has** lots of great new features.

PRICE

5

$159.00

$289.99

FEATURES

It's **a** camera, **a** phone, and **a** GPS. It's **an** amazing deal!

- ☑ Talk!
10
- ☑ Text.
- ☑ Play games!
- ☑ Listen to music!

It's **a** phone, **a** browser, **a** camera, **a** TV player, and it has **an** assistant to help you!

- ☑ Send texts, emails, photos and videos anytime, anyplace.
- ☑ Read news and weather updates.
- ☑ Shop online.
- ☑ Play games.
- ☑ Watch movies and TV or listen to music.

REVIEWS

15
Jen: I'm a busy person, and this is a great phone for me at college. It's perfect for students.

Mei: I'm an artist, and I need a good camera. This phone has **an** excellent camera for photos and video.

★★★☆☆

Niki: I like the size, and it's good for 20 texting and making calls, but the camera isn't very good.

★★★☆☆

Pedro143: The battery life is only **10 hours** (talk time), so that's not great. But it's a good phone.

[1]**feature:** an important characteristic

2 Nouns; *A/An*

Grammar Presentation

Nouns are words for people, places, and things.	*I'm an artist.* *It's an electronics store.* *It is a great phone.* *They are great phones.*

2.1 Singular and Plural Nouns

SINGULAR	PLURAL
It's a watch. *It's a good product.*	*They are watches.* *They are good products.*

2.2 Singular Nouns

A Count nouns have singular and plural forms.	*a book – three books one phone – two phones*
B Use *a* before singular count nouns that begin with a consonant sound (*b, c, d, f, g,* etc.).	*a cell phone a web browser* *a screen a camera*
C Use *an* before singular count nouns that begin with a vowel sound (*a, e, i, o, u*).	*an address book an advertisement* *an email an update*
Note: Some nouns that begin with the letter *u* have a consonant sound ("you").	*a unit a university*

▶▶ Indefinite and Definite Articles: See page A19.

2.3 Plural Nouns

A Add *-s* to most singular nouns to form plural nouns.	*a model – two models a device – two devices* *a key – keys a student – students*
B Add *-es* to nouns that end in *-ch, -sh, -ss, -z,* and *-x*.	*watch – watches class – classes* *dish – dishes tax – taxes*

2.3 Plural Nouns *(continued)*

C With nouns that end in consonant + *y*, change the *y* to *i* and add *-es*.	*battery – batteries* *accessory – accessories*
D With nouns that end in *-ife*, change the ending to *-ives*.	*life – lives* *knife – knives*

2.4 Irregular Plural Nouns

A Some plural nouns have irregular forms. 📊 These are the most common irregular plural nouns in academic writing.	*man – men* *woman – women* *child – children* *person – people* *foot – feet* *tooth – teeth*
B Some nouns have the same form for singular and plural.	*one fish – two fish* *one sheep – two sheep*
C Some nouns are only plural. They do not have a singular form.	*clothes* *jeans* *scissors* *headphones* *pants* *sunglasses*

▸▸ Spelling Rules for Noun Plurals: See page A2.

2.5 Proper Nouns

Proper nouns are the names of specific people, places, and things. They begin with capital letters.	*Jenny* *Mr. Johns* *Ms. Thorson* *Canada* *Dallas* *Chester College* *San Francisco Herald*

▸▸ Capitalization and Punctuation Rules: See page A1.

🖥 Grammar Application

Exercise 2.1 *A or An*

A Write *a* or *an* next to each noun.

1	*a* pencil	5	*an* address book	
2	*an* eraser	6	*a* calculator	
3	*a* camera	7	*a* wallet	
4	*a* laptop	8	*a* notebook	

B Over to You Ask and answer questions about things in the classroom. Use *a* or *an*. Make a list of the new words you learn.

A *What's the word for this in English?* *an*

B *It's a desk. / I don't know. Let's ask the teacher.*

A Look at this store advertisement. Write the plural form of the nouns. For nouns that have only one form, leave the space blank.

Shop at THE MART

This Week's Sale Prices

Electronics

battery _ies_	$15
calculator_s_	$129
headphones_____	$5–$65
cell phone _s_	$60–$200
computer _s_	$800–$4,000
video camera _s_	$400–$1,000

School Supply _ies_

dictionary _ies_	$19–$49.95
scissors_____	$2.95–$10
notebook _s_	$2.99–$17.99

Clothes and Accessory_____

dress _es_	$49–$239
belt _s_	$24–$89
sunglasses_____	$19.99–$289
purse _s_	$29.99–$239
jeans_____	$39–$160

B Pair Work Practice asking and answering questions about the items in A with a partner.

A *How much are the belts?*
B *They're $24–$89.*

For nouns that end in the sounds /s/, /ʃ/, /tʃ/, /dʒ/, /ks/, and /z/, say /əz/ in the plural. These nouns have an extra syllable in the plural form.	**/əz/** /s/ cla**ss** – classes /ʃ/ di**sh** – dishes /tʃ/ wat**ch** – watches /dʒ/ messa**ge** – messages /ks/ bo**x** – boxes /z/ qui**z** – quizzes
For most other nouns, say /s/ or /z/ in the plural.	**/s/ or /z/** boo**k** – books pho**ne** – phones accessor**y** – accessories

A Listen. Check (✓) the nouns with an extra syllable in the plural form.

☑ **1** purse – purses   ☐ **4** door – doors   ☐ **7** page – pages

☐ **2** bag – bags   ☐ **5** size – sizes   ☐ **8** closet – closets

☐ **3** map – maps   ☐ **6** computer – computers   ☐ **9** phone – phones

B Write the plural form of these nouns. Do they have an extra syllable? Check (✓) *Yes* or *No*.

	Extra Syllable?				Extra Syllable?	
	Yes	**No**			**Yes**	**No**
1 desk _desks_	☐	☑	**8** brush brushes		☐	☐
2 tax taxes	☐	☐	**9** dictionary dictionaries	☐	☐
3 monitor monitors	☐	☐	**10** match matches	☐	☐
4 case cases	☐	☐	**11** chair chairs	☐	☐
5 orange oranges	☐	☐	**12** quiz quizes	☐	☐
6 penny pennies	☐	☐	**13** pen pens	☐	☐
7 student students	☐	☐	**14** garage garages	☐	☐

Exercise 2.4 Proper Nouns

Write answers to the questions. Use proper nouns.

1 What's the capital of the United States? _It's Washington, D.C._

2 What's your last name? _Maldonado_

3 What's the name of the street where you live? _Sunset maple trail_

4 What's the name of your hometown? _Michoacan_

5 What's the name of your favorite movie? _Scary movies_

3 *Be* with *A / An* + Noun

Grammar Presentation

3.1 Using *Be* with *A / An* + Noun

A You can use *be* with *a / an* + noun to tell:	*It's a watch. It's an activity tracker, too.*
• what something is.	*It's a great phone.*
• what something is like.	*Jon is a friend from college.*
• who someone is.	*He's a nice guy.*
• what someone is like.	
B You can use *be* + *a / an* + noun to say a person's occupation.	*Jenny is a businesswoman.* *Pedro is an architect.*
C Don't use *a / an* with plural nouns.	*They're cell phones.* NOT *They are a cell phones.*

Pronunciation note: *A* and *an* are not usually stressed. *a* = /ə/ and *an* = /ən/
/ə/ CELL phone   /ən/ ARchitect

Grammar Application

Exercise 3.1 A/An + Noun

Complete the conversation with *a* or *an*.

A Is that __*a*__ regular watch? Is it ___an___ activity
   (1)   (2)
tracker, too?

B Both, It's my new toy. It's ___a___ smart watch.
                                  (3)

A Cool. Oh, look! Is that ___a___ message?
                              (4)

B No, it's ___a___ text from Jeff.
           (5)

A Jeff? Is he ___a___ friend?
              (6)

B Yes, from high school. He's now ___an___ engineering student at ___an___ university in
                                      (7)   (8)
Florida. He's in town with his brother, Dan. Dan's ___an___ artist.
                                                    (9)

A Wow. So, where are they?

B They're at ___a___ coffee shop near here. Let's go see them.
             (10)

A That sounds like fun. Let's get ___a___ taxi.
                                      (11)

Exercise 3.2 A/An + Noun: Occupations

A Match the occupations and the pictures. Write the correct letter next to the names. Then complete the sentences below. Make some occupations plural.

| a chef | b electrician | c engineer | d mechanic | e pharmacist | f receptionist |

1 Mike __c__   **2** Carl __a__   **3** Julia __f__   **4** Jody and Bryan __d__

1 Mike *is an engineer.*

2 Carl is a chef

3 Julia is a receptionist

4 Jody and Bryan are mechanics

5 Sarah is a pharmacist

6 Ana is an electrician

5 Sarah __e__   **6** Ana __b__

B Over to You Write sentences about people you know.

1 I am *a student. I'm also a part-time salesclerk.*

2 My friend is a doctor.

3 My neighbor is an attorney / is a lawyer.

4 My friends are mechanics and scientists. They are very busy.

5 My classmate's name is musa . He/She is tall and smart.

6 My mother is a housewife.
(family member)

4 Have

Grammar Presentation

Have can show possession. It can also mean "to experience."	He **has** a nice apartment. (possession) My friends and I **have** a good time together. (experience)

4.1 Have

Subject	Have	
I We You They	**have**	a camera.
He She It	**has**	

4.2 Using Have

A Use *have* + noun to show: • possession or ownership. • relationships. • parts of a whole.	I *have* a car. She *has* a friend from Chile. The website *has* helpful links.
B It can also mean "to experience" or "to take part in an activity."	We *have* fun in class. They *have* lunch at 12:30.

Grammar Application

Complete the sentences. Use *have* or *has*.

1 Big Electric is an electronics store. It usually __has__ good prices.

2 The store is very large. It __has__ four floors.

3 The first floor __has__ computers and phones.

4 The second floor __has__ video game consoles and video games.

5 The third and fourth floors __have__ TVs, sound systems, and entertainment systems.

6 Big Electric also __has__ a website.

7 The website sometimes __has__ special sale prices.

8 Customers __have__ a lot of fun shopping here.

Exercise 4.2 *Have and Be*

Complete the sentences from a student essay. Use *have*, *has*, *am*, *is*, or *are*.

My Favorite Gadget

Let me tell you about my computer. It __is__ an old laptop, but it __is__ a good
(1)   (2)
computer. It only weighs two pounds, so it __is__ not very heavy. It __has__
(3)   (4)
great speakers, and it also __has__ a bright, colorful screen. It __is__ great for
(5)   (6)
movies and music. It __is__ also good for email. I __am__ a student, so my
(7)   (8)
laptop __is__ very important for me. I use it to do almost all my homework.
(9)
Of course, this laptop also __has__ a webcam, so I use it to talk to my friends in
(10)
Mexico. I __have__ a lot of friends there, and we __are__ always happy to see each
(11)   (12)
other and talk. Sometimes I __have__ problems with my laptop. For example, the
(13)
battery __is__ not very good, and the hard drive __is__ slow. I want a new one,
(14)   (15)
but good laptops __are__ expensive.
(16)

5 Avoid Common Mistakes ⚠

1 **Use *a* or *an* to say a person's job.**

        an
Jody is artist.

2 **Use *a* or *an* to say what kind of a person someone is.**

        a
She's nice person.

3 **Use *are* after plural nouns. Remember: *people*, *men*, *women*, and *children* are plural.**

        are
The people in my class is nice.

        are
His children is smart.

4 **Use *are* with two nouns joined with *and*.**

        are
My phone and my laptop is on my desk.

5 **Use *has* with a singular subject.**

        has
Tom have a great laptop.

Editing Task

Find and correct nine more mistakes about the Lim family.

                                    are
1 The people in my neighborhood is nice.

                    are
2 My neighbors is very friendly.

                      are
3 Tom and Nancy Lim is my neighbors.

           a
4 Nancy is computer programmer.

       a
5 Tom is cell phone designer.

                are
6 Their children is Joe and Cathy.

                are
7 Joe and Cathy is students at Hatfield College.

      a
8 Joe is student in the computer department.

       has
9 He have a lot of classes this year.

             a
10 Cathy is busy architecture student.

4 Demonstratives and Possessives

12/16/20

The Workplace

1 Grammar in the Real World

A Can you name five things that you use in an office? Read the conversation. How many different office things do the speakers mention in the conversation?

B Comprehension Check Match the two parts of the sentences about the conversation.

1 Claudia __c__   **a** are in the cabinets.

2 Keung __e__   **b** are his sister's children.

3 The little girls in the photograph __b__   **c** is a new employee.

4 Office supplies __a__   **d** is in the conference room.

5 The meeting __d__   **e** is on her team.

C Notice Find the sentences in the conversation and circle the correct words.

1 The paper is in **these**/ **this** *drawers* below the printers.

2 **Those**/**That** *photograph* on the left is great.

3 **That**/**Those** little *girls* are my sister's children.

4 It's **this**/ **these** *way*, down the hall.

Now look at the nouns in *italics*. What words come before the singular nouns? What words come before the plural nouns?

FIRST DAY AT THE OFFICE

Robert Hello, Claudia. I'm Robert. Welcome to **our** company!

Claudia Hello, Robert. It's nice to meet you.

5 **Robert** **This** is **your** desk. **That's** the closet for **your** coat. Let me show you around.

Claudia Thanks.

Robert Office supplies, like paper,
10 folders, and pens, are in **those** cabinets over there. The printers are here, and **this** is the only copy machine. The paper is in **these** drawers below
15 the printers.

Claudia Thanks. **That's** good to know.

Robert Now, let me introduce you to Keung. He's on **your** team. Keung, **this** is Claudia. She's
20 **our** new sales manager.

Keung Nice to meet you, Claudia.

Claudia Nice to meet you, Keung. **Those** photographs are beautiful. Are you a photographer?

Keung Well, photography is **my** hobby. 25 **Those** pictures are from **my** trip to Thailand.

Claudia **That** photograph on the left is great. What is it?

Keung It's the Royal Palace in Bangkok, 30 **my** favorite place.

Claudia **That's** a great picture, too.

Keung **Those** little girls are **my sister's** children. She lives in Bangkok.

Robert Sorry to interrupt, but we have 35 a management meeting in 10 minutes. It's in the conference room. It's **this** way, down the hall. Let's get some coffee before the meeting. 40

Claudia OK. See you later, Keung.

Keung Wait. Robert, are **these your** reports?

Robert Yes, they are. Thanks. I need them for the meeting. 45

2 Demonstratives (*This, That, These, Those*)

Grammar Presentation

The demonstratives are *this, that, these,* and *those.* We use demonstratives to "point to" things and people.	**This** is my desk. **Those** desks are for new employees.

2.1 Demonstratives with Singular and Plural Nouns

SINGULAR

This/That	Noun	Verb	
This	drawer	is	empty.
That			for paper.

PLURAL

These/Those	Noun	Verb	
These	cabinets	are	for supplies.
Those			locked.

2.2 Demonstratives Used Without Nouns

SINGULAR

This/That	Verb	
This	is	for you.
That		my desk.

PLURAL

These/Those	Verb	
These	are	from your co-workers.
Those		for us.

2.3 Using Demonstratives with Singular and Plural Nouns

A Use *this* for a person or thing <u>near</u> you (a person or thing that is <u>here</u>).	*This* desk is Amanda's. *This* paper is for the printer.
B Use *that* for a person or thing <u>not near</u> you (a person or thing that is <u>there</u>).	*That* desk is Janet's. *That* printer is a 3D printer.
C Use *these* for people or things <u>near</u> you (people or things that are <u>here</u>).	*These* reports are for the meeting. *These* students are in your English class.

2.3 | Using Demonstratives with Singular and Plural Nouns *(continued)*

D Use *those* for people or things <u>not near</u> you (people or things that are <u>there</u>).	*Those folders are the sales reports.* *Those soccer players are great.*
E Use *this, that, these,* and *those* before nouns to identify and describe people and things.	*This photo is my favorite.* *That little girl in the photo is my sister's daughter.* *These charts are helpful.* *Those papers are important.*

2.4 | Using Demonstratives with *Be*

A You can use *this, that, these,* and *those* as pronouns to identify things.	*This is the only copy machine.* *= This copy machine is the only copy machine.* *That is the color printer.* *= That printer is the color printer.* *These are the reports for the meeting.* *= These reports are the reports for the meeting.* *Those are my keys.* *= Those keys are my keys.*
B You can only use *this* and *these* as pronouns to introduce people.	**A** *This is Claudia.* **B** *Hi, Claudia! Nice to meet you.* **A** *These are my co-workers, Mena and Liz.* **B** *Hello. Nice to meet you.*
C In informal speaking, use the contraction *that's* instead of *that is.*	*That's a nice picture.*

2.5 | Questions with Demonstratives

A To identify people, ask questions with *Who is . . . ?* If it's clear who you are talking about, you can omit the noun.	*Who is that new teacher?* *Who is that?*
B To identify things, ask questions with *What is . . . ?* If it's clear what you are talking about, you can omit the noun.	*What is that noise?* *What is that?*

C To ask about a price, use *How much is / are . . . ?* If it's clear what you are talking about, you can omit the noun.	*How much is* this printer? *How much is* this? *How much are* these printers? *How much are* these?
D After questions with *this* and *that*, answer with *it* for things and *he* or *she* for people.	"*How much is* **this** copier?" "**It**'s $400." "*Who is* **that** woman?" "**She**'s my boss."
E After questions with *these* and *those*, answer with *they*.	"*Are* **these** your reports?" "Yes, **they** are." "*Who are* **those** people?" "**They**'re my co-workers."

Grammar Application

Help Margo describe her office. Write *this* or *these* for things that are near her, and *that* or *those* for things that are **not** near her.

1 _**This**_ phone is old.
2 _That_ closet is for her coat.
3 _Those_ books are about business.
4 _This_ computer is old.
5 _These_ pens are very good.
6 _That_ window is open.
7 _These_ papers are for the meeting.
8 _That_ cabinet is for paper clips, folders, and general office things.
9 _That_ picture is a photograph of her family.
10 _These_ folders are for the sales reports.

Exercise 2.2 More Demonstratives with Singular and Plural Nouns

Pair Work What's in your pocket? What's in your bag? Tell your partner using *this* and *these*. Then your partner repeats everything using *that* and *those*.

A *This is a cell phone. These are keys. This is a pen. These are pencils. This is a paper clip.*

B *OK. That's a cell phone. Those are keys. That's a pen. Those are pencils. That's a paper clip.*

Exercise 2.3 Demonstratives Without Nouns

A Which noun isn't necessary? Cross out the noun. Check (✓) the sentences where you cannot cross out the noun.

Jane	How much are these (1) ~~flash drives~~?
Salesclerk	$30.
Jane	Thank you. That's a nice (2) *computer*. ✓
Lisa	Yes, it has a big screen. What's that (3) *thing* on the front?
Salesclerk	It's the webcam. And here's the headphone jack.
Jane	Yeah. Is this (4) *model* a new model?
Salesclerk	No. This (5) *model* is an old model. That's why it's on sale. That's (6) *the new model* over there.
Jane	Oh, I see. Hey, these (7) *headphones* are great headphones.
Lisa	Yeah? Buy them!
Jane	Hmm . . . They're $250. No, thank you!

 B Listen to the conversation and check your answers.

Exercise 2.4 Questions and Answers with Demonstratives

Circle the correct words.

1 **A** How much is **these /(that)** printer, please? **B** (**It's**)**/ They're** $220.

2 **A** Excuse me, how much are (**these**)**/ this** scanners? **B** **It's /(They're)** $250.

3 **A** How much is **those /(this)** projector? **B** (**It's**)**/ They're** $899.

4 **A** Excuse me, how much are **that /(those)** pens? **B** **It's /(They're)** $7.99.

5 **A** How much are (**these**)**/ that** laptops? **B** **It's /(They're)** on sale. **It's /(They're)** $1,100.

6 **A** How much is **those /(that)** digital photo frame? **B** (**It's**)**/ They're** $80.

Pair Work Look around your classroom. In each box, write the names of three more things you see.

	Near Me	Not Near Me
Singular	a desk, . . .	a map, . . .
Plural	books, . . .	windows, . . .

Ask your partner *Yes/No* questions about the things above. Answer with *it* (singular) or *they* (plural).

A Is **that** a map of Iowa?

B No, **it**'s not. **It**'s a map of Illinois.

A Are **these** books new?

B Yes, **they** are.

You can use short responses with *That's* + adjective in conversations.	A I have a new job.	A My printer is broken.
	B *That's* great! / *That's* good!	B *That's* too bad.
Here are common adjectives to use with *that's*.	excellent good great interesting nice OK terrible too bad wonderful	

Write a response with *That's* + adjective. Use the adjectives above.

1 It's a holiday tomorrow. *That's nice.*

2 We're on the same team! That's great

3 Business isn't very good this year. That's terrible

4 Patricia's not here today. She's sick. That's too bad

5 I have a new laptop! That's excellent

6 This phone has a dictionary app. That's interesting

3 Possessives and *Whose*

Grammar Presentation

Possessives show that someone possesses (owns or has) something.	**A** *Is this Diane's desk?* **B** *No, it's my desk. Her desk is in the other office. Her boss's desk is in that office, too.*

3.1 *My, Your, His, Her, Its, Our, Their*

Subject	Possessive	
I	my	I'm not ready for the meeting. *My* presentation isn't finished.
you	your	You are very organized. *Your* space is so neat.
he	his	He is a new employee. *His* old job was in Hong Kong.
she	her	She isn't in the office now. *Her* computer is off.
it	its	It is a technology start-up. *Its* CEO is Prima Janesh.
we	our	We have the reports. *Our* boss wants to read them now.
you	your	You are co-workers. *Your* office is on the second floor.
they	their	They are at the office. *Their* boss is on vacation.

▶▶ Subject and Object Pronouns: See page A18.

3.2 Possessive Nouns

A Add 's to singular nouns to show possession.	The *manager's* name *(one manager)* The *boss's* ideas *(one boss)*
B Add an apostrophe (') to plural nouns ending in -s to show possession.	The *managers'* names *(more than one manager)* The *bosses'* ideas *(more than one boss)*
C For irregular plural nouns, add 's to show possession.	The *men's* books *(more than one man)* The *children's* room *(more than one child)*
D *My, your, his, her, our,* and *their* can come before a possessive noun.	*my friend's* job *our parents' names*

▶▶ Capitalization and Punctuation Rules: See page A1.

3.3 Whose?

A We can use *whose* to ask who owns something. We can use it with singular and plural nouns.

Whose jacket is this?
I think that's Kana's jacket.

B We often use *whose* with *this, that, these,* and *those.*

Whose papers are those?
Oh! They're my papers. Thank you.

3.4 Using Possessives

A Use the same possessive form before a singular noun or a plural noun.

SINGULAR	PLURAL
my friend	*my friends*
her report	*her reports*
the boss's report	*the boss's reports*

B Use a possessive to show that someone owns something.

her pen   *their folders*   *Rachel's car*

C Use a possessive to show that someone has something.

your name   *my birthday*   *Jared's job*

D Use a possessive to show relationships between people.

my sister   *his boss*   *Claudia's co-worker*

E Use a possessive noun to talk about places and countries.

The city's population
Japan's prime minister

Grammar Application

Exercise 3.1 Possessives

Ben sends an e-mail to Dora and attaches some pictures. He describes them. Complete the e-mail. Use the possessive form of the pronoun in parentheses – *my, his, her, its, our, their* – or *'s*.

Hi Dora,

Here are the photos of __*our*__ (we) end-of-semester party
(1)

for _____ (we) English class. The first photo is Juliana
(2)

and Sue-jin. Is Juliana in _____ (you) math class?
(3)

5 She's sometimes _____ (I) partner in pair work.
(4)

Sue-jin is _____ (she) best friend.
(5)

Then, in the second photo, the woman in the white

shirt is Sally. She's _____ (Juliana) sister. _____
(6) (7)

(They) family is in Chicago, but Sally is here, too. The tall

10 man is Mr. Donovan. He's _____ (we) new teacher.
(8)

_____ (He) first name is Howard, and he's very
(9)

friendly. In this photo we're in the hall near _____
(10)

(Mr. Donovan) office. Send me some pictures of

your class.

15 Ben

Exercise 3.2 Possessive 's or s'?

A Circle the correct form of the possessive ('s or s') in the sentences.

1 My **co-worker's** / **co-workers'** name is Krista.

2 **Krista's** / **Kristas'** last name is Logan.

3 She has two managers. Her **manager's** / **managers'** names are Tom and Sara.

4 **Sara's** / **Saras'** family is from Colombia.

5 She has two brothers. Her **brother's** / **brothers'** names are José and Carlos.

6 **Tom's** / **Toms'** wife is from New Jersey. Her name is Jessica.

7 Jessica and Tom have a daughter. Their **daughter's** / **daughters'** name is Danielle.

8 They have two cats. The **cat's** / **cats'** names are Sam and Max.

B Pair Work Tell a partner about someone you know at work or about a friend at school.
Use the sentences in A as a model.

A Complete the questions about the people in the photos with *Whose* and *Who's*. Then answer the questions.

Name: Ling Yang
Nationality: Chinese
Birthday: October 2
Best friend: Leila
Major: Nursing
Interests: yoga, art

Name: Ki-woon Do
Nationality: South Korean
Birthday: June 5
Best friend: Nora
Major: Business
Interests: soccer, movies

Name: Missolle Beauge
Nationality: Haitian
Birthday: April 7
Best friend: Lona
Major: Computers and Technology
Interests: music, cooking

1 ___*Whose*___ best friend is Leila?   *Leila is Ling's best friend.*

2 _____ birthday is in June? _____

3 _____ Chinese? _____

4 _____ major is Business? _____

5 _____ Haitian? _____

6 _____ from South Korea? _____

7 _____ major is Nursing? _____

8 _____ birthday is in October? _____

9 _____ interested in soccer? _____

10 _____ interests are music and cooking? _____

B Pair Work Ask and answer other questions about the people in A.

A *Whose best friend is Nora?*
B *Nora is Ki-woon's best friend.*

4 Avoid Common Mistakes ⚠

1 **Use *this* and *that* for singular things and people.**

~~These~~ *This* printer is $179.

~~Those~~ *That* man is my manager.

2 **Use *these* and *those* for plural things and people.**

~~This~~ *These* folders are for the meeting.

~~That~~ *Those* women are on my team.

3 ***Its* is possessive. *It's* is a contraction for *it is.***

He works for a small company. ~~It's~~ *Its* name is Z-Tech. ~~Its~~ *It's* on Main Street.

4 **Use *'s* (singular) or *s'* (plural) with possessive nouns.**

Tomorrow is her ~~mother~~ *mother's* birthday.   I don't know my ~~co-workers~~ *co-workers'* birthdays.

5 **Use the same possessive form before a singular noun or a plural noun.**

Justine enjoys spending time with ~~hers~~ *her* co-workers.

Editing Task

Find and correct eight more mistakes in this conversation.

A Hi. I'm sorry to interrupt you, but where's the manager*'s* office?

B Its next to Claudia office.

A Where is those? I don't know Claudia.

B Oh, it's down these hallway right here. Turn left after you pass that two elevators.

A Oh, OK. You mean its near the two assistants office.

B That's right. Do you know them?

A Yes, I do.

B Then please give them a message. Theirs folders are on my desk.

Descriptive Adjectives

Skills and Qualities for Success

1 Grammar in the Real World

A Do you use a social networking website? Which one? Read the web article about a social networking site for jobs. Are these websites useful for employers?

B Comprehension Check Answer the questions. Use the article to help you.

1 What is JobsLink?

2 Is Julia a student or an instructor?

3 Is Ricardo an employee or an employer?

4 Who has an interview with Ricardo?

C Notice The nouns in each sentence are underlined. Circle the word that describes each noun. These words are adjectives.

1 Companies can find new <u>workers</u>.

2 He has a small <u>business</u>.

3 Julia is a hardworking <u>student</u> at a large <u>community college</u>.

4 Julia has a new <u>job</u>.

Do the adjectives come before or after the nouns?

USING SOCIAL MEDIA
FOR JOBS

Sometimes, social networking websites[1] are for sending news, messages, and photos to friends. They're like **big** bulletin boards on the Internet. Now social networking websites are for work, too. **Unemployed**[2] people can find jobs there, and companies can find **new** 5 workers. Some sites also have a lot of very **useful** information about jobs and careers.

Here is the story of two people who use JobsLink, a social networking website for business professionals.

Julia is a **hardworking** student at a **large** community college. She's 10 very **busy** with her courses, but she is also **ambitious**.[3] Her career goal is to be an accountant. She has a profile on JobsLink. Her profile has a link[4] to her résumé.

Ricardo is an employer. He has a **small** business. His accounting office needs a **new** accountant. He's interested in Julia's profile on 15 JobsLink. She's **young**, but she's an **excellent** student. Ricardo contacts Julia by e-mail. She has an interview with Ricardo. He thinks that Julia is **friendly** and **smart**. Soon, Julia has a **new** job. Julia and Ricardo are **happy** with JobsLink.

[1]social networking websites: places on the Internet for meeting and talking to people

[2]unemployed: not having a job that earns money

[3]ambitious: wanting success

[4]link: a word or image on a website that can take you to another document or website

2 Adjectives

Grammar Presentation

Adjectives describe or give information about nouns – people, places, things, and ideas.	I found a *good* job. (*Good* describes *job*.) This website is *helpful*. (*Helpful* describes *this website*.)

2.1 Adjectives

A Adjectives can come before nouns.

		ADJECTIVE	NOUN
He owns a		*small*	*business*.
She has a		*new*	*job*.

B Adjectives can come after the verb *be*. They describe the subject.

SUBJECT	BE	ADJECTIVE
Julia	*is*	*smart*.
They	*are*	*young*.

C Adjectives have the same form when they describe singular or plural nouns.

	ADJECTIVE	NOUN (SINGULAR)
He needs a	*good*	*accountant*.

	ADJECTIVE	NOUN (PLURAL)
He needs two	*good*	*accountants*.

2.2 Using Adjectives

A When using an adjective before a singular noun:
- use *a* before adjectives that begin with a consonant[1] sound.

They work for *a big* company.
She has *a long* résumé.
A new student is in my class.

- use *an* before adjectives that begin with a vowel[2] sound.

He has *an interesting* blog.
She's *an ambitious* businessperson.
That's *an excellent* idea!

B You can use adjectives to describe:
- color
- age
- size
- shape
- opinions
- length of time

a *blue* suit	an *orange* skirt
a *new* website	an *old* résumé
a *tall* building	a *small* phone
a *wide* street	a *round* window
a *great* job	an *excellent* student
a *short* meeting	a *long* vacation

C You can use *very* to make the adjective stronger.

The meeting was *very long*.

Reminder:
[1]**Consonants:** the letters *b, c, d, f, g, h, j, k, l, m, n, p, q, r, s, t, v, w, x, y, z*
[2]**Vowels:** the letters *a, e, i, o, u*

Data from the Real World

These adjectives are used after the verb *be*. Do *not* use them before a noun.

afraid, alone, asleep, awake
Ahmed is asleep.
NOT Ahmed is ~~the asleep man~~.

Grammar Application

Exercise 2.1 Adjective + Noun

A Rewrite the sentences with the adjectives in parentheses.

1 James is an engineer. (unemployed) *James is an unemployed engineer.*

2 James is a person. (hardworking) _____

3 This is a website. (useful) _____

4 It has jobs. (interesting) _____

5 This is a company. (large) _____

6 James can send his résumé. (new) _____

B Write sentences about the people and things in parentheses. Use your own ideas and some of the adjectives from the box. Remember to put the adjectives before the nouns.

ambitious	busy	friendly	interesting	popular	unusual
big	difficult	good	kind	smart	useful

1 (company) *Microsoft is a big company.* _____

2 (person) _____

3 (website) _____

4 (job) _____

5 (employer) _____

6 (student) _____

asleep / awake	good / bad	old / new (things)	*My office isn't loud. It's quiet.*
big / little	happy / sad	old / young (people or animals)	*Please be early. Don't be late.*
big / small	hot / cold	short / long	*This résumé is old, but that one*
early / late	loud / quiet	short / tall	*is new.*

Note: *Big* has two opposites, *little* and *small*. *Short* has two opposites, *tall* and *long*. *Tall* is for height. *Long* is for length, distance, or time.
Old has two opposites, *new* and *young*. *New* is for things, and *young* is for people or animals.

A Complete the sentences with their opposites. Use adjectives from the Vocabulary Focus box.

1 I'm not asleep right now. I'm ___*awake*___ .

2 This is a _____ resumé.
   It's not old.

3 The office is very _____ .
   There are only two people here.
   It isn't big.

4 The office building is _____ .
   It isn't short. It has 50 floors.

5 Today isn't bad. This is a _____ day!
   I have a new job!

6 Do you have a _____ ruler?
   This one is short.

B Pair Work Work with a partner. Make sentences with adjectives from the Vocabulary Focus box. Your partner makes sentences with the opposite adjectives. Take turns.

A *This isn't a little book.*
B *It's a big book.*

A *I'm tall.*
B *Maria is short.*

C Complete the e-mail. Use the adjectives from the box.

~~excited~~	happy	interesting	long	young
friendly	helpful	late	old	

Hi Ramon,

How are you? I'm very ___*excited*___ about my new job. My work hours are _____ .
                        (1)   (2)
For example, I usually work from 8:00 a.m. until 6:00 p.m.

But I'm _____ because it's an _____ job. I am a research assistant
        (3)   (4)
in a hospital. My office is on the tenth floor. It's an _____ building.
                                                        (5)
It's 60 years old. My boss is _____ – he's only 30. He's _____ and
                              (6)   (7)
_____ when I have questions.
(8)
That's all for now. It's _____ at night and I'm tired. Please write soon.
                         (9)

Take care,

Jack

Exercise 2.3 Vocabulary Focus: Nationality Adjectives

Ending in -*an* or -*ian*		Ending in -*ish*	Ending in -*ese*	Ending in -*i*
African	Indian	British	Chinese	Iraqi
American	Indonesian	Danish	Japanese	Israeli
Australian	Italian	English	Lebanese	Kuwaiti
Austrian	Korean	Irish	Portuguese	Omani
Brazilian	Mexican	Polish	Sudanese	Pakistani
Canadian	Nigerian	Scottish	Vietnamese	Qatari
Chilean	Peruvian	Spanish		Saudi
Egyptian	Russian	Swedish		Yemeni
Ethiopian	Syrian	Turkish		
German	Venezuelan			

Exceptions: Dutch (from the Netherlands), Filipino (from the Philippines), French (from France), Greek (from Greece), Swiss (from Switzerland), Thai (from Thailand)

A Complete the sentences. Use nationality adjectives.

1 Paula is from Brazil. She's _____*Brazilian*_____ .

2 My co-workers are from Chile. They're _____ .

3 Hakim is from Kuwait. He's _____ .

4 Alex is from Germany. He's _____ .

5 Vinh is from Vietnam. He's _____ .

6 Sarah is from England. She's _____ .

B Over to You Write three sentences about yourself. Then write sentences about three people from other countries. Remember to capitalize the names of countries and languages.

My name is Claudia. I'm from Mexico. I'm Mexican.

3 Questions with *What . . . like?* and *How + Adjective*

Grammar Presentation

Questions with *What . . . like?* and *How +* adjective ask for a description. They are usually answered with an adjective.	**A** *"What is Arizona like?"* **B** *"It's beautiful."* **A** *"How deep is the Grand Canyon?"* **B** *"It's very deep."*

3.1 Questions with *What . . . like?*

What + Be	Subject	*Like*	Answers with Adjectives
What is **What's**	New York	**like?**	It's **big**.
What are	the restaurants		They're **expensive**.

3.2 Questions with *How + Adjective*

How	Adjective	*Be*	Subject	Answers with Adjectives
How	**old**	is	the company?	It's 40 years **old**.
	tall	is	Jack?	He's 6 feet (1.80 meters) **tall**.
	long	are	the lines?	They're not **long**. They're very **short**.
	cold	is	the water?	It's not very **cold**. It's **warm**.

Grammar Application

Exercise 3.1 Questions with *What . . . like?*

A Complete the conversation about the city of St. Louis. Use *What . . . like* in the questions. Then choose an answer from the box.

> It's very cold, and it's snowy. They're good and not too expensive.
> It's an old Midwestern city in Missouri. They're very friendly.

John I have exciting news! I have a new job!

Erica That's great!

John Well, the bad news is this: It's in St. Louis. It's not here in Chicago.

Erica Wow! <u>*What's*</u> St. Louis <u>*like*</u> ?
(1)(1)

John _____
(2)

Erica _____ the weather _____
(3)(3)
in the winter?

John _____
(4)

Erica _____ the people _____?
(5)(5)

John	_____
	(6)

Erica _____ the restaurants _____?
      (7)   (7)

John _____
                    (8)

 B Listen to the conversation and check your answers.

C Over to You Write questions with *What . . . like in your city?* Then answer the questions with *It's* or *They're.*

1 (the weather)

    A *What's the weather like in your city?*

    B *It's very hot in the summer.*

2 (the traffic)

    A _____

    B _____

3 (the people)

    A _____

    B _____

4 (the shopping)

    A _____

    B _____

5 (the restaurants)

    A _____

    B _____

6 (the nightlife)

    A _____

    B _____

7 (the winters)

    A _____

    B _____

8 (the public transportation)

    A _____

    B _____

D Pair Work Ask and answer questions with a partner.

Exercise 3.2 Questions with *How* + Adjective

A Complete these questions with *How* and an adjective from the box.

bad	cold	crowded	expensive	hot	old

1 _____*How old*_____ is your city?

2 _____ is it in the summer?

3 _____ is it in the winter?

4 _____ is the downtown area with people?

5 _____ are the apartments?

6 _____ is the traffic?

B Write the answers to the questions above about your city. Then ask and answer the questions with a partner.

1 _____

2 _____

3 _____

4 _____

5 _____

6 _____

A *How old is your city?*   **B** *It's really old. It's about 200 years old.*

C Pair Work Write six questions about a city to ask your partner. Write two with *What . . . like?* and three with *How + adjective*. Your partner chooses a city. Then you ask the questions and guess the city.

1 What *are winters like in this city?* _____

2 What _____

3 What _____

4 How _____

5 How _____

6 How _____

7 Let me guess. Is this city _____

4 Avoid Common Mistakes ⚠

1	**An adjective can come before the noun it describes or after the verb be.**
	long meeting *is* I have a ~~meeting long~~ every Wednesday. This meeting important.

2	**Adjectives do not have plural forms.**
	wonderful I have three ~~wonderfuls~~ employees.

3	**Use *an* before adjectives that begin with a vowel sound. Use *a* before adjectives that begin with a consonant sound.**
	an *a* My sister is ~~a~~ ambitious person. She's ~~an~~ hardworking employee.

4	**Nationality adjectives begin with a capital letter.**
	Danish Sven is from Denmark. He's ~~danish~~.

Editing Task

Find and correct nine more mistakes in these profiles from a social networking website.

Brazilian

My name is Enrique. I'm ~~brazilian~~. My company is called WeMeet. We connect people with similars interests. Users find a interesting topic and sign up to go to a meeting. Some travelers business use WeMeet to find customers, but most people go to make news friends.

My name is Miho. I Japanese. I'm a saleswoman in a japanese robotics company. We make helpfuls robots. We have a ambitious plan to give everyone a robot personal for their home.

Around the House

1 Grammar in the Real World

A What's it like to have a houseguest? Maya is away, but her friend Cathy is her houseguest for the weekend. Read Maya's note to Cathy. Do you think Cathy is happy right now?

B Comprehension Check **Match the two parts of the sentences about the note.**

1 Maya is _b_   a on the floor.

2 The car is _d_   b at her sister's house.

3 The cat food is _a_   c in the closet.

4 Clean towels are _c_   d out of gas.

5 Cathy is _e_   e in the apartment.

C Notice **Complete the sentences. Use the note to help you.**

Where 1 Clean towels and sheets are _in_ the closet.

Where 2 The car keys are _on top of_ the refrigerator.

Where 3 The remote control is _on_ the counter _next to_ the coffee maker.

When 4 See you _on_ Sunday evening.

When 5 My bus arrives _at_ 5:30 p.m.

Which sentences tell you *when* (Time) something happens? Which sentences tell you *where* something is?

Location
Place

Maya's Mess

Hi Cathy,

I'm happy you're in the apartment this weekend. My cat Fluffy is glad you're here, too. Please use my bedroom. Clean towels and sheets
5 are in the closet. There's an extra blanket **in** the drawer **under** the bed.

I'm sorry the refrigerator's empty, but the supermarket's **across** the street. The car keys are **on top of** the refrigerator. The car's out of gas,[1]
10 but the gas station's close, just two blocks away on Main Street.

The TV's **in** the cabinet **near** the window. The remote control's **on** the counter **next to** the coffee maker. (I think the batteries are dead. ☹)

15 I'm sorry about the cat food **on** the floor. Fluffy's very messy. ☺ The vacuum cleaner's **in** the closet. It's old, but it works. The cleaning supplies are **behind** the plant. The garbage cans are **outside** the front door, **in front of**
20 the garage.

See you **on** Sunday evening. My bus arrives **at** 5:30 p.m, so expect me **between** 6:00 and 7:00.

Love,

25 Maya

P.S. I'm **at** my sister's house. Her phone number is (212) 555-8749.

[1]**out of gas**: without gas

2 Prepositions of Place: Things at Home and in the Neighborhood

Grammar Presentation

Prepositions can show place. They can tell you where someone or something is.	*The remote control is next to the coffee maker.* *My home is near the train station.*

2.1 Things at Home

in

The vacuum cleaner is *in* the closet.

on / on top of

The bottle is *on* the refrigerator.
The bottle is *on top of* the refrigerator.

above

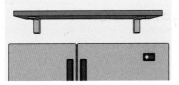

The shelf is *above* the refrigerator.

in front of

The garbage can is *in front of* the garage.

under

The shoes are *under* the bed.

behind

The cleaning supplies are *behind* the plant.

next to / near

The book is *next to* the lamp.
The lamp is *near* the window.

between

The car keys are *between* the watch and the wallet.

2.2 Things in the Neighborhood

in front of

The man is in front of the bakery.

behind

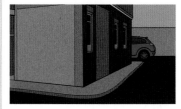

The car is behind the building.

next to / near

The coffee shop is next to the post office.
The coffee shop is near the bakery.

at

The children are at the zoo.

between

The bank is between the restaurant and the delicatessen.

across from

The woman is across from the bank.

outside

The garbage can is outside the door.

inside

The ATMs are inside the bank.

Grammar Application

A Complete the sentences with prepositions of place and the words in the box. Use the picture to help you. Sometimes more than one answer is possible.

| coffee maker | counter | door | floor | gym bag | refrigerator | table |

Sean I need my cell phone. Where is it?

Jon It's _on the table_ .
(1)

Sean Thanks. Now, where's my gym bag?

Jon It's on the floor.
(2)

Sean OK. Oh, and I need my wallet. Where's that?

Jon It's under the table
(3)

Sean And my keys. Where are my keys?

Jon They're on/on top of the gym bag
(4)

Sean Now, where's my laptop? I need my laptop.

Jon It's on top of the refrigerator
(5)

Sean Is the newspaper outside the front door?

Jon No, it's behind the door
(6)

Sean And where are my books for school?

Jon They're on the kitchen counter
(7)

Sean Hey. How about a cup of coffee?

Jon Sure. Where's the coffee?

Sean It's inside the coffee maker
(8)

B Write questions with *Where* and answers. Use the picture in A to answer the questions.

1 (radio) *Where's his radio? It's on/on top of the refrigerator.*
2 (watch) Where's his watch? It's on the table.
3 (glasses) Where are his glasses? They're on/on top of the coffee
4 (headphones) Where are the headphones? They're under the chair.
5 (notebook) Where's the notebook? It's under the textbook

C Pair Work Ask your partner about where things are in his or her home. Write six questions. Then answer your partner's questions. Use the words from the box.

| bed | coffee maker | desk | remote control | sofa |
| clothes | computer | refrigerator | rug | |

A *Where's your TV?* **B** *It's in the living room. It's next to the bookshelf.*

Exercise 2.2 Prepositions of Place: Things in the Neighborhood

A Write sentences about the places in this neighborhood. Use four more of the prepositions from the box.

| above | at | ~~between~~ | ~~next to~~ |
| across from | behind | ~~in front of~~ | ~~outside~~ |

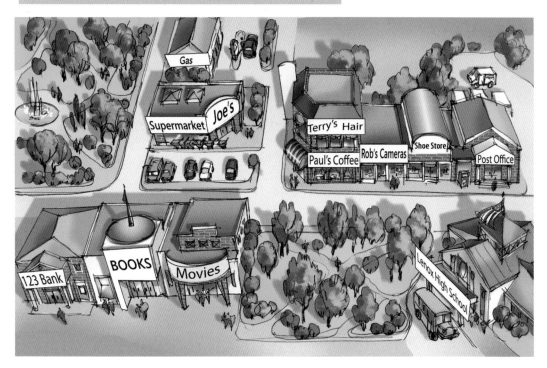

1 the gas station / the supermarket *The gas station is behind the supermarket.*
2 the camera store / the shoe store and the coffee shop ___is between___
3 the red car / the gas station ___is front of___
4 the shopping carts / the supermarket ___are outside___
5 the bookstore / the bank ___is next to___

B Listen. Where are these places? Write sentences. Use and reuse the prepositions from the box in A.

1 The parking lot is *in front of the supermarket.*
2 The hair salon is ___above the coffee shop___
3 The movie theater is ___across from the supermarllet___
4 The park is ___next to the school___
5 The post office is ___across from the school___

C Pair Work Ask and answer questions about your school and the area around the school.

A *Where's the post office?*
B *It's across from the school.*

A *Is the school across from the bank?*
B *No, it's next to the library.*

3 Prepositions of Place: Locations and Other Uses

Grammar Presentation

Certain prepositions commonly appear with some locations.	Maya's sister lives *in San Diego*. She lives *on Market Street*. Her home is *at 606 Market Street*.

3.1 *In*, *On*, and *At* with Locations

in + neighborhood . . . + city / town . . . + state . . . + country	*I live in Midtown*. *I live in Miami*. *My hometown is in Ohio*. *Montreal is in Canada*. *What state is Seattle in?*
on + street	*I live on Main Street*. *The restaurant is on Grand Avenue*. *What street is the movie theater on?*
at + address	*I live at 1298 Seventh Avenue*. *We met at 405 Broadway*.

3.2 Ordinal Numbers with Streets and Floors

1 first	7 seventh	13 thirteenth	19 nineteenth
2 second	8 eighth	14 fourteenth	20 twentieth
3 third	9 ninth	15 fifteenth	21 twenty-first
4 fourth	10 tenth	16 sixteenth	30 thirtieth
5 fifth	11 eleventh	17 seventeenth	31 thirty-first
6 sixth	12 twelfth	18 eighteenth	32 thirty-second

Use ordinal numbers with some streets.	*I live on Third Avenue*. *My apartment is on Ninth Street*.
Use *on* + *the* + ordinal number + *floor*.	*The doctor's office is on the second floor*. *I live on the fifteenth floor*.

3.3 Common Expressions with Prepositions

at home (or home)	Maya is not at home this weekend. NOT Maya is not ~~at the home~~ this weekend.
at work	She is not at work today. NOT Maya is not ~~at the work~~ today.
at school/college in school/college	It's 10:30. Cathy's at school right now. (= in the building) I'm a student. I'm still in school. (= still a student)
in class/in a meeting	Tom is in class. (= in the classroom)
on campus	The bookstore is on campus.
across the street	The student center is across the street.

Grammar Application

Exercise 3.1 In, On, and At with Locations

A Pair Work **Complete the questions with the correct prepositions. Then write the full answers to the questions. Use your own ideas. Check your answers with a partner.**

1 Are we __in__ Canada right now? _No we aren't_
2 What town or city are we __in__ ? _In atlanta_
3 Are we still __on__ Broad Street? _No, we aren't_
4 Are you __at__ 25 Madison Avenue? _No, we aren't_
5 Are the restrooms __on__ the first floor? _Yes, they are_
6 What street is this school __on__ ? _On new peachtree rd_

B **Complete the paragraphs about a student. Use in, on, or at.**

My name is Blanca González, and I am from Mexico. My hometown is __in__ Mexico. Now I live
(1)
__In__ the United States. I live __in__ Waltham,
(2)   (3)
Massachusetts. It's near Boston. My apartment is
__at__ 399 Moody Street. My parents also live in
(4)
Waltham, __at__ 147 Hope Avenue. They are only
(5)
two minutes away from my apartment.

I have three roommates. Our apartment is __on__ the third floor. There
(6)
is a large supermarket __on__ my street. There are also several gas stations
(7)
__In__ my neighborhood. It's noisy __on__ the street, but it's OK __in__ our
(8)   (9)   (10)
apartment. During the day I study accounting. In the evenings I work at a restaurant
__in__ Watertown. That's a town next to Waltham.
(11)

A Over to You Complete the information about your home and school. Use the information in parentheses.

1 My hometown is ____*in*____ ____*Illinois*____ .
  (preposition)   (state or country)

2 My hometown is between _____ and _____ .
  (one city/town)   (another city/town)

3 Now I live _____ _____ .
  (preposition)   (neighborhood)

4 My home is _____ _____ .
  (preposition)   (street name)

5 I live _____ _____ .
  (preposition)   (address – You can give an imaginary address.)

6 My home is near _____ .
  (a place or building)

7 My classroom is _____ _____ _____ floor.
  (preposition)   (+ *the*)   (ordinal number)

8 My school is across the street from _____ .
  (a place)

B Pair Work Share your information with a partner.

Complete the cell phone conversations. Use *in*, *on*, or *at*. Sometimes more than one answer is possible.

1 **Ashley** Hi, this is Ashley.

  Sarah Hi. This is Sarah. Where are you?

  Ashley I'm __*at*__ work. How about you? Are you ___at___ home?

  Sarah No, I'm ___at___ the movie theater ___on___ Fourth Street, and I'm cold.

  Ashley Oh, sorry. I'm late. I'm on my way.

2 **Rodrigo** Hi, it's me.

  Bob Hi. Where are you? Are you ___at___ class?

  Rodrigo No. Class starts in two minutes. I'm ___on___ campus, but I think my backpack's ___in___ my closet. Can you bring it?

  Bob Sure. No problem. I'm still ___in___ the apartment.

3 **Alan**   Hey. Where are you? Are you ___in___ class?

Inga   No. I'm ___on___ campus. Class starts in five minutes.

Alan   OK. I'm ___at___ home, but I'll be ___at___ work tonight.

Inga   OK, thanks for the reminder. I won't wait for you for dinner.

4 **Joseph**   Mike? It's Joseph. Are you ___at___ school today?

Mike   Hi, Joseph. Yes. I'm ___in___ the library.

Joseph   Well, I'm ___in___ the coffee shop ___on___ Sullivan Street. Are you free?

Mike   Sure. See you in five minutes.

4 Prepositions of Time

Grammar Presentation

Prepositions can tell you about when something happens.	Maya returns on Sunday. Her bus arrives at 5:30 p.m. Cathy expects her between 6:00 and 7:00.

4.1 In, On, At

Use *in* + parts of the day	*Cathy always goes for a walk* in the afternoon. *On Mondays, I work* in the morning. *Time of day*
Use *in* + month	*My birthday is* in December. *Month* *Vietnam is beautiful* in April.
Use *in* + season	*Waltham is very cold* in the winter. *Season* *Please visit me* in the spring.

📊 People also say, for example, "in winter" and "in spring," but "in the winter" and "in the spring" are more common.

Use *on* + date In dates, write the number, but say the ordinal number.	*I'll see you* on July 1. (on July first) *Date* *My class ends* on May 20. (on May twentieth)

📊 People also say, for example, "the twentieth of May," but "May twentieth" is more frequent.

Use *on* + day	*See you* on Monday. *Day* *Our class begins* on Friday.
Use *at* + specific time	*The bank opens* at 7:00. (at seven / at seven o'clock) *Clock* *I usually wake up* at 5:30. (at five-thirty / at half past five) *Time*

4.2 Questions with Days, Dates, and Times

You can ask questions about days, dates, or times with: *When is / are . . .* *What day is . . .* *What time is . . .* You can give shorter or longer answers to questions about days, dates, and times.	*"When is Independence Day?"* *"It's on July 4. / On July 4. / July 4."* *"What time is your class?"* *"It's at 8:00. / At 8:00. / 8:00."*

 ## Grammar Application

Exercise 4.1 *In, On, At with Time*

A Circle the correct preposition.

1 In my state, it's very cold **at / (in)** the winter and very hot **at / (in)** the summer.

2 The warm weather usually starts **on / (in)** April.

3 Unfortunately, it rains a lot **(in)/ on** the spring.

4 The first day of summer is **(in)/ on** June.

5 In the summer, the sun goes down late **at /(in)** the evening.

6 It's still sunny when I finish my class **on /(at)** 7:00.

7 I usually stay up late **(on)/ in** Fridays and look at the stars.

8 I like to wake up **on /(at)** 6:30 on Saturdays because the weather is still cool **(in)/ at** the morning.

📊 **Data from the Real World**	
People often give approximate times with *around* or *about*.	*See you around 6:30.* (= 6:20–6:40) *Call me about 6:15.* (= 6:10–6:20)
You can use *between* + two times.	*I'll see you between 6:00 and 7:00.*

B Complete the conversation. Use *in, on, at, around,* or *between.* Sometimes more than one answer is possible.

Alex Let's get together next week. Let's have lunch ___on___ Monday. I'm free ___between___
     (1)   (2)
12:30 and 2:30.

Sam Monday? That's my brother's birthday. We always have lunch

together ___on___ my brother's birthday.
     (3)

Alex How about ___on___ Tuesday?
     (4)

Sam Well, I have class ___in___ the afternoon on Tuesday. It's ___at___ 1:00.
     (5)   (6)
It usually finishes ___at___ 2:15. Let's meet ___on___ Wednesday.
     (7)   (8)

Alex Great. Let's meet ___on___ Wednesday then, ___at___ 1:00.
     (9)   (10)

C Over to You Write six sentences about dates that are special for you. Then share your sentences with a partner.

	Date	Why is this date special?
	July 16	*My mother's birthday is on July 16.*
1	Dec 14	My favorite daughter was born
2	July 5	Sandra's birthday is on july 5
3	April 19	
4	April 4	
5	June 20	
6	June 28	

A *So July 16 is a special date. It's my mother's birthday.*

B *Really? My mother's birthday is in April. It's on April 17.*

A Unscramble the words to make questions about the Expo.

1 the / Expo / is / When

When is the Expo?

2 day / What / is / the concert

What day is the concert?

3 the students / do / a break / When / have

When do the students have a break?

4 the Career Fair / What / is / day

What day is the Career Fair?

5 is / lunch / When

When is lunch?

6 the welcome / is / time / What

What time is the welcome?

VALE COMMUNITY COLLEGE

MUSIC INDUSTRY
EXPO

Thursday, April 22, 7 p.m.–10 p.m.

CONCERT

Friday, April 23, 9 a.m.–5 p.m.

FRIDAY

9:00 Welcome
9:30 "The Business of Music"
10:30 "Becoming a Songwriter"
11:15–11:30 Break
11:30 Talk by Sound Engineer
12:30–1:30 Lunch
1:30 "Writing Music for the Movies"
2:30–4:30 Career Fair
4:30 New Music Software

B Pair Work **Ask and answer the questions in A with a partner.**

A *When is the Expo?*
B *It's on Thursday, April 22.*

5 Avoid Common Mistakes ⚠

1	**Use *in* + month, but use *on* + date or day.**
	on .... *in* .... *on*
	My birthday is in May 10. My sister's birthday is on May, too, but it's not in the same day.

2	**Use *at* + time.**
	at
	My bus arrives 9:00.

3	**Use *on* + street name. Use *at* + address.**
	on .... *at*
	My house is in Gorge Avenue. It's on 1276 Gorge Avenue.

4	**Use *on* + *the* + ordinal number + *floor*.**
	on the
	My office is in third floor.

Editing Task

Find and correct nine more mistakes in this e-mail about a birthday celebration.

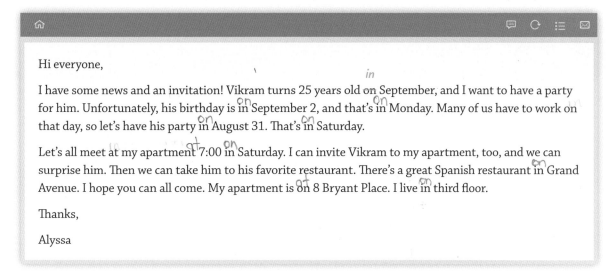

Hi everyone,

I have some news and an invitation! Vikram turns 25 years old on [in] September, and I want to have a party for him. Unfortunately, his birthday is in [on] September 2, and that's in [on] Monday. Many of us have to work on that day, so let's have his party in [on] August 31. That's in [on] Saturday.

Let's all meet at my apartment 7:00 [at] in [on] Saturday. I can invite Vikram to my apartment, too, and we can surprise him. Then we can take him to his favorite restaurant. There's a great Spanish restaurant in [on] Grand Avenue. I hope you can all come. My apartment is on [at] 8 Bryant Place. I live in [on] third floor.

Thanks,

Alyssa

There Is and There Are

Local Attractions

1 Grammar in the Real World

A Do you know a lot about the old areas of your town? Read the blog about a historic street in Los Angeles. What are some fun things to do there?

B Comprehension Check Match the two parts of the sentences about Olvera Street.

1 Olvera Street was _e_   a little shops in the area.

2 It's a tourist attraction   b interesting things to do.

3 There are a lot of   c at noon.

4 There are some   d in downtown Los Angeles.

5 The last tour is   e a small village in 1781.

C Notice Find these words in the text. Do they come after *there is* or *there are*? Write the words in the correct columns.

a lot of interesting things to do	27 historic buildings
traditional music	a statue of King Carlos III
restaurants	

There is . . .	There are . . .

Now circle the correct words in these two sentences about *there is* and *there are*.

The writer uses **_There is_ / _There are_** with singular nouns. She uses **_There is_ / _There are_** with plural nouns.

Historic Olvera Street

By Marta Ruiz

What is Olvera Street? It's the birthplace of Los Angeles! In 1781, this marketplace was a small village of 44 Mexican settlers.[1] Now it's a popular tourist attraction.[2] It is only one block, but **there are** a lot of interesting things to do.

5 **There are** 27 historic buildings on Olvera Street. **There is** a house that is about 200 years old. **There is** a statue of King Carlos III of Spain and a statue of Felipe de Neve, the first governor[3] of California, in a beautiful plaza.

There are some little shops in the area that sell Mexican clothes, toys, and 10 jewelry. **There are** restaurants with delicious Mexican foods such as *churros* and *enchiladas*. **There is** traditional music and folk dancing on the weekends.

Olvera Street is in downtown Los Angeles, across the street from Union Station. **There are** free tours on most days. Just go to the visitor's center at the Sepulveda House.

15 Come to Olvera Street! Learn about history and experience Mexican culture!

Comments [4]

WorldTraveler78: Are there any public parking lots in the area?

Marta_Ruiz: Yes, **there's** one on Alameda Street, 20 and **there's** one on North Main Street.

LAgirl: Are there any tours in the evening?

Marta_Ruiz: No, **there aren't**. The last tour is at noon.

[1] **settler**: a person who moves to a new country or area
[2] **tourist attraction**: something that makes people want to go to a place
[3] **governor**: a person in charge of a large organization, like a state

2 There Is / There Are

Grammar Presentation

There is and *There are* tell you that something or someone exists or that something is a fact.	*There's* a statue of King Carlos III in this plaza. *There are* free tours on most days.

2.1 Affirmative Statements

There	Be	Subject	Place/Time	Contraction
There	is	a parking lot a free tour	on Alameda Street. at 10:00.	There is → There's
	are	some little shops free tours	in the area. on most days.	

2.2 Negative Statements

There	Be + Not/No	Subject	Place/Time
There	isn't	a bank	in Union Station.
	is no	bank	
	isn't	a show	at 8:00.
	is no	show	
	's no	bank	in Union Station.
		show	at 8:00.
	aren't	any cars	on Olvera Street.
	are no	cars	
	aren't	any tours	in the evening.
		tours	

2.3 Using *There Is / There Are*

A Use *There is/There are* to say that something or someone exists or to introduce a fact or a situation.	*There are* a lot of interesting things to do in this area. *There's* an article by Marta Ruiz on this website. *There are* two questions from readers.
B Use *There is/There are* to tell the location of something or someone.	*There's* a parking lot on the corner. *There are* some Mexican restaurants on the next block. *There's* a tour guide at the door.

2.3 Using *There Is / There Are* (continued)

C	Use *There is / There are* to tell when an event happens.	*There's an art show at 8:00.* *There are concerts on the weekend.*
D	Use the full forms in academic writing, but in speaking, use contractions.	*There's music in the plaza.* *There's no free parking on this street.*
	In informal speech, people often say *There're* instead of *There are*, but don't write it.	*There are a lot of museums in Los Angeles.* NOT ~~*There're*~~ *a lot of museums in Los Angeles.*
E	Use *There is* when there are two or more nouns and the first noun is singular.	SINGULAR NOUN PLURAL NOUN *There's a <u>jewelry store</u> and two <u>restaurants</u> on this street.*
	Use *There are* when there are two or more nouns and the first noun is plural.	PLURAL NOUN SINGULAR NOUN *There are two <u>restaurants</u> and a <u>jewelry store</u> on this street.*
F	You can use *some* with a plural noun after *There are*.	*There are some shops around the corner.*
G	For negative statements, you can use *There isn't* and *There aren't*. The full forms *is not* and *are not* are not often used. OR You can use *There is / There are* + *no*.	*There isn't a bad restaurant on this street.* *There aren't any parking spaces here.* *There's no fee at this parking lot.* *There are no hotels around here.*
	You can use *any* in negative statements with *There aren't*.	*There aren't any traffic lights on Olvera Street.*
H	You can use *There is* and *There are* to introduce new people, places, and things.	INTRODUCTION MORE INFORMATION *There is an old house on the street. It's now a museum.*
	You can use *It is / It's* and *They are / They're* to give more information.	*There are a lot of shops on Olvera. They are all very nice.*

Grammar Application

A Complete the sentences from an e-mail. Use *There's* or *There are*.

Hi Naoko,

I'm so happy about your visit to Santa Monica. From Los Angeles airport (LAX), *there are* (1) several buses to Santa Monica. Please call me from the bus. I can meet you at the Santa Monica bus station. _____ (2) a lot of things to see and do here. First, _____ (3) the famous beach. It has a historic pier[1] and some nice restaurants. On the beach, _____ (4) volleyball, swimming, and biking. In fact, _____ (5) even a volleyball competition on Saturday. I know you like surfing, so _____ (6) a surfing school you can check out. _____ (7) also the Santa Monica Pier Aquarium. My other favorite place is the Third Street Promenade. _____ (8) some great concerts there on the weekend. _____ (9) great stores on the Promenade, too.

See you soon!

Kim

[1]pier: a structure over the water where boats can dock

B Over to You What is your favorite city? Fill in the chart with some of the interesting places in your favorite city.

There is . . .	*There are . . .*

C Pair Work Tell your partner what is in your favorite city. Use your information from B. Take turns.

A *There's an art museum.*

B *There are several big parks.*

Exercise 2.2 Affirmative and Negative Statements

A Look at the hotel information. Complete the sentences. Use *There is / There are* and *There isn't / There aren't*.

✳ COMFORT HOTEL ✳

- $54 parking (for 24 hours)
- $14.99 wireless Internet service (per day)
- Free breakfast
- Free coffee in the lobby
- Outdoor pool
- Fitness room
- Business services
- Conference center
- Meeting rooms (4)
- Ice machines in the hallways
- Park views
- Restaurant

1 *There isn't* free parking.

2 *There are* business services.

3 _____ an indoor pool.

4 _____ six meeting rooms.

5 _____ any free wireless Internet service.

6 _____ any ocean views.

7 _____ a fitness room.

8 _____ any refrigerators in the rooms.

9 _____ a restaurant.

10 _____ a conference center.

B Over to You What doesn't exist in your town or city? Look at the places in the box. Add your own ideas. Write six sentences about your town or city. Use *There is no* and *There aren't any*.

aquarium	cheap restaurants	historic houses	park	statues
beach	free parking	library	public pool	tourist attractions
bus station	gas stations	museums	river	train station

1 *There aren't any gas stations.*

2 _____

3 _____

4 _____

5 _____

6 _____

7 _____

A Read Mi-Sun's description of her town on her blog. Complete the sentences. Use *There's*, *There are*, *It's*, or *They're*.

Hi, my name is Mi-Sun. My hometown is Concord, MA. It's a small historic town near Boston.

___There are___ some historic buildings in Concord. ___They're___ very old.
(1)   (2)

_____ also a lot of small shops. _____ usually
(3)   (4)

expensive.

_____ an old hotel. _____ called the Colonial Inn.
(5)   (6)

_____ a popular place for lunch and dinner. _____ a
(7)   (8)

lot of special events at the hotel, like weddings and meetings. _____
                                                                (9)

often live music at night. I like to go and listen to jazz.

_____ a national park by the Concord River. _____
(10)   (11)

beautiful and peaceful. _____ always a lot of tourists at the park.
                        (12)

It has a famous bridge – Old North Bridge. Also, _____ a very famous
                                                 (13)

statue of a minuteman next to the bridge. The soldier was called a "minuteman"

because he could get ready in a minute. A historic battle happened there in 1775.

I often walk there with friends.

B Listen to Mi-Sun and check your answers.

C Over to You Write four pairs of sentences about your town or city. Use *There's / There are* in the first sentence. Use *It's* or *They are* in the second sentence to add more information.

There's a big park in my city. It's on State Street.

1 _____

2 _____

3 _____

4 _____

3 Yes / No Questions with *There Is / There Are*

Grammar Presentation

Yes / No Questions with *There is / There are* can ask about people, things, and events.	*Is there a tour guide in this museum?* *Are there any concerts on Friday?*

3.1 *Yes / No* Questions and Short Answers

Be	There	Subject	Place / Time	Contraction
Is	there	a visitor's center	on Olvera Street?	Yes, **there is.**
		a performance	at 6:00?	No, **there isn't.**
Are		any parking lots	in the area?	Yes, **there are.**
		any tours	in the evening?	No, **there aren't.**

3.2 Using *Yes / No* Questions and Short Answers with *There Is / There Are*

A You can use *any* with a plural noun in *Yes / No* questions with *Are there*.	"*Are there any hotels on Alameda Street?*" "*Are there any concerts on weekdays?*"
B In affirmative short answers, don't use the contractions *there's* or *there're*.	"*Yes, there is.*" NOT "*Yes, ~~there's~~.*" "*Yes, there are.*" NOT "*Yes, ~~there're~~.*"
C You can use *It is / They are* to say more after a short answer.	"*Is there a visitor's center on Olvera Street?*" "*Yes, there is. It is at the Sepulveda House.*" "*Are there any parking lots in the area?*" "*Yes, there are. They are on Alameda Street.*"

3.3 Longer Answers with *There Is / There Are*

A In longer answers with *There is*, you can use *one* instead of repeating *a* + singular noun.	*Is there a visitor's center on Olvera Street?* *Yes, there's one in the Sepulveda House.* *No, there isn't one on Olvera Street.*
B In longer answers with *There are*, you can use *some / any* instead of repeating *some / any* + plural noun.	*Are there any public parking lots in the area?* *Yes, there are some on Alameda Street.* *No, there aren't any in the area.*

Grammar Application

A Read the TV schedule and complete the questions and answers. Use *Are there any* and *Is there a* for the questions. Then write short answers.

6:30 p.m.	News: *Weather report*	**11:15 p.m.**	Movie: *Where Is Jimmy Jones?*
7:00 p.m.	Talk show: *The Guy Norris Show*	**1:00 a.m.**	Music: *The Dixonville Festival*
8:00 p.m.	Documentary: *Antarctica*	**2:00 a.m.**	Music: *Jazz with Kenny Delmot*
9:00 p.m.	Movie: *The Long Road*	**3:00 a.m.**	Comedy: *The Watson Family*

1 ___*Are there any*___ movies on TV tonight?   Yes, there _____ two movies. There's one at 9:00 and one at 11:15.

2 ___*Is there a*___ talk show?   Yes, _____ one at 7:00.

3 _____ music shows?   Yes, there _____ . There's

one at _____ and one at

_____ .

4 _____ sports shows?   _____ .

5 _____ documentary?   _____ one at 8:00.

6 _____ kids' show?   _____ .

7 _____ comedy show?   _____ .

8 _____ news program?   _____ .

B Write questions about events in your city or town. Use *Is there a/an* and *Are there any*.

1 (art festival) _____

2 (jazz concerts) _____

3 (baseball game) _____

4 (dance performance) _____

5 (new paintings at the museum) _____

6 (good movies) _____

C Pair Work Ask and answer the questions with a partner. Write the answers to the questions with your partner.

> **A** *Are there any good movies this weekend?*
> **B** *Yes, there are two good movies.*

1 _____

2 _____

3 _____

4 _____

5 _____

6 _____

D Answer each question with *yes* in three different ways. Give information about your own area, if possible.

1 Is there a mall in this town?

Yes, there's one on Westwood Avenue. Yes, there's a mall on Westwood Avenue. Yes, it's on Westwood Avenue.

2 Is there a good coffee shop nearby?

_____

_____

3 Is there an art museum?

_____

_____

4 Is there a nice park?

_____

_____

5 Is there a sports stadium?

_____

_____

6 Is there a big movie theater?

_____

_____

4 Avoid Common Mistakes ⚠

1 **Use *There is* with singular nouns. Use *There are* with plural nouns.**

~~There are~~ *is*
There are a music festival this week.   There is musicians from different countries at the festival. *are*

2 ***There is* and *There are* introduce <u>new</u> people, places, and things.**
It is and *They are* give more information.

There is a small building on Thomas Street. ~~There~~ is the town museum. *It*
~~They~~ *There*
They are three large cities in Texas. They are Houston, San Antonio, and Dallas.

3 **Use the full forms in academic writing. Do not use the contractions.**
There is
~~There's~~ a wonderful museum in downtown Philadelphia.
There is
~~There's~~ no bank in the train station.

4 **In informal speaking, people often say *There are* very quickly, so it sounds like *They're*. Don't confuse them in writing.**
There are
~~They're~~ some great shows this weekend.

Editing Task

Find and correct seven more mistakes in this article about New York City's famous park.

New York City's Central Park

New York City is an expensive place to visit, but there ~~are~~ *is* one place that is always free: Central Park. There is a very big park. In fact, it is about 2.5 miles (4 km) long and 0.5 miles (0.8 km) wide. There is over 843 acres[1] in the park. There is fields, ponds, and lakes. Visitors enjoy different kinds of sports and events here. There are
5 walkers, joggers, skaters, bicyclists, and bird-watchers. There are a zoo and two ice-skating rinks. There's also an outdoor theater. The theater has "Shakespeare in the Park" summer festivals. There is a swimming pool in the summer, too. Throughout the year, they're horse-and-carriage rides. Every year, there is over 25 million visitors. They are happy to visit a fun and free New York City tourist attraction.

[1]**843 acres:** 1.32 square miles or 3.41 square kilometers

Simple Present

Lifestyles

1 Grammar in the Real World

A Is there someone very old in your family? Read the magazine article about places where people live a long time. Why do some people have a long life?

B Comprehension Check **Answer the questions.**

1 Why do people in some areas live so long?

2 Do these people feel stressed?

3 Do they eat much meat?

C Notice **Find the sentences in the article. Complete the sentences with the correct words.**

1 People in these areas _____move_____ around a lot.

2 They _____don't_____ exercise in a gym.

3 They _____walk_____ a lot during the day.

4 _____Every day_____, they _____take_____ time to rest and relax.

Find the places you use *don't*. What words show time?

A Long, Healthy Life

On the Japanese island of Okinawa, many people **live** to be over 100 years old. Researchers[1] **find** this in several places around the world, including Sardinia, Italy; Icaria, Greece; the Nicoya Peninsula of Costa Rica; and Loma Linda, California. Why do people in these areas **live** so long? The answer is lifestyle.[2] This list **shows** six lifestyle habits[3] that **are** common in these places.

1 People in these areas **move** around a lot. They **don't exercise** in a gym, but they **walk** a lot during the day. They **use** their bodies and **live** actively.

2 They **have** a purpose in their lives. Some **spend** time with grandchildren. Others **do** gardening or volunteer work.[4]

3 They **relax**. **Every day**, they **take** time to rest and relax. They **rarely feel** stressed.[5]

4 They **eat** a lot of vegetables, and they **usually don't eat** meat.

5 They **have** many friends. They **are** part of an active social group.

6 They **feel** close to their families.

[1]**researcher:** a person who studies something to learn detailed information about it

[2]**lifestyle:** the way people live; how people eat, sleep, work, exercise

[3]**habit:** something you do or the way you act regularly

[4]**volunteer work:** work without pay, usually to help other people or an organization

[5]**stressed:** very nervous or worried

2 Simple Present: Affirmative and Negative Statements

Grammar Presentation

The simple present describes habits, routines, and facts.	*In some cultures, people live to be 100 years old. These people exercise and eat very well.*

2.1 Affirmative Statements

SINGULAR

Subject	Verb	
I You	**eat**	vegetables every day.
He She It	**eats**	

PLURAL

Subject	Verb	
We You They	**eat**	vegetables every day.

2.2 Negative Statements

SINGULAR

Subject	*Do / Does* + *Not*	Base Form of Verb	
I You	**do not** **don't**	**eat**	a lot of meat.
He She It	**does not** **doesn't**		

PLURAL

Subject	*Do + Not*	Base Form of Verb	
We You They	**do not** **don't**	**exercise**	in the morning.

2.3 Using Simple Present and Time Expressions

A Use simple present to talk about things that regularly happen, such as habits and routines.	*Okinawans usually eat fruits and vegetables.* *We don't eat meat.* *He doesn't drive to work.*

2.3 Using Simple Present and Time Expressions *(continued)*

B When you talk about things that regularly happen, use time expressions such as *every day, every* + day, *in the morning/afternoon/evening, at night,* and *at 6:30.*	*They take long walks* every day. *She takes long walks* every Saturday. *We take naps* in the afternoon. *I watch TV* at night. *Our family eats dinner* at 6:30.
An *-s* after the day of the week/*morning/afternoon/evening* or *weekend* means the action or event always happens.	On Saturdays, *I work in a restaurant.* *I take long walks* on weekends.
Use *from . . . to . . .* to say how long something happens.	*I work* from 8:00 to 5:00.
C Time expressions usually come at the end of the sentence. If the time expression is at the beginning of the sentence, use a comma after it.	*I visit my grandparents* in the summer. In the summer, *I visit my grandparents.* In June, *I take a break from school.*
D You can also use the simple present to talk about facts.	*Okinawans* live long lives.

2.4 Spelling Rules for Adding *-s*, *-es*, and *-ies* to Verbs

A Add *-s* to most verbs. Add *-s* to verbs ending in a vowel[1] + *-y.*	*drinks, rides, runs, sees, sleeps* *buys, pays, says*
B Add *-es* to verbs ending in *-ch, -sh, -ss, -x.* Add *-es* to verbs ending in a consonant[2] + *-o.*	*teaches, pushes, misses, fixes* *does, goes*
C For verbs that end in a consonant + *-y,* change the *y* to *i* and add *-es.*	*cry* → *cries* *study* → *studies*
D Some verbs are irregular.	*be* → *am / are / is* *have* → *has*

Reminder:
[1]**Vowels:** the letters *a, e, i, o, u*
[2]**Consonants:** the letters *b, c, d, f, g, h, j, k, l, m, n, p, q, r, s, t, v, w, x, y, z*
Spelling and Pronunciation Rules for Simple Present: See page A20.

📊 Data from the Real World

Here are some of the most frequent simple present verbs:

be	do	get	know	see	come	want
have	say	go	think	make	take	give

Grammar Application

Complete the sentences with the correct form of the verbs in parentheses.

1 My grandparents __*live*__ (live) healthy lifestyles.

2 My grandfather ____goes____ (go) for a walk every morning.

3 In the afternoon, he ____checks____ (check) his e-mail and ____works____ (work) in his garden.

4 My grandmother ____is____ (be) also active.

5 She ____works____ (work) part-time in a hotel.

6 She ____does____ (do) volunteer work at a local school three days a week.

7 Before dinner, they ____relax____ (relax) in the living room.

8 They ____eat____ (eat) healthy food, and they ____don't smoke____ (not smoke).

Complete the statements with the affirmative or negative form of the verbs in parentheses.

1 Tran and his roommate, Edgar, __*have*__ (have) a lot to do every week.

They 2 They often _____ (feel) stressed during the week.

He 3 Tran ____works____ (work) long hours at a department store.

He 4 He ____doesn't see____ (not see) his family very much.

They 5 Tran and Edgar both ____take____ (take) night classes at the community college.

They 6 They usually ____don't have____ (not have) time to cook dinner.

They 7 For dinner, they often ____eat____ (eat) fast food like hamburgers and French fries.

He 8 Edgar ____doesn't have____ (not have) a job.

He 9 Every morning, he ____goes____ (go) online to look at job listings.

He 10 Edgar usually ____runs____ (run) in the afternoon.

They 11 On the weekends, Edgar and Tran ____relax____ (relax) with friends.

Exercise 2.3 More Simple Present Statements

A Over to You Complete the sentences about yourself. Use affirmative or negative forms of the verbs in the box.

do	eat	feel	live	sleep
drink	exercise	have	read	spend

1 I ___feel___ stressed during the week.

2 I ___have___ good friends in my town.

3 I ___live___ very actively.

4 I ___exercise___ in a gym.

5 I ___eat___ a lot of meat.

6 I ___sleep___ about eight hours every night.

7 I ___spend___ a lot of time online or on the computer.

8 I ___do___ volunteer work in my area.

9 I ___drink___ a lot of water every day.

10 I ___read___ the news in the morning.

B Pair Work Share your sentences with a partner. Then change partners. Tell your new partner about your classmate.

A *Ari feels stressed during the week.*

B *Maria doesn't feel stressed during the week.*

Exercise 2.4 Pronunciation Focus: -s and -es

Say /s/ after /f/, /k/, /p/, and /t/ sounds.	*laughs, drinks, walks, sleeps, writes, gets, texts*
Say /z/ after /b/, /d/, /g/, /v/, /m/, /n/, /l/, and /r/ sounds and all vowel sounds.	*grabs, rides, hugs, lives, comes, runs, smiles, hears, sees, plays, buys, goes, studies*
Say /əz/ after /tʃ/, /ʃ/, /s/, /ks/, /z/, and /dʒ/ sounds.	*teaches, pushes, kisses, fixes, uses, changes*
Pronounce the vowel sound in *does* and *says* differently from *do* and *say*.	*do* /duː/ → *does* /dʌz/ *say* /seɪ/ → *says* /sez/

A Listen and repeat the verbs in the chart above.

SHE = Verb + s/es

B Read about Staci's week. Underline the verbs that end in *-s* or *-es*.

Staci goes to school from Monday to Friday from 7:30 a.m. to 11:30 a.m. Then she rushes to work. She works at a hospital until 8:00 p.m. In the evening, Staci catches a bus to go home. On her way home, she listens to music and relaxes. She eats a quick dinner with her family. Then she reads to her children and checks their homework. If she isn't too tired, she finishes her own homework. Staci usually falls asleep by 10:00 p.m.

C Listen to the information about Staci's week and check (✓) the sounds of the verbs in the boxes below. Then practice saying the verbs.

	/s/	/z/	/əz/
1 goes		✓	
2 rushes			✓
3 works	✓		
4 catches			✓
5 listens	✓		
6 relaxes			✓
7 eats	✓		
8 reads		✓	
9 checks	✓		
10 finishes			✓
11 falls	✓		

D Pair Work Ask and answer the questions with a partner. Then tell the class about your partner.

1 What are two of your healthy habits?

2 What do you do to relax?

Paulo eats healthy food, and he doesn't smoke or drink. To relax, he listens to music.

Exercise 2.5 Using Time Expressions with Simple Present

Allie's Schedule

	Sunday	Monday	Tuesday	Wednesday	Thursday	Friday	Saturday
Morning	Off	Get up 6:30 a.m. Work 7:30 a.m.–2:30 p.m.	Get up 6:30 a.m. Work 7:30 a.m.–2:30 p.m.	Get up 6:30 a.m. Work 7:30 a.m.–2:30 p.m.	Get up 6:30 a.m. Work 7:30 a.m.–2:30 p.m.	Get up 6:30 a.m. Work 7:30 a.m.–2:30 p.m.	Off
Afternoon	Visit parents	Yoga		Yoga			Do homework
Evening			Class 7:15–9:45 p.m.		Class 7:15–9:45 p.m.		
	Bed at 11:00 p.m.	Bed at 11:00 p.m.	Bed at 11:00 p.m.	Bed at 11:00 p.m.	Bed at 11:00 p.m.	Bed at 11:00 p.m.	

A Look at Allie's schedule and complete the sentences about it. Use the correct time expressions.

Time	Part of Day / Day of Week
at (time)	*in the* (morning / afternoon / evening)
from (time) *to* (time)	*on* (day of week)

Use *at* (time) and *from* (time / day) *to* (time / day) to indicate exact times and days.

Use *on* (day of week) or *in the* (morning / afternoon / evening) to indicate the day or part of day.

1 Allie goes to yoga *on Mondays and Wednesdays* . (days)

2 She works *from Monday to Friday* . (days)

3 She works from 7:30 am to 2:30 p.m . (times)

4 She has classes on tuesdays and Thursdays . (days)

5 Her classes are from 7:15 to 9:45 p.m . (times)

6 Her days off are on Sunday and Saturday . (days)

7 She visits her parents on Sunday afternon . (day)

8 During the week, she usually goes to bed at 11:00 pm and
   wakes up at 6:30 am . (times)

9 She does her homework on Saturdays . (day)

B Over to You Think about your schedule. Complete the sentences below. Make them true for you.

1 I take classes (days) _on Mondays, Tuesdays, Wednesdays, and Thursdays_ .

2 My classes are (time) _from 6 pm to 10 pm_ .

3 I work (days) _From Monday to Friday_ .

4 I work (time) _from 9 am to 3 pm_ .

5 During the week, I go to sleep (time) _At 11:00 pm_ .

6 On the weekends, I go to sleep (time) _At 12:00_ .

7 On Sundays, I get up (time) _At 11 am_ .

8 I do my homework (time) _At any time possible_ .

3 Statements with Adverbs of Frequency

Grammar Presentation

Adverbs of frequency describe how often something happens.	Our neighbors *never drive* to work. They *always ride* their bikes.

3.1 Adverbs of Frequency

Negative
0%

Positive
100%

never   rarely   sometimes   often   usually   always

Rarely is not frequently used.

3.2 Adverbs of Frequency · Adverbs of Frequency with *Be*

RULE 1

Subject	Adverb of Frequency	Verb	
I You We They	always usually often sometimes	work	10 hours a day.
He She It	rarely never	works	

RULE 2

Subject	*Be*	Adverb of Frequency	
I	am		
You We They	are	always usually often sometimes	tired.
He She It	is	rarely never	

3.3 Using Adverbs of Frequency

A	Adverbs of frequency usually come after the verb *be*.	*I am often busy in the afternoon.* *She is usually tired in the morning.*
B	Adverbs of frequency usually come before other verbs.	*My parents rarely eat meat.* *Cristina often rides her bike to work.* *He doesn't usually watch TV.*
C	*Sometimes, usually,* and *often* can come before the verb OR at the beginning or end of a sentence.	*We sometimes cook for our family.* *Sometimes we cook for our family.* *We cook for our family sometimes.*
D	Do not begin or end sentences with *always* and *never*.	*Your grandparents are always active.* NOT *Always your grandparents are active.* NOT *Your grandparents are active never.*

Grammar Application

Exercise 3.1 Adverbs of Frequency with Simple Present

Unscramble the words to make sentences.

1 happy / My / always / is / brother / at work.
   My brother is always happy at work.

2 music. / He / listen to / does / not / often
   He does not listen to music.

3 slows down. / never / He
   He never slows down.

4 sometimes / He / seven / works / a week. / days
   He sometimes works 7 days a week.

5 takes / He / a day off. / rarely
   He rarely takes a day off.

6 starts / in / work / He / at 3:00 / usually / the afternoon.
   He usually stars work at 3:00 in the afternoon.

7 until 1:00 a.m. / doesn't / He / usually / finish
   He usually doesn't finish unit 1:00 am.

8 is / tired. / rarely / My brother
   My brother is rarely tired.

A Over to You **Read the sentences and check (✓) the boxes. Make them true for you.**

Talk About Your Lifestyle

	NEVER	SOMETIMES	OFTEN	USUALLY	ALWAYS
1 I get eight hours of sleep at night.		✓			
2 I fall asleep easily.	✓				
3 I wake up at night.		✓		✓	
4 I exercise three times a week.	✓				
5 I have dinner with friends on the weekend.	✓				
6 I watch TV at night.					✓
7 I go to the library one day a month.	✓				
8 I go away for vacation.					✓

B Pair Work **Take turns saying your sentences from A with a partner.**

A *I never get eight hours of sleep at night. How about you, Olga?*

B *I sometimes get eight hours of sleep at night.*

4 Avoid Common Mistakes ⚠

1 For affirmative statements with *he/she/it*, use the base form of the verb + *-s / -es.*

relaxes
He ~~relax~~ after lunch.

2 For affirmative statements with *I/you/we/they* or a plural noun, use the base form of the verb.

go
My parents ~~goes~~ out to dinner every Friday night.

3 In negative statements, use *do not / don't* or *does not / doesn't* + the base form of the verb.

jog
Maria does not ~~jogs~~ after dark.

he/she/it = no s/es Quest. po Negative
he/she/it = s/es (affirmative)

4 Do not use *do* or *does* in negative statements with *be.*

am not
I ~~don't be~~ active on social media.

5 Do not use *be* with a simple present verb.

I ~~am~~ exercise on Tuesdays.

Editing Task

Find and correct 10 more mistakes in the letter.

Dear Pedro,

How are you? I'm fine. I'm in Vermont with my aunt and uncle. They ~~lives~~ *live*
on a farm. The lifestyle here is very different. They are dairy farmers, so they
~~are~~ work hard every day. They usually get up at 4:30 a.m. They go to the barn

5   and milk the cows. Cows ~~makes~~ a lot of noise in the morning, so they usually
~~wakes~~ me up. Of course, I do not ~~gets~~ up until about 7:00 a.m. At 9:00, my
uncle ~~cook~~ a wonderful breakfast. We all eat together. After that, he and I *we*
~~goes~~ to the barn and ~~works~~ there. My aunt usually ~~stay~~ in the house. In the
afternoon, there is more work. At night, I am really tired, so I always ~~goes~~ to

10   bed at 8:30! Usually my aunt and uncle ~~don't be~~ tired. They usually go to bed
late!   *are not*

I hope your vacation is fun. See you soon!

Your friend,

Oscar

Simple Present *Yes/No* Questions and Short Answers

Daily Habits

1 Grammar in the Real World

A Do you get enough sleep? Do you have trouble sleeping? Read the news article about sleeping habits. Answer the survey questions.

B Comprehension Check Circle the correct answer.

1 This article is about **health /(sleep)** habits.

2 Sleep is a **(problem)/ hobby** for many people.

3 Many people believe poor sleep can affect their **(work)/ friends**.

C Notice Find the questions in the news article, and choose the correct word to complete the questions. Then underline the subject of each sentence.

1 **(Do)/ Does** most adults think sleep is important?

2 **Do /(Does)** productivity improve after a good night's sleep?

3 **(Do)/ Does** you feel good about your sleep habits?

Notice the use of *do* and *does*. Which word do you use for singular subjects? Which word do you use for plural subjects?

Do most people get
ENOUGH SLEEP?

If you think "no," you are correct. The National Sleep Foundation's 2010 Sleep in America™ poll[1] shows that sleep is a problem for many people. About 75 percent agree that poor sleep can affect their work or family relationships. How are your sleep habits? To find out, answer the
5 survey[2] questions below.

[1]**poll:** a short questionnaire, usually one question

[2]**survey:** a set of questions to find out people's habits or beliefs about something

[3]**suffer from insomnia:** find it difficult to get to sleep or to sleep well

		Yes	No
1	**Do** you **fall asleep** in 30 minutes or less?	☐	☑
2	**Do** you **have** trouble falling asleep?	☐	☑
3	**Do** you **suffer** from insomnia?[3]	☑	☐
4	**Does** stress **keep** you awake?	☐	☑
10 5	**Do** you **take** any sleep medication?	☐	☑
6	**Do** you **wake up** during the night?	☐	☑
7	**Do** you **wake up** too early in the morning?	☑	☐
8	**Do** you **feel** very tired in the morning?	☐	☑
9	**Do** you **get** at least seven hours of sleep each night?	☐	☑
15 10	**Do** you **get** more sleep on the weekends?	☑	☐

2 Simple Present Yes/No Questions and Short Answers

Grammar Presentation

You can use simple present questions to ask about habits, routines, and facts.	*Do you wake up early?* *Does she suffer from insomnia?*

2.1 Yes/No Questions

Do / Does	Subject	Base Form of Verb	
Do	I you we they	**fall asleep**	**in 30 minutes?**
Does	he she it		

2.2 Short Answers

AFFIRMATIVE

Yes	Subject	Do / Does
Yes,	I you we they	**do.**
	he she it	**does.**

NEGATIVE

No	Subject	Do / Does + Not
No,	I You We They	**do not.** **don't.**
	he she it	**does not.** **doesn't.**

2.3 Using Simple Present Yes/No Questions and Answers

A For simple present Yes/No questions, use *Do* or *Does* with the base form of the verb.	*Do you feel tired every morning?* *Does he wake up during the night?*
B People usually use contractions in negative short answers.	*"Do you watch TV all night?"* *"No, I don't."*
Be careful! Negative full forms are very strong. You can sound angry.	*"No, I do not!"* (This can sound angry.)

2.3 Using Simple Present *Yes/No* Questions and Answers (continued)

C You can give longer answers to *Yes/No* questions. It's friendly to give more information.	"Do you fall asleep easily?" "Yes, I usually fall asleep in about 15 minutes." "No, I often stay awake for an hour."
You can also give a short answer and then give more information in a separate sentence.	"Yes, I do. I usually fall asleep in about 15 minutes." "No, I don't. I often stay awake for an hour."
D Some questions do not have a simple *yes* or *no* answer. You can answer *Well, . . .* and give a longer answer in speaking.	"Do you live with your family?" "*Well*, I live with my aunt and uncle."
Do not use *Well, . . .* to answer questions in academic writing, for example in compositions or tests.	"Does the average college student get a lot of sleep?" "The average student gets about six hours of sleep." NOT "~~Well~~, the average student gets about six hours of sleep."

Grammar Application

Exercise 2.1 *Yes/No* Questions and Short Answers

A Complete the questions with *Do* or *Does*. Then write short answers. Make them true for you.

1 __Do__ you get up early? _Yes, I do./No, I don't._

2 __Does__ the sun wake you up? Yes, I do.

3 __Does__ your alarm play music? Yes, I do.

4 __Do__ you often go back to sleep? Yes, I do

5 __Do__ you like mornings? Yes, I do

6 __Do__ you sleep until noon on the weekends? Yes, I do

7 __Do__ you usually stay up past midnight? No, I don't.

8 __Do__ you study late at night? Yes, I do.

B Pair Work Ask and answer the questions in A. Give short answers to your partner's questions.

A *Do you get up early?*

B *No, I don't.*

A Complete the conversation about other habits. Write questions with the words in parentheses. Then complete the short answers.

Q **Lucy** *Do you and your brother share*
(1)
(you and your brother/share) the cooking?

A **Malia** No, we don't . I'm always busy with school.
(2)

Q **Lucy** So, does your brother do all the cooking?
(3)
(your brother/do) all the cooking?

A **Malia** Yes, he does . He's a great cook.
(4)

Q **Lucy** Does he work in a restaurant (he/work)
(5)
in a restaurant?

A **Malia** No, he doesn't .
(6)

Q **Lucy** Oh, Does he go to cooking school ?
(7)
(he/go) to cooking school?

A **Malia** No, he doesn't . He just loves food.
(8)

B Pair Work Practice the conversations in A with a partner.

> In speaking, people often say *Do you* very fast.
> It can sound like one word ("D'you").
> Always write *Do you* as two words, but say it fast so it sounds like one word ("D'you").

A Listen to the questions about people's music habits. Repeat the questions. Say *Do you* fast, as one word.

Do you fall asleep with music on?

Do you like loud music?

Do you dance when you listen to music?

Do you listen to music all the time?

Do you study with music on?

Do you sing along to music?

Do you have a television in your bedroom?

B Pair Work Ask and answer the questions in A. Give a short answer first, and then give more information in a second sentence. Use *Well, . . .* for some answers.

A *Do you like loud music?*
B *No, I don't. I prefer soft music.*

A *Do you listen to music all the time?*
B *Well, I don't listen to music when I'm in class.*

Exercise 2.4 *Yes / No Questions in a Survey*

A Over to You Write questions for these habits. Then ask your classmates these questions. Write their names in the chart.

Who . . . ?			Name
falls asleep with the TV on	1	*Do you fall asleep with the TV on?*	
falls asleep to music	2		
talks in his or her sleep	3		
dreams a lot	4		
remembers his or her dreams	5		
walks in his or her sleep	6		

B Pair Work Tell a partner about four classmates and their sleeping habits.

Delia talks in her sleep.

3 Avoid Common Mistakes ⚠

1 **Use *Do* with plural subjects and with *you*.**

　　Do
　~~Does~~ your roommates stay up late?

2 **Use *Does* with singular subjects (except *you*).**

　　Does
　~~Do~~ this this coffee maker have a timer?

3 **Use *Do / Does* in simple present questions with *have*.**

　　Do you have
　~~Have you~~ a website?

4 **Do not use *Do / Does* in questions with *be*.**

　　Is
　~~Do~~ your phone new?

5 **Do not use *Be* with other simple present verbs.**

　　Do
　~~Are~~ you agree?

Editing Task

Find and correct seven more mistakes in these questions about sleeping habits.

　　Do you have
1 ~~Have you~~ trouble falling asleep?

Do 2 ~~Are~~ you sleep on your stomach, your back, or your side?

Do you 3 Have ~~you~~ a TV in your bedroom?

4 Doe~~s~~ you dream in color or in black-and-white?

Does 5 ~~Do~~ a dream ever scare you?

6 Doe~~s~~ loud noises wake you up at night?

Are you 7 ~~Do you~~ a light sleeper or a deep sleeper?

8 Doe~~s~~ you fall asleep quickly?

10

Simple Present Information Questions

Cultural Holidays

1 Grammar in the Real World

A What is your favorite holiday or celebration? Read the interview about a Mexican holiday. What is the Day of the Dead?

B Comprehension Check **Choose the correct answers.**

1 On the Day of the Dead, people remember _b_ .
   a their parents   b their dead relatives   c their children

2 People put pictures of the dead _a_ .
   a on altars   b on sweets   c on skulls

3 The Day of the Dead takes place _c_ .
   a every month   b one day a year   c on November 1 and 2

4 People _a_ their ancestors' graves.
   a decorate   b paint   c celebrate

C Notice **Answer the questions with the correct question word. Use the interview to help you.**

1 Which word asks a question about **time**?   What   (When)   Where

2 Which word asks a question about **places**?   What   When   (Where)

3 Which word asks a question about **things**?   (What)   When   Where

What word comes after *when*, *where*, and *what*? = do

Coffee Time

Today's Topic:
MEXICO'S DAY of the DEAD

[1]**ancestor:** any member of your family from long ago

[2]**altar:** a type of table that people use in religious ceremonies

[3]**grave:** a place where you bury a dead person or people, usually under the ground

[4]**skull:** the bones of the head around the brain

[5]**symbolize:** use a sign or mark to represent something

[6]**rebirth:** a new period of growth of something

Michelle Hello, everyone! This is *Coffee Time*. Our topic today is celebrations around the world. Today our guest is Elena Lopez, from a university in Mexico. She's here to tell us about the Day of the Dead. Welcome, Dr. Lopez!

5 **Dr. Lopez** Thank you. It's nice to be here.

Michelle First of all, **where do people celebrate the Day of the Dead?**

Dr. Lopez They celebrate it in many parts of the world, such as in Mexico.

10 **Michelle** **When do people celebrate it, and how do they celebrate it?**

Dr. Lopez Well, the Day of the Dead takes place on two days: November 1 and 2. We remember our dead relatives – our ancestors[1] – and friends. People build little altars[2]
15 in the home and in public schools. They also clean and decorate the graves.[3]

Michelle **What do they put on these altars and graves?**

Dr. Lopez They put candles, food, drinks, flowers, and pictures of the dead. There are sweets in the shape of skulls,[4] too.
20 The traditions are a little different in every region of Mexico.

Michelle **What do the different things mean?**

Dr. Lopez Well, for example, the candles are a guide for our ancestors. They guide them home. There are bells, too.
25 They call the dead.

Michelle **What do the skulls symbolize?**[5] Do they symbolize death?

Dr. Lopez Well, yes. But they also symbolize rebirth,[6] according to the first Day of the Dead thousands of years ago.

2 Simple Present Information Questions

Grammar Presentation

Information questions begin with a *Wh-* word (*Who, What, When, Where, Why,* or *How*). They ask for information and cannot be answered with a simple *yes* or *no*.

Where do people celebrate the Day of the Dead?
When do Americans celebrate Independence Day?

2.1 Information Questions

Wh- word	Do / Does	Subject	Base Form of Verb	
Person *People* **Who**		I	see	at school?
things **What**	**do**	you	eat	at parties?
time **When**		we	celebrate	that holiday?
time **What time**		they	begin	the celebration?
Place *location* **Where**		he	study	for school?
reason *because* **Why**	**does**	she	live	at home?
Method *Style – manner* **How**		it	meet	new people?

2.2 Using Simple Present Information Questions

A	Use a *Wh-* word with *do* before *I, you, we, they,* and plural nouns.	*When do you celebrate the holiday?* On dec 25
	Use a *Wh-* word with *does* before *he, she, it,* and singular nouns.	*Why does she study Spanish?* Because she wants to go to Spain
B	Use simple present information questions to ask for specific information.	*"Where do you live?"* *"I live in Mexico City."* *"What time do you start work?"* *"8:30."*
C	Use simple present information questions to ask about habits, facts, traditions, and regular activities.	*"When do they celebrate the Day of the Dead?"* *"In November."* *"Why does she travel to Mexico every year?"* *"Because she has family there."*
D	You can answer information questions with a short or long answer.	*"What do you eat on Thanksgiving?"* Short answer: *"Turkey and pie."* Long answer: *"I eat turkey and pie."*

2.3 Using *Wh-* Words

A	Use *Who* to ask about people.	*"Who do you remember on the Day of the Dead?"* *"I remember my grandmother."*
B	Use *What* to ask about things.	*"What do you study?"* *"Spanish and history."*
C	Use *When* to ask about time (days, months, years, seasons, parts of the day).	*"When do you celebrate Chinese New Year?"* *"In January or February."*
D	Use *What time* to ask about clock time.	*"What time does your class finish?"* *"4:30. / Five o'clock."*
E	Use *Where* to ask about places.	*"Where does she work?"* *"At the University of Mexico."*
F	Use *Why* to ask about reasons.	*"Why do you like celebrations?"* *"Because they're always fun."*
G	Use *How* to ask about manner – the way people do something.	*"How do you celebrate your birthday?"* *"We eat at my favorite restaurant."*

Grammar Application

Exercise 2.1 Questions with *Who, What, When, Where, How*

A Complete the questions with *Who, What, When, Where,* or *How* and *do* or *does.*

1 **A** __*Where*__ __*do*__ people celebrate the Day of the Dead?
   B In Mexico.

2 **A** __When__ __do__ they celebrate the Day of the Dead?
   B On November 1 and 2.

3 **A** __Who__ __do__ they remember?
   B Their dead relatives and friends.

4 **A** __What__ __do__ they decorate?
   B Graves and altars.

5 **A** __Where__ __do__ they put pictures of the dead?
   B On altars.

6 **A** __How__ __do__ they decorate the graves?
   B With flowers, candles, food, and drinks.

B Over to You Unscramble the words and add *do* or *does* to make questions. Then write answers that are true for you.

1 what celebration / you / like / the best / ?

   A *What celebration do you like the best?*

   B Christmas / Ramadan.

2 when / you / celebrate / it / ?

   A When do you celebrate it?

   B On Dec. 25th

3 who / you / celebrate / it / with / ?

   A Who do you celebrate it with?

   B Whit my family and friends.

4 what / you / usually / do / ?

   A What do you usually do?

   B We usually cook, eat, drink.

5 where / you / celebrate / it / ?

   A Where do you celebrate it?

   B At home.

6 what / you / usually / eat / ?

   A What do you usually eat?

   B Every thing.

7 when / it / usually / end / ?

   A When does it usually end?

   B Whe everyone is tired and sleepy.

C Pair Work Ask and answer the questions in B with a partner.

Exercise 2.2 Questions with *When* and *What Time*

A Complete the questions with *When* or *What time* and *do* or *does*.

1 A <u>*When*</u> <u>*do*</u> you graduate? B On June 15.

2 A <u>What time</u> ^{do} you have the ceremony? B At 3:30.

3 A <u>When does</u> Sandi turn 21? B Next Saturday.

4 A <u>What time</u> ^{does} her birthday party start? B At 7:00.

5 A <u>When do</u> you celebrate Thanksgiving in the United States? B At the end of November.

6 A <u>When does</u> your family usually have the meal? B In the late afternoon.

7 A <u>What time do</u> you usually start cooking on that day? B At about 8:00 a.m.

B Pair Work Ask and answer the questions in A with a partner.

Exercise 2.3 Asking Information Questions

A Read the paragraph about a holiday celebration in Massachusetts. Write information questions using the words in parentheses. Find the verbs in the paragraph, and use the information to write your questions. Remember to use *do* and *does* in your questions.

One of my favorite holidays is Patriots' Day in the Boston, Massachusetts, area. Every year, Boston residents celebrate Patriots' Day on the third Monday of April. On this day, people remember the beginning of the American Revolutionary War. Many towns have parades and speeches.[1] The second important event is the Boston Marathon.[2] The marathon happens every year on Patriots' Day. The race starts around 10:00 a.m. in Hopkinton and ends in Boston. Thousands of people watch runners from all over the world. The third event is the special Patriots' Day baseball game. The Boston Red Sox play a team from another town. The game starts around 11:00 a.m. in Boston.

¹speech: a formal talk | **²marathon:** a race in which people run 26 miles and 385 yards (42.195 kilometers)

1 (what / people / celebrate) ^{do} <u>*What do people celebrate on the third Monday of April?*</u>

2 (what / people / remember) ^{do} _____

3 (what / towns / have) ^{do} _____

4 (when / marathon / happen) ^{does} _____

5 (what time / marathon / start) ^{does} _____

6 (where / marathon / start) ^{does} <u>in Hopkinton</u> _____

7 (who / people / watch) ^{do} _____

B Pair Work Ask and answer the questions in A with a partner.

    A *What do people celebrate on the third Monday of April?*

    B *They celebrate Patriots' Day.*

In information questions, our voice usually *goes down*. We call this falling intonation.	Where do you go on va**ca**tion? Why do you stay **home**? When do you see your **re**latives?
In *Yes/No* questions, our voice often *goes up*. We call this rising intonation.	Do you celebrate Me**mo**rial Day? Is that your favorite day of the **year**? Does she work at **night**?

A Listen to the questions and answers. Mark the questions with ↗ for rising intonation and ↘ for falling intonation.

  1 **A** Excuse me. Are you from Japan? ↗

     B Yes, I am. I'm from Tokyo.

  2 **A** Can I ask you some questions? _____

     B Sure!

  3 **A** What's your favorite holiday in Japan? _____

     B New Year's Day.

  4 **A** Why is it your favorite? _____

     B Because we have special food for the holiday, and we relax all day.

  5 **A** Do you help your mother with the cooking? _____

     B Yes, I do. We also see all our relatives on New Year's Day.

  6 **A** Do you play any special games? _____

     B No, not really. But we watch some special TV programs.

  7 **A** What else do you do on New Year's Day? _____

     B Well, we read all our holiday cards then.

  8 **A** Do you really save all the cards to open on the same day? _____

     B Yes, it's a special custom.

B Listen and repeat the questions.

Exercise 2.5 Information Questions in Titles

📊 Data from the Real World

We often use information questions in the titles of academic articles and books. The article or book answers the question.

Why Do We Laugh?

How Does a Computer Work?

When Do People Watch TV?

Titles with *How? What?* and *Why?* are very frequent.

How do/does? ▐▐▐▐▐▐▐

What do/does? ▐▐▐▐▐▐

Why do/does? ▐▐▐

A Read the quotations from academic articles. Choose a title for each article from the box.

A Why Do People Celebrate Holidays?

B How Do People Make New Friends?

C When Does a Child Become an Adult?

D Why Do We Dream?

E What Do Teens Search for on the Internet?

F Why Does a Bird Learn to Sing?

G ~~What Do Children Like to Eat?~~

H Why Do We Grow Old?

1 G *What Do Children Like to Eat?*
"Children prefer food that is not very hot or very strong in flavor."

2 F
"Birds need to communicate with other birds."

3 A
"We need to bring people together to remember good and bad events in our cultures."

4 H
"Our body is a machine. It works hard every day, year after year."

5 E
"Most searches are about movie stars, singers, and sports personalities."

6 B *Why do people make new f*
"We make friends with people we have something in common with, often at work or school."

7 D
"We dream because our minds need to rest."

8 C
"Teenagers are young adults, and the years 16 to 18 are very important."

B Over to You Do you know more about the topics in A? Tell a partner.

A lot of children don't like spicy food.

3 Questions with *How Often*

Grammar Presentation

Questions with *How often* ask about how many times something happens.	*How often does she travel to Mexico?* *How often do you see your family?*

3.1 Questions with *How Often*

How Often	Do/Does	Subject	Base Form of Verb	
How often	do	I/you/we/they	take	a vacation?
	does	he/she/it	receive	a gift?

(handwritten annotations: "2 o mas" next to "do"; "1 nomas" next to "does")

3.2 Using Questions with *How Often*

A Use questions with *How often* to ask how many times something happens.	*How often do you run in a marathon?* *How often does your family eat together?*	
B The answers are often frequency expressions.	*All the time.* *Every day.* *Every weekend.* *Every other week.* *Once a week.* *Twice a month.* *Three times a month.* *Several times a year.* *A few times a year.* *Once in a while.* *Almost never.*	

Grammar Application

Exercise 3.1 Questions with *How Often*

A Use the words to write questions with *How often*. Write true answers. Then ask and answer questions with a partner.

1 you/drink coffee

Question: _How often do you drink coffee?_

Answer: _Every day._

2 you/drink soda

Question: How often do you drink soda?

Answer: Every day.

3 you/eat breakfast alone

Question: How often do you eat breakfast alone?

Answer: Once time a week.

4 your family / go out to a nice restaurant

Question: _How often does your family go out to a nice restaurant?_

Answer: _twice a month._

5 your friends / eat at a fast-food restaurant

Question: _How often does your friends eat at a fast food restaurant_

Answer: _Almost never. ck_

6 your relatives / visit your home

Question: _How often dos your relatives visit your home?_

Answer: _Once a month._

B Over to You Use *How often* to write your own questions on a separate piece of paper. Use words from the box and your own ideas. Then ask your partner the questions.

board game	hiking	movie	swimming	TV
gym	library	music concert	text message	

How often do you watch TV past midnight?

4 Avoid Common Mistakes ⚠

1 In simple present information questions, use *do* or *does* before the subject.

do
Where you work?

does
Why he drink so much coffee?

2 Use *do* or *does*, not *is* or *are*, with the verb.

does
What time is the concert begin?

3 Do not use *-s* on the verb with *he / she / it* or a singular noun.

go
Where does Tom goes to school?

Editing Task

Find and correct seven more mistakes in these questions about Thanksgiving.

do
1 How you celebrate Thanksgiving?

2 Where do you celebrates Thanksgiving?

3 What are you does during Thanksgiving Day?

4 What you watch on TV?

5 What time are you usually have your meal?

6 What you do on the Friday after Thanksgiving?

7 Why people celebrate Thanksgiving?

Conjunctions: *And, But, Or; Because*

Time Management

1 Grammar in the Real World

A Do you have enough time for school, work, and family? Read the article. What is one way to manage your time well?

B Comprehension Check **Answer the questions. Use the article to help you.**

1 What do most adults not have enough of?

2 What are two ways to manage your time?

3 What happens when people make plans and complete them?

C Notice **Find the words** *and, but, or,* **and** *because* **in the article. Then complete the sentences.**

1 They are busy with work, family, and school.

2 People feel stressed because there is not enough time to do it all.

3 Some people don't like schedules, lists, _____ weekly plans.

4 Put a reminder for the task on your phone, _____ don't forget to do it!

TIME FOR EVERYTHING

Many adults say they want more time. They are busy with work, family, **and** school, **and** they often don't get everything done. People feel stressed **because** there is not enough time to do it all. However, there are some simple ways to manage your time well **and** avoid stress.

5 One way is to identify the important **or** necessary tasks for that day. Then create a schedule **or** a "to do" list.[1] When you finish your important tasks, you can move on to the next, less important ones. Soon your tasks are done, **and** there is hopefully some extra time for fun activities.

Another way is to do important tasks on the same days every week.
10 For example, you can do your laundry every Monday, **and** go to the gym on Tuesday and Thursday mornings before work or school. Always do the tasks on the same days. That way, you can plan around these important tasks **and** have time for other things. Some people don't like schedules, lists, or weekly plans. Instead, they use the notes or calendar
15 features on their cell phones. Put a reminder[2] for the task on your phone, **but** don't forget to do it!

These ideas can help you improve your time management.[3] When you make plans and complete them, you feel good **and** can do more.

[1]**"to do" list:** a list of things you need to do

[2]**reminder:** something that helps someone remember, like an alarm on a phone

[3]**time management:** being in control of your time; planning and using your time well

Things to Do!
1.
2.
3.

Monday's Tasks
9:00 a.m.
10:00 a.m.
11:00 a.m.
12:00 p.m.

2 *And, But, Or*

Grammar Presentation

And, but, and *or* are coordinating conjunctions. They connect words, phrases, and clauses.	People are busy with family *and* work. I like to exercise, *but* I don't have time for it every day. She studies in the morning *or* after work.

2.1 *And, But, Or* for Connecting Words and Phrases

Connecting Words	*Time and money* are valuable. She sleeps only *five or six* hours a night.
Connecting Phrases	I always *make a schedule and look at it often*. I have "to do" lists *on my refrigerator but not on my phone*. Do you work *during the day or at night*?

2.2 *And, But, Or* for Connecting Clauses

First Clause		Second Clause
You have more time in your day,	**and**	you feel less stressed.
Some people use their time well,	**but**	other people do not.
You can make a list,	**or**	you can schedule tasks on the same days.

2.3 Using *And, But, Or*

A Use *and, but*, and *or* to connect words, phrases, and clauses.	Time *and* money are valuable. He has time *but* not money. Do you use schedules, *or* do you make "to do" lists?
B Use *and* to join two or more ideas.	Maria makes time for school, family, *and* work. I study *and* work every day. I make a "to do" list, *and* I check the list often during the day.
C Use *but* to show contrast or surprising information.	José works hard, *but* he also has fun. He always makes a schedule, *but* he rarely follows it.

2.3 | Using *And, But, Or* (continued)

D Use *or* to show a choice of two alternatives.	You can make lists *or* schedules. I exercise *or* do laundry after I study. Is he at school *or* at work?
E Use a comma when *and*, *but*, and *or* connect two clauses.	My family gets together at night, *and* we talk about our day. Sonya wakes up early, *but* she is always late for work.

Grammar Application

Exercise 2.1 Choosing *And, But, Or*

A Read the sentences about two types of people. Complete the sentences with *and*, *but*, or *or*. Add commas where necessary.

The Organized Person

1 Every day I wake up**, and** I make a long "to do" list.

2 I usually use the "notes" feature on my phone for important tasks _____ I always do them.

3 I don't like to forget appointments _____ be late.

4 I like to be busy _____ I feel good when I get things done.

The Disorganized Person

5 Sometimes I make lists _____ I usually lose them.

6 I have a lot of appointments _____ a lot of things to do every day.

7 I try to be on time _____ I am often late for appointments.

8 I am always busy _____ I don't get things done.

B Over to You Read the sentences in A with a partner. Which statements are true for you? Tell your partner.

Exercise 2.2 Punctuating Sentences with *And, But, Or*

A Correct the sentences below about ways to add time to a busy day. Add capital letters, periods, and commas as necessary.

1 a Jane wants to read more but she doesn't have the time

   Jane wants to read more, but she doesn't have the time.

   b now she listens to audiobooks in the car and during her breaks at work

   _____

   c she listens to a book or a podcast every day and feels good about herself

   _____

2 **a** James is very busy and often doesn't do his homework or study

_____

b he worries about his grades and gets very upset

_____

c finally, he talks about his problem with a classmate and they decide to help each other

_____

d he and his classmate now talk on the phone every day and work on their homework together

_____

B Group Work Make a list of four study tips. Use *and*, *but*, and *or* in your sentences.

Exercise 2.3 More *And, But, Or*

Good time management includes time for fun activities. Complete the sentences with your ideas about things you do for fun. Use *and*, *but*, or *or*.

1 On the weekends, I _watch TV and garden_____.

2 Once a day, I _____.

3 In the evenings, I _____.

4 Sometimes I _____.

Exercise 2.4 Vocabulary Focus: Expressions with *And* and *Or*

📊 Data from the Real World

English has many expressions using *and* and *or*. The nouns usually occur in the order they appear below.	Do you like peanut butter and jelly? NOT ~~Do you like jelly and peanut butter?~~	
Common "noun *and* noun" expressions for food	cream *and* sugar salt *and* pepper bread *and* butter	peanut butter *and* jelly fish *and* chips
Common "noun *and* noun" expressions for relationships	mom *and* dad brother *and* sister husband *and* wife	Mr. *and* Mrs. father *and* son mother *and* daughter
Other common "noun *and* noun" expressions	night *and* day men *and* women name *and* address	ladies *and* gentlemen boys *and* girls
Common expressions with *or*	cash *or* credit	coffee *or* tea
Common "adjective *and* adjective" expressions	black *and* white old *and* new	nice *and* warm

A Complete the questions.

1 Do you like ___*cream*___ and sugar with your coffee?

2 Do your _____ and dad live in the United States?

3 Do you have brothers and _____ ?

4 Do you work _____ and day?

5 Do you like black and _____ movies?

6 Do you think _____ and women have really different interests?

7 Do you put salt and _____ on your food?

8 Do you usually pay with _____ or credit?

9 Do you ever eat peanut butter and _____ sandwiches?

10 Do you prefer _____ or tea?

B Pair Work Take turns asking and answering the questions in A with a partner. Use complete sentences in your answers.

A *Do you like cream and sugar with your coffee?*
B *I like sugar, but I don't like cream.*

3 Because

Grammar Presentation

Because introduces the reason for or cause of something.	EFFECT CAUSE *People feel stressed because there is not enough time.*

3.1 *Because* for Connecting Clauses

A *Because* shows a cause-and-effect relationship.	EFFECT CAUSE *I am always late because I don't like to get up early.*
Clauses with *because* must have a subject and a verb.	SUBJECT VERB *Some people send e-mail reminders because they want to remember their tasks.*

B A clause with *because* is <u>not</u> a complete sentence. It needs the main clause to form a complete sentence.	MAIN CLAUSE *I am always late because <u>I don't like to get up early</u>.* NOT *I am always late. Because <s>I don't like to get up early.</s>*
C *Because* can come before or after the main clause. Use a comma when *because* comes first in a sentence.	MAIN CLAUSE *Because <u>I don't like to get up early</u>, I am always late.* MAIN CLAUSE *I am always late because I don't like to get up early.*
D In speaking, you can answer a question starting with *because.* Do not do this in writing.	*Why are you at school?* Say: *Because I want to learn English.*

Grammar Application

Match the effect on the left with the cause on the right.

1 John is tired __c__
2 Tanya is usually late _____
3 Dan is often hungry _____
4 Eric walks slowly _____
5 Sue takes her brother to school _____
6 Maya and Sara sleep late _____
7 Jack takes classes at night _____

a because his foot hurts.
b because he never eats breakfast.
c because he doesn't sleep enough.
d because he works during the day.
e because she doesn't put reminders on her phone.
f because their mother doesn't have time.
g because they work until midnight.

Put *because* in the correct place in each sentence. Add commas where necessary. Then listen and compare your answers.

Bob, Jamal, Tony, and Leo are roommates. They study at the local community college. Each roommate has a problem with time.

because

1 Leo works at night ∧ he goes to school during the day.

2 Tony can only study in the mornings he thinks more clearly then.

3 Bob's bus arrives after 8 o'clock he is always late.

4 Jamal can't study at home his roommates are too noisy.

5 Leo forgets to write his assignments down he often misses them.

6 Tony and Jamal sometimes miss class they play basketball instead.

Exercise 3.3 Combining Sentences with *Because*

Label each clause with *C* for "cause" and *E* for "effect." Then combine the sentences with *because*. Do not change the order of the clauses.

1 _*E*_ Brendon does well in class.   _*C*_ He studies every day.

   Brendon does well in class because he studies every day.

2 _*C*_ Tanya forgets to set her alarm.   _*E*_ She is often late for work.

   Because Tanya forgets to set her alarm, she is often late for work.

3 ____ Alan has three reminders about   ____ He doesn't want to forget about it.
   the meeting on his phone.

   _____

4 ____ Wanda is always hungry at work.   ____ She doesn't have time for lunch.

   _____

5 ____ Karin starts work very early.   ____ She drinks a lot of coffee.

   _____

6 ____ Blanca works during the day.   ____ She takes night classes.

   _____

7 ____ Jared keeps a "to do" list.   ____ He has a lot of work.

   _____

Complete the sentences. Make them true for you.

1 I take English classes because _____ .

2 I wake up at _____ because _____ .
    (time)

3 I live in _____ because _____ .
    (town/city)

4 I like _____ because _____ .
    (class)

5 I go to bed at _____ because _____ .
    (time)

4 Avoid Common Mistakes ⚠

1 **Do not use a comma when you join two words or two phrases.**

Lisa creates a schedule ~~,~~ and a list every day.

2 **Use a comma when you join two clauses with *and*, *but*, and *or*.**

I need to study for the test ‸ and then I have to work!

3 **Use *and* to add information. Use *but* to show a contrast. Use *or* to show a choice.**

                                but
Sam is always late, ~~and~~ he gets his work done.

4 **Do not use a comma if *because* is in the second part of the sentence.**

Jake is always on time ~~,~~ because he takes the 8:00 bus to school every day.

But do use a comma if *because* is in the first part of the sentence.

Because Lily makes a daily schedule ‸ she never forgets to do her tasks.

5 **Use *because* to state the reason (cause) for something. The other part of the sentence states the result (effect).**

Because Kylie writes her assignments on her calendar,

~~Kylie writes her assignments on her calendar because~~ she doesn't forget them.

Kylie doesn't forget her assignments because

~~Because Kylie doesn't forget her assignments,~~ she writes them on her calendar.

Editing Task

Read the story about Professor Kwan's class on time management. Find and correct nine more mistakes.

A Useful Class

Every year, Professor Kwan teaches a class on time management. Many students like to take her class. Sometimes the class fills up quickly / because it is so popular. Students know that they need to register early – in person and online. This is the first lesson of the time-management class.

5   In this class, Professor Kwan talks about different ways for students to organize their time. Her students often complain about the stress they have but how little time they have. Professor Kwan always tells her students to buy a calendar. She says students can use an electronic calendar but a paper calendar. Because her students get organized they use their calendar every day. She tells students to find time to

10   study at least once a day – either after school and at night. When students plan their time well, they feel in control and confident.

This is not the only thing that Professor Kwan teaches in the class. Students have a lot of stress because it is also important to find time to relax, and exercise. Professor Kwan's class is so popular, because all students need help with time management. At the

15   end of her class, students have less stress and they have great time-management skills!

Simple Past Statements

Success Stories

Sok ses storiz

1 Grammar in the Real World

A Do you know people who don't give up easily? Read the article. What do you learn about this band?

B Comprehension Check Are these sentences true or false? Use the article to help you. Correct the false sentences.

1 The executive traveled to London in December 1961.	True	<u>False</u>
2 The executive invited the band to London.	<u>True</u>	False
3 The band went to London and played on New Year's Eve.	True	<u>False</u>
4 The company didn't call the band immediately.	<u>True</u>	False
5 The band signed a contract with another company.	<u>True</u>	False

C Notice Answer the questions. Use the article to help you.

1 Can you find the past forms of these verbs in the article?

Present	travel	invite	play	wait	sign
Simple Past	traveled	invited	played	waited	signed

2 What do the simple past verbs in question 1 have in common?

3 Can you find the past forms of these verbs in the article?

Base Form	go	think	have	tell	become
Simple Past	went	thought	had	told	became

4 How are these simple past verbs different from the verbs in question 1?

A Band That Didn't Give Up[1]

Writers, artists, singers, and inventors[2] often feel discouraged[3] when others tell them they are not good enough. Some people give up. Others, like a group of young musicians in the 1960s, don't let it stop them.

5   In December 1961, a record company executive[4] **traveled** to Liverpool, England. He **went** to listen to a new rock 'n' roll band. The executive **thought** the band **had** talent and **invited** them to an audition[5] in London. The group **went** to London and **played** on New Year's Day 1962. After the audition, they **went** home and **waited** for a phone call.
10 They **didn't hear** any news for weeks.

    Finally, the company executive **told** the band manager, "Guitar groups are on the way out,[6] Mr. Epstein." So the record company **didn't give** the band a contract.[7]

    But the band **didn't give up**. In the end, they **signed** a contract with 15 another company and **became** a very famous band: The Beatles.

bicam

[1]**give up:** stop trying
[2]**inventor:** someone who designs or create new things
[3]**discouraged:** not confident to try again
[4]**executive:** person in a high position in a company who manages and makes decisions
[5]**audition:** short performance given to show ability
[6]**out:** not fashionable; not popular
[7]**contract:** written legal agreement

2 Simple Past Statements: Regular Verbs

Grammar Presentation

The simple past describes events that started and ended before now.	In 1961, he *traveled* to Liverpool. The band *played* for two hours. They *didn't hear* any news for weeks.

2.1 Affirmative Statements

Subject	Simple Past Verb	
I You We They He / She / It	**started**	in 1962.

2.2 Negative Statements

Subject	Did + Not	Base Form of Verb	
I You We They He / She / It	**did not** **didn't**	**sign**	a contract.

2.3 Using Simple Past Statements

A Use the simple past for events that started and ended in the past.	the past now
It can be one event or repeated events.	He *traveled* to Liverpool. The band *played* in clubs every week. They *didn't hear* any news.
B You can use the simple past to describe a feeling in the past.	He *didn't like* the band.

2.4 Spelling: Regular Simple Past Verbs

A For most verbs, add -ed.	work → work**ed**
B For verbs ending in e, add -d.	live → live**d**
C For verbs ending in consonant + y, change y to i and add -ed.	study → stud**ied**

2.4 Spelling: Regular Simple Past Verbs *(continued)*

D For verbs ending in vowel + *y*, add *-ed*.	*play → play*ed
E For one-syllable verbs ending in consonant-vowel-consonant, double the consonant.	*plan → plan*ned
F Do not double the consonant if the verb ends in *-x* or *-w*.	*show → show*ed
G For two-syllable verbs ending in consonant-vowel-consonant and stressed on the first syllable, do not double the consonant.	*travel → trave*led
H For two-syllable verbs ending in consonant-vowel-consonant and stressed on the second syllable, double the consonant.	*control → control*led
📊 Here are some of the most common regular simple past verbs.	called wanted started happened worked lived tried moved looked talked liked decided

▸ Spelling and Pronunciation Rules for Regular Verbs in Simple Past: See page A21.
▸ Common Regular and Irregular Verbs: See page A15.

Grammar Application

Exercise 2.1 Affirmative Simple Past Statements: Regular Verbs

Complete the sentences about The Beatles. Use the simple past form of the verbs in parentheses.

1 The Beatles first _visited_ (visit) the United States in 1964.

2 They _landed_ (land) in New York on February 7, 1964.

3 The door of the plane _opened_ (open).

4 The Beatles _appeared_ (appear).

5 The fans _cheered_ (cheer) and _shouted_ (shout).

6 Some fans _screamed_ (scream) and others _cried_ (cry).

7 The Beatles _played_ (play) on *The Ed Sullivan Show* on TV.

8 About 74 million people _watched_ (watch) the show.

9 Their long hair _shocked_ (shock) the country.

10 They _changed_ (change) popular music forever.

A Complete the first paragraph of this biography with negative simple past verbs. Use the full form *did not*.

This child **did not talk** (talk) before the age

of four. He _did not learn_ (learn) to read before
(2)

the age of seven. He _did not like_ (like) his
(3)

high school, and he _did not pass_ (pass) the
(4)

entrance exam for the Swiss Federal Polytechnic School,

a university in Zurich. One teacher _did not believe_
(5)

(believe) that he was intelligent at all. However, this boy

did not stop (stop) working hard. His teachers
(6)

_did not ___>_ (recognize) his genius, but he
(7)

did not listen (listen) to their discouraging words.
(8)

B Complete the rest of the biography with simple past forms of the verbs in the box.

enjoyed	explained	~~not perform~~ did not	studyied
entered	graduated	showed	worked

He **did not perform** well in school, but he _showed_ an interest in
(1)   (2)

science, and he _enjoyed_ math. He _studied_ for a high school
(3)   (4)

diploma, and finally he _entered_ the university. He _graduated_
(5)   (6)

four years later and then _worked_ on a Ph.D. He later _explained_
(7)   (8)

the laws of the universe. Who is he? _Albert einstein_ [The answer is on page 128.]

Exercise 2.3 Pronunciation Focus: Saying Simple Past Verbs

When the verb ends in /t/ or /d/, say -ed as an extra syllable /ɪd/ or /əd/.	/ɪd/ or /əd/ /t/ wai**t** → waited	/d/ deci**de** → decided
When the verb ends in /f/, /k/, /p/, /s/, /ʃ/, and /tʃ/, say -ed as /t/.	/t/ /f/ lau**gh** → laughed /k/ loo**k** → looked /p/ sto**p** → stopped	/s/ mi**ss** → missed /ʃ/ fini**sh** → finished /tʃ/ wat**ch** → watched
For verbs that end in other consonant and vowel sounds, say -ed as /d/.	/d/ list**en** → listened cha**nge** → changed li**ve** → lived	pl**ay** → played agr**ee** → agreed borr**ow** → borrowed

A Listen and repeat the verbs in the chart above.

B Pair Work Add simple past endings to the verbs below. Then read the sentences aloud with a partner. Do the verbs have an extra syllable? Check (✓) Yes or No.

	Yes	No
1 A friend **call**_ed_ me last night.		✓
2 I **invite**_d_ her to dinner.	✓	
3 We **talk**_ed_ about music.		✓
4 She **want**_ed_ to get an old album from the 1960s for her grandfather.		✓
5 We **laugh**_ed_ about the old-fashioned records.		✓
6 We **look**_ed_ for the album on the Internet.		✓
7 I **download**_ed_ the music files.		✓
8 We **play**_ed_ them.		✓
9 They **sound**_ed_ funny.		✓
10 We **forward**_ed_ the music files to her grandfather.		✓
11 He **listen**_ed_ to the songs.		✓
12 Then he **delete**_d_ them. Not all music from the 1960s is good.	✓	

C Over to You Tell a partner about four things you did last night. Use some of the verbs in this exercise.

I watched TV last night.

yesterday	last . . .	. . . ago	Prepositions
yesterday	last night	two days ago	in 2007
yesterday morning	last week/month/year	six weeks ago	on June 19
yesterday evening	last Friday/June/	10 months/years ago	at 7:30
	spring	a long time ago	before/after the audition

Time expressions usually come at the end of a sentence.	*I listened to a Beatles album last night.* *The Beatles became famous in 1962.*
Time expressions can also come at the start of a sentence when they are very important.	*After the audition, they went home and waited.* *In 1961, a record company executive traveled to Liverpool.*

Complete the sentences about a famous poet. Use the words from the box. Some words are used more than once.

after	ago	in	last	on

1 I borrowed a book of poems from the library __*last*__ week.
2 The poet lived in Massachusetts over 100 years _ago_ .
3 She published only seven poems _in_ her lifetime.
4 She died at the age of 55 _on_ May 15, 1886.
5 _After_ the poet's death, her sister discovered over 1,800 poems in her room.
6 Her first book of poems appeared four years after she died, _in_ 1890.
7 T. H. Johnson published a complete collection of her poems _in_ 1955.
8 I prepared a presentation about her for class _last_ night.

1830–1886

Pair Work **When was the last time you or a friend did these things? Ask and answer questions with a partner. Write sentences about your partner.**

1 borrow a book from the library *Marie borrowed a book from the library three weeks ago.*
2 listen to a podcast _Ms Eno listened to podcast last Saturday._
3 laugh or cry at a movie _Islam laughed at a movie long time ago_
4 move to another apartment or house _Jumping moved to another house._
5 try really hard to do something _We tried really hard to speak English._
6 travel to another city _Gloria traveled to Mexico 2 weeks ago._

Exercise 2.6 *Did Not* and *Didn't* in Writing

📊 Data from the Real World

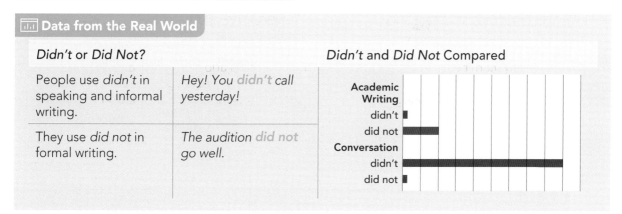

Didn't or *Did Not*?		*Didn't* and *Did Not* Compared
People use *didn't* in speaking and informal writing.	Hey! You *didn't* call yesterday!	
They use *did not* in formal writing.	The audition *did not* go well.	

Rewrite these sentences about the famous poet Emily Dickinson for academic writing. Change the contractions.

1 Emily Dickinson didn't publish a lot of poems in her lifetime.

Emily Dickinson did not publish a lot of poems in her lifetime.

2 Even her family didn't know about the 1,800 poems in her room.

Even her family did not know about the 1,800 poems in her room.

3 In the nineteenth century, some critics didn't like her work, but she continued to write for herself.

did not

4 She didn't write like other poets.

She did not write like other poets.

5 She didn't use correct punctuation.

She did not use correct punctuation.

6 In the 1950s, poetry experts published her work again. This time, they didn't edit it.

In the 1950s, poetry experts published her work again. This time, they did not edit it.

3 Simple Past Statements: Irregular Verbs

Grammar Presentation

Irregular simple past verbs don't end in *-ed*.	In 1961, he **went** to Liverpool. The company **made** a big mistake.

3.1 Irregular Verbs

AFFIRMATIVE STATEMENTS		
Subject	Simple Past Irregular Verb	
I You We They He / She / It	**became**	popular.

NEGATIVE STATEMENTS			
Subject	*Did + Not*	Base Form of Verb	
I You We They He / She / It	**did not** **didn't**	**become**	popular.

3.2 Using Irregular Simple Past Verbs

A 📊 Here are the most common irregular verbs.	come → came make → made do → did put → put get → got read → read go → went say → said have → had see → saw
B Be careful with the verb *do*.	I *did* my homework last night. I *didn't do* my homework this morning.

➤➤ Irregular Verbs: See page A16.

▸ Grammar Application

Exercise 3.1 Simple Past Statements with Irregular Verbs

A Make guesses about things your partner did yesterday. Use the verbs in parentheses. Write affirmative and negative sentences.

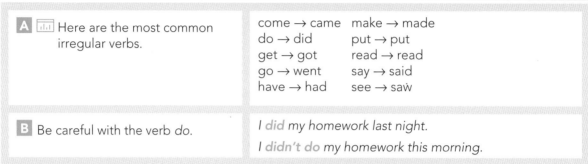

1 You ___*didn't do*___ (do) your homework last night.
2 You _____ (read) your e-mail after dinner.
3 You _____ (get up) late yesterday morning.
4 You _____ (come) to school early today.
5 You _____ (go) to work last night.
6 You _____ (make) a wonderful dinner yesterday.
7 You _____ (see) a movie in a theater last weekend.
8 You _____ (read) the news this morning.
9 You _____ (have) breakfast this morning.
10 You _____ (see) the weather report this morning.

Yes, I did
No, didn't
DID

B Pair Work Read the sentences to your partner. Are your guesses correct?

A You didn't do your homework last night.
B That's true. I did my homework this morning! / That's not true. I did my homework after dinner.

Exercise 3.2 Pronunciation Focus: Saying Irregular Simple Past Verbs

Sometimes the spelling of two verbs is the same, or similar, but the pronunciation is different.	read → read say → said BUT pay → paid hear → heard
Sometimes the letters *gh* are not pronounced.	buy → bought think → thought
When you learn an irregular verb, learn the pronunciation, too.	

A Listen and repeat the verbs in the chart above. Notice the pronunciation of the irregular past forms.

B Tell a partner about something . . .

1 you bought last week.

2 you read recently.

3 your teacher said in the last class.

4 you thought about today.

5 you paid a lot of money for years ago.

6 you heard on the news today.

Exercise 3.3 More Irregular Simple Past Verbs

A Complete the descriptions with the verbs below. Can you match the pictures to the texts?

Vincent van Gogh

J. K. Rowling

Marilyn Monroe

Abraham Lincoln

1

see	not get	come
saw	*didn't get*	*came*

In 1944, Norma Jean Baker ___*came*___ to see the director of a modeling agency for a job interview. Unfortunately, Baker ___*didn't get*___ the job. The next time the director ___*saw*___ her, she had a different name and was a famous movie star. Who was she? *Marilyn Monroe*

2

buy	make	pay
bought	*made*	*paid*

This artist ___*made*___ over 800 paintings, but only one person ___*bought*___ one in his lifetime. The sister of a friend ___*paid*___ 400 francs (about $1,600 today) for it. Who was he? *Vincent van Gogh*

3

~~became~~	~~went~~	~~read~~	~~lost~~	~~didn't have~~
become	go	read	lose	not have

This man ___didn't have___ a lot of money as a child. He ___went___ to school for only 18 months, but he ___read___ hundreds of books. As a politician, he ___lost___ his first election. Later, he ___became___ an important president in U.S. history. Who was he? _Abraham Lincoln_

4

~~became~~	~~said~~	~~wrote~~	~~told~~	~~bought~~
become	say	write	tell	buy

This single mother ___wrote___ her first book in a café. Twenty publishers ___told___ her they didn't want it. Finally, one publisher ___said___ "Yes." Millions of people ___bought___ the book, and it ___became___ a successful movie. Who is she? _J. K. Rowling_

B Group Work Discuss the famous people in this unit. Who is the most interesting to you? Why?

Answer to Exercise 2.2B, p. 122: Albert Einstein

4 Avoid Common Mistakes ⚠

1 Use simple past verbs to write or talk about the past.

started
He ~~starts~~ his career in 2002.

ate
I ~~eat~~ at a restaurant last night.

2 After *did not / didn't*, use the base form of the verb. Do __not__ use the past form.

earn
They didn't ~~earned~~ a lot of money.

I didn't EAT
COOK
_GO_

3 For the negative, write *did not* as two words.

did not
She ~~didnot~~ get the job.

I did not VISIT
We " " COME
He " " TRAVEL

4 Use the correct spelling for simple past verbs.

~~bought~~	~~took~~	~~read~~	~~studied~~	~~dropped~~	~~paid~~
buyed	taked	red	studyed	droped	payed

stop – ped
drop – "
shop – "

5 The simple past negative of *have* is *did not / didn't have*. The simple past negative of *do* is *did not / didn't do*.

did not have / didn't have

didn't have
He ~~had not~~ a successful career.

did not do
She ~~did not~~ her homework last night.

did not do / didn't do

Editing Task

Find and correct 10 more mistakes in this paragraph about the inventor of the lightbulb.

Thomas Edison was born in 1847 in Milan, Ohio. He ~~had not~~ *did not have* very much education in school. His mother taught him reading, writing, and math. Like many children at the time, he ~~droped~~ *dropped* out of school and got a job. At age 13, he ~~sells~~ *sold* newspapers and candy

5 at a railroad station. Thomas continue to learn about science by reading. At age 16, he ~~become~~ *became* a telegraph operator.[1] Later, he ~~start~~ *started* to invent things. In 1869, he moved to New York City. One of his inventions earned him $40,000, so he opened his first research laboratory[2] in New Jersey. He tried hundreds of times to make the

10 first lightbulb, but he ~~had not~~ *did not have* success. However, Thomas Edison ~~didnot~~ *did not* give up. He ~~learn~~ *learned* from his mistakes. In 1879, he introduced his greatest invention, the electric light for the home. He told a reporter, "I didn't ~~failed~~ *fail* 1,000 times. The lightbulb was an invention with 1,000 steps."

[1]**telegraph operator:** a person who worked with a communication device that sent and received signals
[2]**research laboratory:** a building with equipment for doing scientific tests

1 Grammar in the Real World

A Do you know a business owner? Read the conversation between two students. What is unusual about Blake Mycoskie's business?

B Comprehension Check **Answer the questions.**

1 Did Blake Mycoskie win *The Amazing Race* on TV?

_____

2 When did he start TOMS Shoes?

_____

3 How many pairs of shoes did he distribute by the end of September 2010?

_____

4 What are two problems for children without shoes?

_____

C Notice **Find the questions in the conversation. Complete the questions.**

1 Did you _____finish_____ your report for class tomorrow?

2 What did he _____do_____ ?

3 Did you _____say_____ "shoes"?

4 Why did he _____decide_____ to sell shoes?

What form of the verb did you use to complete the questions?

A WORLD OF SHOES

Greg Hey, Liliana. **Did you finish** your report for class tomorrow?

Liliana No, but I found a really interesting businessman, Blake Mycoskie. Do you
5   remember him from that reality TV show, *The Amazing Race*?

Greg No, not really. **Did he win?**

Liliana No, he didn't, but that's not important. My report is on his *business*. It's really unusual.

10 **Greg** Why? **What did he do?** Let me guess . . . He started a cool company, and he made millions from his idea.

Liliana He started a cool company, and it helps fight poverty. He sells shoes, and . . .

15 **Greg** **Did you say** "shoes"?

Liliana Yes, he started TOMS Shoes in 2006. For every pair of shoes he sells, he donates a pair to a child in need.[1] By the end of September 2010, he distributed[2] his one
20   millionth pair.

Donate = doneit
25 *pair = peh*

Greg Hmm. Interesting. But **why did he decide to sell shoes?**

Liliana During *The Amazing Race*, he traveled with his sister all over the world. He saw a lot of very poor people and a lot of children without shoes. A lot of these children had diseases because they walked barefoot.[3] The schools did not allow children to attend without shoes.
30   So he came up with this concept[4] of selling and donating shoes. In the future, he plans to expand[5] his business and make other products, too.

Greg Oh, I see. He's a social entrepreneur.
35   He wants to make money, but he also wants to help people.

---

[1] **in need:** not having enough money
[2] **distribute:** give something to many people
[3] **barefoot:** not wearing any shoes or socks
[4] **concept:** idea
[5] **expand:** make something bigger

2 Simple Past *Yes / No* Questions

Grammar Presentation

Simple past *Yes / No* questions ask about actions and events that happened before now.	*Did you **finish** your report?* *Did he **do** something fun?*

2.1 *Yes / No* Questions

Did	Subject	Base Form of Verb	
Did	I you we they he / she / it	**finish**	the report?

2.2 Short Answers

AFFIRMATIVE

Yes	Subject	*Did*
Yes,	I you we they he / she / it	**did.**

NEGATIVE

No	Subject	*Did + Not*
No,	I you we they he / she / it	**did not.** **didn't.**

2.3 Using Simple Past *Yes / No* Questions

A	Questions in the simple past often use definite past-time expressions.	*Did Blake go to college **in the 1990s**?* *Did he start his company **11 years ago**?*
B	Use the contraction *didn't* in negative short answers. The full form *did not* is very formal.	*"Did Blake win The Amazing Race?"* *"No, he didn't."*
C	Use pronouns in short answers.	*"Did Blake start a shoe company?"* *"Yes, he did."*
	To give extra information, you can also answer *Yes / No* questions with long answers.	*"Yes, he started TOMS shoes in 2006."*

Grammar Application

Liliana heard about Blake Mycoskie and then went to a trade show[1] for entrepreneurs. Complete the questions in the simple past. Use the words in parentheses.

Liliana _Did you have_ (you/have) a good weekend?
(1)

Simon Yeah, pretty good. How about you?

Liliana Yes, very good.

Simon _Did you go out_ (you/go out)?
(2)

Liliana Yeah. I went out with Aisha on Saturday.

Simon Oh, _did you go_ (you/go) somewhere
(3)
interesting?

Liliana Yeah. We went to a trade show. There were lots of exhibits[2] from new companies.

Simon A trade show? I didn't know you were interested in business!

Liliana Yes, I'm very interested in it. _Did I tell_ (I/tell) you about my
(4)
grandmother's company?

Simon No.

Liliana My grandmother had her own clothing design company, so I want to do something like that.

Simon Really? _Did you see_ (you/see) any design companies there?
(5)

Liliana Yeah. We saw some. A lot of the companies' owners are young entrepreneurs.

Simon _Did you speak_ (you/speak) with any interesting people?
(6)

Liliana Yeah. I spoke with the owner of a men's tie company. He designs his own fabric.[3]

Simon Hmm. _Did you have_ (he/have) any good ideas for you?
(7)

Liliana Yes. He told me one thing: find a good business partner. What do you say? Do you want to be my business partner?

[1]**trade show:** a large event at which companies show and sell their products and try to increase their business
[2]**exhibit:** a collection of things people can see in public
[3]**fabric:** cloth or material

A Read Liliana's notes for her report on Blake Mycoskie. Then write the questions.

Questions About Blake Mycoskie

1 Second in "The Amazing Race"?
2 Other businesses before TOMS?
3 Sister – start the business with him?
4 Any experience in fashion?
5 Company – difficulties at the beginning?

1 he/finish _Did he finish second in "The Amazing Race"?_

2 he/have _____

3 his sister/start _____

4 he/have _____

5 the company/have _____

B Read some more information about Blake. Then answer the questions in A. First, write one short answer, and then write one long answer with extra information for each question.

   When Blake Mycoskie competed in *The Amazing Race* with his sister Paige, they finished third. They lost the race by only four minutes. His sister helped him with the concept of TOMS Shoes, but he started the business by himself. He had previous experience in business, but he didn't have any experience in fashion. But he liked to design things. Before TOMS shoes, he started five other businesses, including a college laundry business and a reality TV channel. When he started TOMS, he had a lot of problems with the shoe factory.[1] Now the factory runs well, and a lot of people work for him.

[1]**factory:** a building where people use machines to produce things

1 a _No, he didn't._

b _No, he finished third._

2 a _____

b _____

3 a _____

b _____

4 a _____

b _____

5 a _____

b _____

C Pair Work Ask and answer the questions about Blake with a partner.

A Over to You Write questions to ask a partner about last weekend. For question 5, use your own verb.

1 (do) _Did you do anything interesting?_

2 (work) Did you work

3 (have) Did you have

4 (go out) Did you go out on Saturday?

5 _____

B Pair Work Ask and answer the questions with your partner. Give your partner additional information.

A *Did you do anything interesting?*   **A** *Did you go out on Saturday?*

B *No, not really. I stayed home.*   **B** *Yes, I went to . . . /No, I worked all day.*

3 Simple Past Information Questions

Grammar Presentation

Simple past information questions ask about people, things, times, and places that happened before now.

What did he do?
Why did he decide to make shoes?

3.1 Information Questions

Wh- Word	Did	Subject	Base Form of Verb	
Who			write	about?
What		I	do	yesterday?
When		you	finish	our report?
What time	did	we	begin	writing?
Where		they	visit	on vacation?
Why		he	start	a company?
How		she	save	enough money?
		it		

3.2 Using Simple Past Information Questions

A Use simple past information questions to ask for specific information about something that happened in the past.	*"**Where did** she **study** business?"* *"She studied at Florida State."* *"**When did** she **graduate**?"* *"She graduated in 2012."*
B Use *Wh-* words with *did* to ask about habits and regular activities.	*"**What did** she **do** every summer?"* *"She worked at a restaurant."*

3.3 Using *Wh-* Words in Simple Past Information Questions

A Use *Who* to ask about people.	*Who did you start your company with?*	*My sister.*
B Use *What* to ask about things.	*What did you make?*	*Shoes.*
C Use *When* to ask about time (days, months, years, seasons, parts of the day).	*When did you have this idea?*	*Last week.*
D Use *What time* to ask about clock time.	*What time did you start work today?*	*At seven o'clock.*
E Use *Where* to ask about places.	*Where did you go to business school?*	*In Boston.*
F Use *Why* to ask about reasons.	*Why did you open a restaurant?*	*Because I love food.*
G Use *How* to ask about manner.	*How did you save enough money?*	*I saved some every month.*

⌨ Grammar Application

Exercise 3.1 Simple Past Information Questions and Answers

A Shelly Hwang, an entrepreneur, started a chain of frozen yogurt stores called Pinkberry. Unscramble the words to make questions about her.

1 Why / she / to / move / did / the United States?

   Why did she move to the United States?

2 What / after / she / did / college? / do

   _____

Shelly Hwang,
founder of Pinkberry

3 Who / she / with? / develop / the concept / did

_____

4 When / open / store? / she / did / her first

_____

5 What / have? / the store / did / flavors

_____

B Listen to an instructor talk about Hwang. Then write short answers to the questions in A.

1 _To study business._   **4** _____

2 _____   **5** _____

3 _____

4 Avoid Common Mistakes ⚠

1 Use *did* + subject + base form of the verb.

    did   *graduate*
When you ~~graduated~~ from business school?

2 In information questions, use *did* and the base form of the main verb. Do <u>not</u> use the past form.

           open   *become*
Where did you ~~opened~~ the first store? Did it ~~became~~ a success?

3 When *do* is the main verb, use *did* + subject + *do* (base form of verb).

    do
What did you at the company?

Editing Task

Find and correct the mistakes in these questions about your work experience.

        work
1 Did you ~~worked~~ for a relative?

2 Who you worked for?

         do
3 What did you?

              do
4 How many hours did you worked each week?

             do
5 How much money did you earned each week?

6 You enjoyed your job?

7 What you learned from this job?

      do
8 Why did you stopped working?

1 Grammar in the Real World

A What were you like as a child? Read the magazine article about Sheryl Sandberg. What was she like as a child?

B Comprehension Check Do these words describe Sheryl Sandberg as a child or as an adult? Check (✓) the correct answers. Some words describe both. Use the article to help you.

	As a Child	As an Adult
1 very famous	☐	☑
2 successful	☐	☑
3 busy	☑	☑
4 interested in friends	☑	☐

C Notice Read the sentences. Circle *was* or *were*. Use the article to help you.

1 Her father **was** / **were** an eye doctor.

2 Her mother **was** / **were** a teacher.

3 Her parents **was** / **were** busy.

4 Sheryl **was** / **were** a good student.

5 She **was** / **were** always busy.

6 People **was** / **were** interested in the Internet.

When do you use *was*? When do you use *were*?

Sheryl Sandberg:
A BUSINESS SUCCESS STORY

Sheryl Sandberg is a very famous business person. She worked at Google and **was** the first woman to be a director at Facebook. She wrote two very popular books. Today she is a billionaire. However, Sheryl Sandberg started her life in an
5 ordinary family. She **was** born in Washington, D.C. in 1969. Her family moved to Miami, Florida, when she **was** two years old. Her mother **was** an English teacher, and her father **was** an eye doctor. Her parents **were** very busy with their jobs, Sheryl, and her brother and sister.

10 Sheryl **was** a very good student at North Miami Beach High School. She studied a lot and taught exercise classes after school. She had a group of very close friends. Her friends say she **was not** interested in television or movies. She **was** always busy doing things.

15 In 1987, Sheryl went to Harvard University and then worked in Washington, D.C. She moved to California and **was** very successful at Google. People **were** interested in using the Internet to make new friends and write to old friends, so Sheryl got a job at Facebook. She made the company bigger and
20 helped it make more money. Sheryl learned a lot at Google and Facebook, and she wrote a book to help other women who want to be successful in business. More than 2.25 million people bought Sheryl's book.

2 Simple Past of *Be*: Affirmative and Negative Statements

Grammar Presentation

The simple past of *be* describes people, places, or things in the past.	Her home was in Florida. Her parents were busy.

2.1 Statements

AFFIRMATIVE

Subject	Was / Were	
I He She It	**was**	in the computer lab.
We You They	**were**	

NEGATIVE

Subject	Was / Were + Not	
I He She It	**was not** **wasn't**	in class.
We You They	**were not** **weren't**	

2.2 Using Simple Past of *Be*

A Use the simple past of *be* to talk or write about people, places, or things in the past. *Be* has two past forms: *was* and *were*.	She was a director. The students were in their class. I was not in the computer lab. They were not bored.
B Use *was/were* + *born* to say when or where someone was born.	She was born in Washington, D.C. in 1969.
C *Not* comes after *be* in negative statements.	She was not interested in television.
D In speaking, you can use the contractions *wasn't* and *weren't* in negative statements.	Sheryl wasn't interested in television. They weren't happy.
E We often use past time expressions with the simple past of *be*: *ten years ago/yesterday/this morning/last week/ in the past*	In 1987, Sheryl was a student. We were in California last week.
Past time expressions can go either at the beginning of a sentence or at the end of a sentence.	

Grammar Application

Exercise 2.1 Simple Past of *Be*: Affirmative and Negative Statements

A Read the descriptions of three famous women. Complete the sentences with *was/wasn't* or *were/weren't*. Write the names on the lines.

> Oprah Winfrey   Taylor Swift   Penélope Cruz

1 Penelope Cruz

She _____**was**_____ born in Madrid, Spain, in 1974.
(1)
Her father __was__ an auto mechanic[1] and her mother
(2)
__was__ a hairdresser.[2] She studied ballet and jazz dance
(3)
as a child. When she __was__ a teenager, she started
(4)
acting. At 17, she __was__ in her first film.
(5)

[1]**auto mechanic:** someone who repairs cars
[2]**hairdresser:** a person who cuts and styles hair (usually women's hair)

2 Oprah Winfrey

She __was__ born in Mississippi in 1954. Her mother
(6)
and father __were__ very poor. Her father __was__ a
(7)   (8)
barber.[3] When she __was__ in high school, she got her
(9)
first radio job. She __was__ a student at Tennessee State
(10)
University for several years. She got her first TV job in 1972.
By age 32, she __was__ a millionaire.
(11)

[3]**barber:** a person who cuts men's hair

3 Taylor Swift

She __was__ born in Pennsylvania in 1989.
(12)
As a child, she loved to write and wrote in her diary every
day. When she __was__ in the fourth grade, she won a
(13)
poetry contest.[4] She began to write songs, and she sang
at festivals and contests. She __wasn't__ (not) shy, and she
(14)
liked to perform. In high school, she __wasn't__ (not) very
(15)
popular. Other students __weren't__ (not) friendly with her.
(16)
Now she's very popular.

[4]**contest:** a competition to win a prize

B Complete the sentences with *was* and *wasn't*. Use the information in A to help you.

1 Penélope Cruz _wasn't_ born in the United States.

2 As a child, Taylor Swift _wasn't_ a songwriter.

3 Oprah Winfrey's family _wasn't_ wealthy.

4 As a child, Penélope Cruz _was_ a dancer.

5 By age 32, Oprah Winfrey _wasn't_ poor.

6 Oprah Winfrey's father _wasn't_ a TV star.

7 Penélope Cruz _was_ a teenager when she started acting.

Exercise 2.2 Simple Past of *Be*: More Affirmative and Negative Statements

A Over to You What were you like as a child? Write six sentences about you and your family members. Write three sentences with *was/were* and three sentences with *wasn't/weren't*. Use the words in the box and your own ideas.

| a bad student | active | busy | funny | intelligent | short | talkative |
| a good student | bored | friendly | happy | quiet | shy | tall |

I was very shy. I wasn't a good student. My father was a mechanic.

was/were

1 I was a good student.

2 My brother was funny

3 I was short and quiet

wasn't/weren't

1 My parents weren't wealthy

2 _____

3 _____

B Pair Work Tell your partner what you were like as a child and about your family members.

A *I was very shy. I wasn't very talkative.*

B *Really? That's surprising. What about your brothers and sisters?*

A *They weren't shy at all.*

3 Simple Past of *Be*: Questions and Answers

Grammar Presentation

Yes/No questions and information questions with the simple past of *be* ask about people, places, and things in the past.	"*Were* you in college last year?" "No, I *wasn't*." "When *were* you in college?" "I *was* in college three years ago."

3.1 Yes/No Questions

Was / Were	Subject	
Was	I he she it	very smart?
Were	we you they	in college?

3.2 Short Answers

AFFIRMATIVE

Yes	Subject	Was / Were
Yes,	I he she it	**was.**
	we you they	**were.**

NEGATIVE

No	Subject	Was / Were + Not
No,	I he she it	**was not.** **wasn't.**
	we you they	**were not.** **weren't.**

3.3 Using Yes/No Questions with Simple Past of *Be*

A We often use past time expressions in *Yes/No* questions with the simple past of *be*: *ten years ago/yesterday/this morning/last week*

Past time expressions go at the end of a question.

> *Were you in college* last year? Yes, I was
> *Was Bill famous* in 1955? No, he wasn't
> *Was she born* in 2003? No, she wasn't

B Use the contractions *wasn't/weren't* in negative short answers.

> *"Was she a dancer?"* *"No, she wasn't."*
> *"Were they wealthy?"* *"No, they weren't."*

C You can also answer with additional information.

> *"Was she a dancer?"* *"No, she was a songwriter."*
> *"Were they wealthy?"* *"No, they were very poor."*

3.4 Information Questions

Wh- Word	Was / Were	Subject	
Who		your best friend	as a child?
What	**was**	your favorite class	last semester?
When		her birthday party?	
What time		the meeting	on Monday?
Where		his partners?	
Why	**were**	they	successful?
How		the concerts	the other night?
How old		their children	in 2017?

A Use *Who* to ask about people.	*Who* was the first female director at Facebook?	Sheryl Sandberg.
B Use *What* to ask about things.	*What* was your favorite class last semester?	English.
C Use *When* to ask about time (days, months, years, seasons, parts of the day).	*When* was your sister born?	In April.
D Use *What time* to ask about clock time.	*What time* was your class?	At eight o'clock.
E Use *Where* to ask about places.	*Where* were you born?	In Tokyo.
F Use *Why* to ask about reasons.	*Why* were they excited?	Because they won the game.
G Use *How* to ask what something was like.	*How* was the play?	It was great.
H Use *How old* to ask about age.	*How old* was your brother last year?	He was 18.

Grammar Application

Exercise 3.1 Simple Past of *Be: Yes / No* Questions

A Tanya's class assignment is to interview her grandfather. Complete her questions with *Was* or *Were*.

1 _____*Were*_____ you born in New York City?

2 _____*Was*_____ your family large?

3 _____*Was*_____ your brother a good student?

4 _____*Were*_____ you and your brother good friends?

5 _____*Were*_____ your sisters nice to you?

6 _____*Were*_____ you and your sisters the same age?

7 _____*Was*_____ your father's store near the house?

B Pair Work Listen to the conversation between Tanya and her grandfather. Write short answers about the grandfather's life to the questions in A. Then compare your answers with a partner.

1 <u>*No, he wasn't.*</u> He was born in Turkey.

2 Yes, there were 5 girls and 2 boys.

3 No, he wasn't, but he's successful business man now.

4 Yes, we were like best friends.

5 No, not really.

6 No, we weren't.

7 Yes, it was downstairs. We lived upstairs. I was never late for work.

Exercise 3.2 Simple Past of *Be: Yes/No* Questions and Information Questions

A Read the paragraph about a childhood photograph. Then write information questions and answers about the photograph.

My great-grandmother was born in 1901 in Wisconsin. She was born at 12:10 in the morning. She was the first of two children. Her father was a store owner, and her mother was a teacher. They lived in a small town. I once saw a photograph of her

5 house. The house had two floors, and it was very simple. There was no paint on the house, but it was well built. There was a nice front porch with several chairs and some flowers. My great-grandmother and her father were in the photo. Her father was happy, but she was angry because she hated sitting for pictures. She was about

10 three years old in the photo. She was upset but very cute.

1 (When/she born) <u>*When was she born?*</u> <u>*She was born in 1901.*</u>

2 (Where/she born) Where was she born? She was born in Wisconsin.

3 (What time/she born) What time was she born? She was born at 12:10

4 (What/her father's job) What was her father's job?

5 (What/her mother's job) What was her mother's job?

6 (Who/in the photo) Who was in the photo?

7 (What/on the porch) What was on the porch?

8 (Why/she angry) Why was she angry?

9 (How old/she in the photo) How old was she in the photo?

B Over to You Write questions to ask a partner about his or her childhood. Write *Yes/No* questions and information questions. Use *was/were* and the words in the box or your own ideas.

born	favorite family activity	school
brothers	favorite games	sisters
chores[1]	favorite room in your house	your bedroom
father's/mother's job	favorite toys	

Where were you born?

1 _____
2 _____
3 _____
4 _____
5 _____
6 _____
7 _____
8 _____

[1]**chore:** a job that is often boring but that is important, like washing the dishes

C Pair Work Ask and answer the questions about childhood from B. Take turns.

A *Were you born in the United States?*
B *No, I was born in Thailand.*

4 Avoid Common Mistakes ⚠

1 **With *I / he / she / it* or a singular noun, use *was*.**

    was
He ~~were~~ a famous artist.

2 **With *you / we / they* or a plural noun, use *were*.**

    were
My brothers ~~was~~ usually nice to me.

3 **Use the correct form with *born*.**

    were you born   *was born*
When ~~was you born~~?   I ~~born~~ in 1980.

Editing Task

Find and correct seven more mistakes in the questions and answers about Yo-Yo Ma.

A When ~~were~~ *was* Yo-Yo Ma born?

B He *was* born in 1955.

Was A He born in the United States?

B No, he wasn't. He was born in France.

5 A Were his parents French?

B No, they *were* ~~was~~ not. They *were* ~~was~~ Chinese.

A Were his parents musicians?

B Yes, they *were* ~~was~~ talented musicians.

A How old was he when he first played the cello?

10 B He was four.

A How old *was* ~~were~~ he when he moved to New York City?

B He *was* ~~were~~ five.

A How many albums does he have?

B Currently, he has more than 75 albums.

Yo-Yo Ma, cellist

Past Time Clauses with *When, Before,* and *After*

Luck and Loss

1 Grammar in the Real World

A Do you ever get e-mails with the message "You won a contest" or "We need to check your bank account"? Read the web article. Why was Sandra Walters lucky?

B Comprehension Check Circle the correct answers.

1 Where did Sandra receive the e-mail?

   a at home   **b** at work   **c** at the bank

2 How much money did the man ask her to send to a bank outside the United States?

   a $1,000   **b** $2.5 million   **c** $25

3 Why did Sandra give her credit card number to the man?

   a because she didn't have a bank   **b** because it was quick   **c** to pay the fee

4 When did she realize it was a scam?

   a when she got home   **b** after she finished the call   **c** when she called her credit card company

C Notice What did Sandra do first? For each pair of sentences, write *1* and *2*. Use the article to help you.

1 _____ Sandra was surprised.   _____ Sandra read her e-mail.

2 _____ She called the number.   _____ She went home.

3 _____ She said she didn't have $1,000.   _____ The man asked for her credit card number.

4 _____ She began to think.   _____ She put the phone down.

5 _____ She realized her mistake.   _____ She called her credit card company.

INTERNET LOTTERY
SCAM[1]

When Sandra Walters opened her e-mail one day at work last year, she was surprised. One message said, "Congratulations. You are the lucky winner of $2.5 million in the National Millionaire's Contest. Call this number." **When Sandra got home**, she called the number and spoke
5 to a man who seemed very nice. The man told her to send a $1,000 fee[2] to a bank outside the United States. **When Sandra said she didn't have $1,000**, the man said, "No problem. I can charge your credit card." She gave him her credit card number, her bank account number, and her address. The man promised to send her a check for $2.5 million the next
10 day. Then he hung up. **After Sandra put the phone down**, she began to think. What was this contest? She didn't remember entering any contest. How did she win?

Unfortunately, it's a common story. There is no National Millionaire's Contest. In a real contest, you never pay a fee **before you receive your**
15 **prize**. Sandra wasn't a winner. She was the victim[3] of a scam . . . almost. Luckily, Sandra realized her mistake and called her credit card company. They canceled[4] the card **before the criminals[5] used it**.

Don't fall for[6] this scam. An e-mail message that asks for personal information is probably a scam. Just delete it!

[1]**scam:** a dishonest way of making money

[2]**fee:** money you pay for a service

[3]**victim:** someone who suffers from violence, illness, or bad luck

[4]**cancel:** stop something from working

[5]**criminal:** a person who has done something illegal

[6]**fall for:** believe something is true when it's not

2 Past Time Clauses with *When*, *Before*, and *After*

Grammar Presentation

	FIRST EVENT SECOND EVENT
Time clauses show the order of events in the past. They can begin with *when*, *before*, and *after*.	*After Sandra put the phone down, she began to think.*

2.1 Time Clauses

Time Clause	Main Clause
When **Before** **I get to work,** **After**	I check my e-mail.

Main Clause	Time Clause	
I check my e-mail	**when** **before** **after**	**I get to work.**

2.2 Main Clauses and Time Clauses

A A clause has a subject and a verb.	SUBJECT VERB
	   She was surprised.
	
	         SUBJECT VERB
	When Sandra opened her e-mail, . . .

B A main clause is a complete sentence. It has a subject and a verb.	SUBJECT VERB Sandra called the number. SUBJECT VERB She began to think.
C A time clause can begin with *when*, *before*, or *after*. It has a subject and a verb. However, it is <u>not</u> a complete sentence. A time clause always goes with a main clause.	SUBJECT VERB SUBJECT VERB When she got home, she called the number. SUBJECT VERB SUBJECT VERB After Sandra put the phone down, she began to think.
D You can add a time clause to a main clause to say when something happened.	MAIN CLAUSE TIME CLAUSE Sandra called the number when she got home. TIME CLAUSE MAIN CLAUSE After Sandra put the phone down, she began to think.

2.2 Main Clauses and Time Clauses *(continued)*

E A time clause can go before or after the main clause.

When the time clause comes first, use a comma after it.

| TIME CLAUSE | MAIN CLAUSE |
When Sandra opened her e-mail, she was surprised.

| TIME CLAUSE | MAIN CLAUSE |
After Sandra put the phone down, she began to think.

When the time clause comes second, do not use a comma.

| MAIN CLAUSE | TIME CLAUSE |
Sandra was surprised when she opened her e-mail.

| MAIN CLAUSE | TIME CLAUSE |
Sandra began to think after she put the phone down.

⟍ Time clauses are more common after the main clause.

| MAIN CLAUSE | TIME CLAUSE |
They canceled the card before the criminals used it.

2.3 Ordering Events

A *When* means "at almost the same time." Use *when* to introduce the first event.

| FIRST EVENT | SECOND EVENT |
When Sandra opened her e-mail, she was surprised.

| SECOND EVENT | FIRST EVENT |
Sandra called the number when she got home.

B Use *after* to introduce the first event.

| FIRST EVENT | SECOND EVENT |
After Sandra put the phone down, she began to think.

| SECOND EVENT | FIRST EVENT |
She felt much better after she called the bank.

C Use *before* to introduce the second event.

| FIRST EVENT | SECOND EVENT |
She canceled the card before they used it.

| SECOND EVENT | FIRST EVENT |
Before they sent her prize, they asked her to pay a fee.

D *Before* and *after* are also prepositions. You can use them before nouns that do not have verbs after them.

After work, she went home.

She was so excited before the phone call.

Grammar Application

Exercise 2.1 *When, Before, or After?*

A Choose the correct words to complete the sentences about the article.

1 Sandra opened her e-mail **when** / **before** she got to work.
2 **When** / **Before** she read the e-mail, Sandra was surprised.
3 She called the number **after** / **before** she got home.

4 The man and Sandra talked **before / after** he had her personal bank information.

5 **When / Before** Sandra said she didn't have $1,000, the man asked for her credit card number.

6 She gave him her address **after / before** she read out her credit card number.

7 **After / Before** she put the phone down, Sandra realized her mistake.

8 She called her credit card company **before / after** she spoke to the man.

B Pair Work Compare your answers with a partner. Which sentences can use both words?

Exercise 2.2 Ordering Events

A Listen to the story about another scam. Number the pictures in the order the events happened.

a _____

He bought a newspaper.

b _____

_____

c _____

_____

d _____

_____

e __1__

_____

f _____

_____

B Write the sentences under the correct pictures in A.

He bought a newspaper.	He left for work.
He read an e-mail from the bank.	He wrote a note to his wife.
He met a co-worker on the train.	He called his wife.

C Complete the story with *when, before,* and *after.* Then listen again to check your answers.

About a year ago, my friend Leo was almost a scam victim. One morning, he saw an e-mail from his bank **_before_** he went to work.
(1)
_____ he opened the e-mail,
(2)
it said, "You have a new account number. Write your old account number here so we can check your identity." He didn't have time to reply _____ he left home.
(3)
_____ he left for work, he wrote
(4)
a note to his wife, "Please reply to the bank's e-mail." Then he left for work.

_____ he got to the subway station, he bought a newspaper.
(5)
_____ he got on the train, he met a co-worker and they talked.
(6)
_____ he read the newspaper at lunchtime, he read an article about a bank
(7)
Internet scam. He realized the e-mail from the bank was that scam. _____ he
(8)
read the article, he called his wife. Luckily, _____ his wife read the e-mail, she
(9)
realized it was a scam and deleted the e-mail.

Exercise 2.3 Writing Main Clauses and Time Clauses

A Over to You What did you do yesterday? Complete each sentence by adding a main clause with a subject and a verb. For sentences with the time clause first, use a comma.

1 _____ before I left home yesterday morning.

2 After I ate lunch _____ .

3 Before I went home last night _____ .

4 _____ when I got home last night.

5 _____ after I ate dinner.

6 Before I went to bed _____ .

B Over to You **What did you do today? Complete each sentence by adding a time clause with *when*, *before*, or *after*. For sentences with the time clause first, use a comma.**

1 I got dressed _____ .

2 _____ I brushed my teeth.

3 I left the house / apartment _____ .

4 I got to school _____ .

5 _____ I went to the classroom.

6 _____ my English class started.

C Pair Work **Share your sentences with a partner. Did you do any of the same things?**

Exercise 2.4 More Main Clauses and Time Clauses

Pair Work **Tell a story about a scam from this unit or use your own ideas. First make notes to help you. Then share your story with a partner. Ask questions about your partner's scam story.**

A *This happened to a friend last year. When she checked her e-mail, she saw a message from a stranger.*

B *What did it say?*

3 Avoid Common Mistakes ⚠

1 **Check the spelling of *when*, *before*, and *after*.**

When
~~Whin~~ she read the e-mail, she got excited.   *before*
They canceled the card ~~befor~~ the criminals used it.

after
She thought about it ~~afther~~ she put the phone down.

2 **When the time clause comes first, use a comma. Don't use a comma when the main clause comes first.**

When she got home she called the company.   She called the company when she got home.

3 **Don't forget the subject in the main clause and the time clause.**

she
Before Ana called the company, checked the address.

Ana
Before called the company, she checked the address.

Editing Task

Find and correct 13 more mistakes in this story about a scam.

When got home one night two months ago I had a voice mail message.
When I listened to the message, got excited. The message said, "Congratulations.
You are a winner in our contest." Befor I made dinner, called the number.
A woman said, "We called you two weeks ago, but you didn't answer. Please hold."

5   After waited for an hour, I put the phone down.

Whin my wife got home I asked her, "Did you get a message about a prize
drawing?" She said, "Yes, but afther heard it, I deleted it. It's a scam." When she
said that I didn't say anything.

I realized my mistake, when we got the phone bill four days later. When read

10   the bill I didn't believe it. That one-hour call cost $5,000!

Count and Noncount Nouns

Eating Habits

1 Grammar in the Real World

A Do you think your diet is healthy? Read the article from a health magazine. What kinds of food are part of a healthy diet?

B Comprehension Check Answer the questions. Use the article to help you.

1 How do colorful fruit and vegetables help your health?

2 Why is a little dark chocolate good for you?

3 What type of oil is good for you?

4 How much water is good to drink each day?

C Notice Find the sentences in the article, and complete them with *a* or *an* or Ø for no article.

1 When you turn on _____ television or read _____ newspaper, you often find _____ information about healthy eating.

2 _____ food and _____ health get a lot of attention in the news these days.

3 Maybe you think _____ fat is bad for you, but people need a little fat in their diet.

4 It is _____ challenge to change your diet, but even small changes can help you stay healthy and happy.

Look at the noun after each space. Which of the nouns are things you can count? Which are things you cannot count?

Food for Health

When you turn on a television or read a **newspaper**, you often find **information** about healthy eating. **Food** and **health** get a lot of **attention** in the **news** these **days**. Researchers seem to find new **things** about how our **diet** affects us every day.

Everyone knows it is important to eat **fruit** and **vegetables**. Did you know that
5 eating **fruit** and **vegetables** with different colors is especially good for your **health**? Green, red, blue, and orange **fruit** and **vegetables** all have different **vitamins**[1] to help hydrate you, and they help prevent different **diseases**.

Did you know that dark **chocolate** is good for you, too? Research shows that a little **chocolate** helps your **heart** and your **mood**.[2]

10 How about **fat**?[3] Maybe you think **fat** is bad for you, but people need a little **fat** in their diet. One type of healthy **fat** is omega-3 **oil**.[4] It comes from **fish** and helps your **heart**, **skin**, and **brain** stay healthy. For **vegetarians** or non-fish eaters, many **seeds**[5] and **nuts** also contain omega-3 **oil**. Omega-3 **oil** comes in **pills**, too.

Finally, **water** is an important part of a healthy **diet**. Try to drink at least six **glasses**
15 of **water** a day, and you don't need to buy it. In most places, tap **water** from the kitchen **faucet** is just fine and tastes great!

It is a **challenge** to change your **diet**, but even small **changes** can help you stay healthy and happy.

---

[1]**vitamin:** a natural substance in food that is important for good health
[2]**mood:** the way someone feels at a particular time
[3]**fat:** a substance in plants and animals, often used for cooking
[4]**omega-3 oil:** a kind of healthy fat
[5]**seed:** a small hard part of a plant from which new plants can grow

2 Count and Noncount Nouns

Grammar Presentation

Nouns are words for people, places, and things.

There are two types of nouns: count nouns and noncount nouns.

Count nouns name things you can count.
peas, vegetables, eggs, cookies

Noncount nouns name things you cannot count.
spinach, water, cheese, sugar

2.1 Count Nouns

A/An	Singular Count Noun	Singular Verb	
A	**vegetarian**	has	a meatless diet.
An	**apple**	is	a healthy snack.

Plural Count Noun	Plural Verb	
Vegetables	have	different vitamins.
Nuts	contain	healthy substances.

2.2 Noncount Nouns

Noncount Noun	Singular Verb	
Health	gets	a lot of attention in the news.
Water	is	an important part of a healthy diet.

▸▸Noncount Nouns and Containers: See page A17.

2.3 Using Count Nouns

A Count nouns are things that you can count. You can use numbers with count nouns.	*one egg, six eggs* *one banana, two bananas*
B You can use *a/an* with singular count nouns.	*Did you have a banana or a cookie?*
Remember: Use *an* with words that start with a vowel sound.	*I eat an apple and an orange every day.*

2.3 Using Count Nouns (continued)

C Count nouns can be plural. They can end in -s.	*Vegetables* are good for you. *Vitamins* keep you healthy.
Remember: Some plural nouns are irregular.	*People* need good food. Some *children* don't like vegetables.
D A singular count noun takes a singular verb.	*A banana is* good on cereal. *My diet isn't* very healthy.
E A plural count noun takes a plural verb.	*Nuts contain* oil. *Vegetarians don't eat* meat.

2.4 Using Noncount Nouns

A Noncount nouns are things you cannot count. Don't use numbers with count nouns.	*milk, rice, sugar, cheese, spinach, tea, coffee* NOT ~~one milk, one rice~~
You can use numbers with drinks in a restaurant when you mean a cup of the drink.	*Can we have three coffees, please?*
B Don't use *a/an* with noncount nouns.	*Eat spinach. Drink water. Cook shrimp.* NOT ~~a spinach, a water, a shrimp~~
C Noncount nouns don't have a plural form. Don't add -s.	*Spinach is* good for you. NOT ~~Spinaches are~~ good for you.
D A noncount noun takes a singular verb.	*Fish is* good for you. *Fish oil improves* your memory.

Grammar Application

Exercise 2.1 Count and Noncount Nouns

Data from the Real World

Research shows that noncount nouns are often the names of food and drink. The charts below show some of the most common food words in English.

A Which words are count nouns? Which are noncount nouns? Check (✓) the correct column.

	COUNT	NONCOUNT
apples	✓	
beans		
beef		
bread		
butter		
cheese		
cookies		
fish		
garlic		
ice cream		
meat		

	COUNT	NONCOUNT
milk		
potatoes		
rice		
sandwiches		
salt		
seafood		
shrimp		
sugar		
tomatoes		
vegetables		
water		

B Over to You Complete the lists with words from the chart. Write *count* after count nouns and *noncount* after noncount nouns.

I never eat / drink . . .	I often eat / drink . . .
apples – count	

Exercise 2.2 A and An

A Complete the survey questions. Write *a* or *an* before the count nouns.
Write Ø before noncount nouns.

1 Do you usually have ___*a*___ sandwich for lunch?

2 Do you often have _____ snack at bedtime?

3 Do you put _____ salt on your food?

4 Do you eat _____ garlic before a class?

5 How do you drink your tea or coffee? With _____ milk and _____ sugar?

6 Do you usually have _____ cookie with your tea or coffee?

7 Do you like _____ butter on your potatoes?

8 How often do you eat _____ pasta?

9 Which do you prefer: _____ apple or _____ banana?

10 Do you prefer _____ cereal or _____ bread for breakfast?

B Pair Work Ask a partner the survey questions in A.

A *Do you usually have a sandwich for lunch?*

B *No, I usually have an omelet or a Caesar salad.*

Read about the eating habits of these people. Change the singular count nouns in bold to plural nouns. Write Ø next to the noncount nouns.

Sean

I'm a vegetarian.

1 I don't eat **meat**___Ø___ .

2 I eat **egg**_s_____ , but not every day.

3 I also eat **nut**_____ , and I love fresh **vegetable**_____ .

4 I also like **apple**_____ and **cheese**_____ a lot.

I don't like dairy food.

Isabel

5 I don't eat **cheese**_____ or **butter**_____ .

6 I don't drink **milk**_____ .

7 I love **seafood**_____ , but I'm allergic to **shrimp**_____ .

8 My favorite food is **bean**_____ .

9 I eat a lot of **pasta**_____ .

Lin

I love fast food.

10 I love potato **chip**_____ and **cookie**_____ .

11 I don't eat **vegetable**_____ very often.

12 I love desserts with **ice cream**_____ .

13 I'm allergic to **chocolate**_____ !

Exercise 2.4 Singular and Plural Verbs with Nouns

A Complete the sentences from a magazine article about food. Use the correct form of the verbs in parentheses.

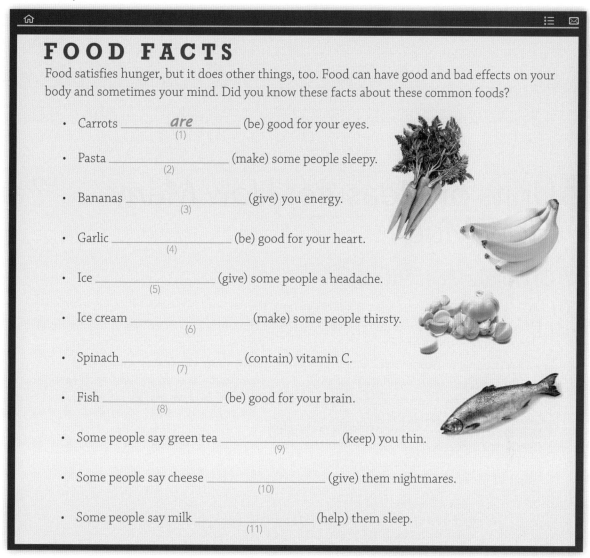

FOOD FACTS

Food satisfies hunger, but it does other things, too. Food can have good and bad effects on your body and sometimes your mind. Did you know these facts about these common foods?

- Carrots _____*are*_____ (be) good for your eyes.
  (1)

- Pasta _____ (make) some people sleepy.
  (2)

- Bananas _____ (give) you energy.
  (3)

- Garlic _____ (be) good for your heart.
  (4)

- Ice _____ (give) some people a headache.
  (5)

- Ice cream _____ (make) some people thirsty.
  (6)

- Spinach _____ (contain) vitamin C.
  (7)

- Fish _____ (be) good for your brain.
  (8)

- Some people say green tea _____ (keep) you thin.
  (9)

- Some people say cheese _____ (give) them nightmares.
  (10)

- Some people say milk _____ (help) them sleep.
  (11)

B Over to You Write four sentences about how different kinds of foods affect you.

Ice cream makes me thirsty.
Soda gives me a headache.

1 _____

2 _____

3 _____

4 _____

3 Units of Measure; *How Many . . . ?* and *How Much . . . ?*

Grammar Presentation

Units of measure help us to tell how much or how many of a noun.	I bought *a cup of* coffee in the cafeteria. We had *a bowl of* soup with lunch.
Questions with *How much . . . ?* and *How many . . . ?* ask about quantities.	*How many* vegetables did you use? *How much* rice do you eat each week?

3.1 Units of Measure

Unit of Measure	Noncount or Plural Count Noun
a cup of	coffee
a bag of	rice
a piece of	cheese
a bottle of	water
a bowl of	soup
two bags of	potato chips
a carton of	eggs
a bunch of	bananas
a pound of	apples
three boxes of	cookies
a loaf of	bread

▶▶ Noncount Nouns and Containers: See page A17.

3.2 Using Units of Measure with Count and Noncount Nouns

A You can use units of measure to count some noncount nouns.	*My mother gave me a bottle of water.* *She drinks a cup of coffee every day.* *Did you eat a piece of cheese?*
You can make these expressions plural.	*She took two bottles of water.* *I drank three cups of coffee today.* *We served some pieces of cheese.*
B You can use units of measure with count nouns.	*I bought a bag of apples.* *David ate a box of cookies!*
You can make these expressions plural.	*We collected some bags of apples.* *Lisa sold six boxes of cookies.*

3.3 How Many . . . ? and How Much . . . ?

How Many	Count Noun	
How many	**apples**	did you eat?
	people	want food?
	bags	do you have?

How Much	Noncount Noun	
How much	**coffee**	do you drink every day?
	sugar	do you put in your coffee?
	money	do we need?

3.4 Using How Many . . . ? and How Much . . . ?

A Use *How many . . . ?* to ask about count nouns.	*How many eggs do you eat every week?* *How many apples do you bring to school every day?*
B Use *How much . . . ?* to ask about noncount nouns.	*How much milk do you drink a day?* *How much meat do you eat in a week?*

Grammar Application

Complete the menu with the units of measure from the box. You can use some units of measure more than once. Sometimes there is more than one correct answer.

a bag of	a bowl of	a glass of	a plate of
a bottle of	a cup of	a piece of	

Welcome to the Class Picnic!
———— Menu ————

Drinks

_____a cup of_____ **coffee or tea**
    (1)

_____ **water or juice**
    (2)

_____ **lemonade or iced tea**
    (3)

Main Course

chicken salad or turkey sandwich

Side Orders

_____ **salad or fresh vegetables**
    (4)

_____ **cheese and crackers**
    (5)

an orange or _____ **watermelon**
    (6)

_____ **potato chips**
    (7)

Dessert

_____ **ice cream**
    (8)

_____ **cookies**
    (9)

Exercise 3.2 *How Much . . . ? and How Many . . . ?*

 A Complete each question about the class picnic with *How much* or *How many*. Then listen to the conversation about the picnic and answer the questions.

1   _How many_   students are there in the class?   _18_

2 _____ money do they have?   _____

3 _____ people want water?   _____

4 _____ juice do they need?   _____

5 _____ people want sandwiches?   _____

6 _____ bags of potato chips do they need?   _____

7 _____ salad do they need?   _____

8 _____ cheese do people want?   _____

9 _____ people want an orange?   _____

10 _____ watermelon do they need?   _____

B Pair Work Plan a class picnic. Use the menu in Exercise 3.1 and the questions in A to help you.

   A *How many students are there in our group?*

   B *There are eight. How many people want water?*

⎍ Data from the Real World

Research shows that these are some of the most common noncount nouns:

equipment	homework	love	music	traffic
fun	information	mail	peace	weather
furniture	insurance	money	software	work

Noncount nouns are the names of:

materials: *oil, plastic, wood*	**Oil** *costs a lot these days.*
groups of things: *money, cash, furniture, jewelry*	*The* **jewelry** *in this store is expensive.*
subjects: *chemistry, geography, psychology*	**Chemistry** *doesn't interest me at all.*
weather: *snow, ice, fog*	*There's always* **snow** *in the winter here.*

Some noncount nouns end in *-s*, but they take a singular verb:

subjects: *economics, physics, politics*	**Economics** *was my best subject in high school.*
activities: *aerobics, gymnastics*	**Gymnastics** *is my favorite sport.*
other: *news*	*The* **news** *is really good.*

Students often make mistakes with noncount nouns, especially these:

information	equipment	advice	research	knowledge	furniture
behavior	work	homework	software	damage	training

A Complete the chart. Use the words in the box.

a check	furniture	a keyboard	music	a~~ ring~~
a couch	homework	knowledge	pop	traffic
equipment	information	money	rain	weather
an exercise	~~jewelry~~	motorcycles		

Category: _jewelry_
(1)

earrings

a necklace

a ring
(2)

Category: _____
(3)

a table

a chair

_____
(4)

Category: _____
(5)

a computer

a printer

_____
(6)

Category: _____
(7)

names

dates

_____
(8)

Category: _____
(9)

cars

trucks

_____
(10)

Category: _____
(11)

an essay

a reading

_____
(12)

Category: _____
(13)

classical

hip-hop

jazz

_____
(14)

Category: _____
(15)

bills

coins

_____
(16)

Category: _____
(17)

snow

ice

_____
(18)

B Group Work Complete the chart with the words in the box. Then add as many words in each category as you can.

4 Avoid Common Mistakes ⚠

1 Do not use *a / an* with noncount nouns.

I'm doing a research on eating habits.

2 Do not make noncount nouns plural or use them with a plural verb.

advice
My teacher gave me some useful advices.

3 Do not use *these* or *those* with noncount nouns.

this information is
I hope these informations are useful.

4 Use *how much* with noncount nouns, and use *how many* with count nouns.

much *many*
How many money do you have? *How much classes did you take?*

Editing Task

Find and correct the mistakes on this school's website.

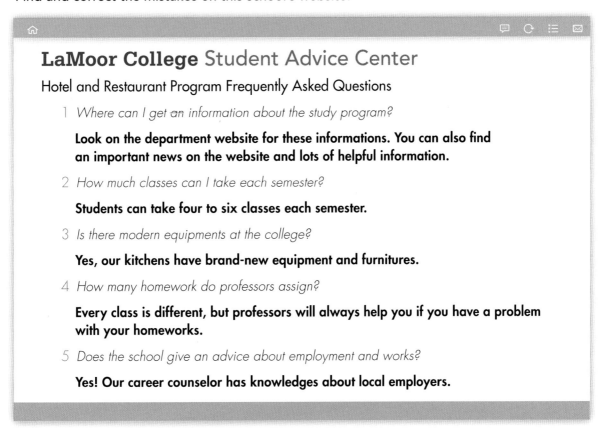

LaMoor College Student Advice Center

Hotel and Restaurant Program Frequently Asked Questions

1 *Where can I get an information about the study program?*

Look on the department website for these informations. You can also find an important news on the website and lots of helpful information.

2 *How much classes can I take each semester?*

Students can take four to six classes each semester.

3 *Is there modern equipments at the college?*

Yes, our kitchens have brand-new equipment and furnitures.

4 *How many homework do professors assign?*

Every class is different, but professors will always help you if you have a problem with your homeworks.

5 *Does the school give an advice about employment and works?*

Yes! Our career counselor has knowledges about local employers.

Quantifiers: *Some, Any, A Lot Of, A Little, A Few, Much, Many*

Languages

1 Grammar in the Real World

A Do you know any words that originally come from another language? Read the article. What languages do some English words come from?

B Comprehension Check Answer the questions. Use the article to help you.

1 From which language did *pajamas* come? _____

2 Which English words are commonly used in China? _____

3 Is *football* an original English word? _____

4 Which language did *ferry* come from? _____

C Notice Find the sentences in the article and complete them with *some* or *any*.

1 Let's go have _____ nachos.

2 Let's get _____ sushi.

3 The server asks, "Do you want _____ drinks?"

Compare the sentences with *some* and *any*. How are they different?

Sushi in the Café

¹**import:** bring something into a country from another country

²**export:** send items to another country for sale or use

A woman says to a friend, "Let's go have **some** nachos." Her friend says, "I don't want nachos. Let's get **some** sushi."
5 After they order their food, the server asks, "Do you want **any** drinks?" "Coffee, please," says the woman. "Cola for me," says her friend. What language did
10 the women speak at the café? English, of course. However, **many** of the words they used are not originally English words. *Nachos, sushi, coffee,*
15 and *cola* all come from other languages. They are called loanwords, words that started as foreign words and then became common.

20 Loanwords are not just names of food. We wear *cotton pajamas*, wash our hair with *shampoo*, and read *magazines*. *Pajamas* and *shampoo* come
25 from Hindi, and *cotton* and *magazines* come from Arabic.

English words are loanwords in other languages, too. For example, the English words
30 *model, baby,* and *computer* are now common in Chinese. In fact, **a lot of** English words are now international. People from **many** different countries understand
35 them. **Some** examples include *football, ferry, flash,* and *Internet.*

Languages import¹ words and export² words because
40 people are always in contact. The next time you learn a new word in English, use a dictionary to check where it comes from. You will be surprised that **a lot**
45 **of** "English" words are really from **many** other languages.

2 Quantifiers: *Some* and *Any*

Grammar Presentation

We use *some* and *any* to talk about an unknown quantity of something.	*Let's go have* **some** *sushi.* *Do you want* **any** *drinks?*

2.1 Affirmative Statements with *Some*

	Some	Noncount Noun
I need		information.
Ricardo had	some	sushi.
We ordered		food.

	Some	Plural Noun
Let's have		nachos.
I know	some	Italian words.
Let's read		examples.

2.2 Negative Statements with *Any*

	Do / Does / Did + Not	Base Form of Verb	*Any*	Noncount Noun
I	don't	want		sushi.
The book	doesn't	have	any	information.
We	didn't	bring		food.

	Do / Does / Did + Not	Base Form of Verb	*Any*	Noncount Noun
I	don't	remember		Italian words.
Yuri	doesn't	want	any	nachos.
We	didn't	see		examples.

2.3 Yes/No Questions with *Some* and *Any*

	Some / Any	Noncount Noun	
Can I have	some	sushi?	
Do you have	any	information	about the English program?
Did you do	any	research	on loanwords?

2.3 Yes/No Questions with *Some* and *Any* (continued)

	Some / Any	Plural Noun	
Can you teach me	**some**	**words**	in Italian?
Do you have	**any**	**books**	on loanwords?
Are there	**any**	**examples**	in the book?

2.4 Using *Some* and *Any* in Statements

A Use *some* with noncount nouns and plural nouns in affirmative statements.	*I found some information about loanwords in this book.*
In affirmative statements *some* refers to small quantities or unknown quantities.	*There are some words in English that come from Arabic, but I don't know how many.*
B Use *some* for small amounts and numbers, not large amounts and numbers.	*There are Latin and Greek words in English.* NOT *There are ~~some~~ Latin and Greek words in English.* (There are thousands!)
C Use *any* with noncount nouns and plural nouns in negative statements.	*There isn't any food in the refrigerator.*
In negative statements, *any* refers to a zero quantity.	*I don't remember any words in Italian.*

2.5 Using Yes/No Questions with *Some* and *Any*

A Use *some* with noncount nouns and plural nouns to ask for something or to offer something that is there.	*Can I get some information from you about Portuguese, please?* (The person asking knows the other person has information about Portuguese.) *Do you want to use some words from Russian for your paper about English loanwords?* (The person asking has words to give to the writer.)
B Use *any* with noncount nouns and plural nouns to ask for unknown quantities.	*Did you make any progress with your paper?* (The questioner doesn't expect progress.) *Are there any English words that come from Swahili?* (There may be <u>no</u> English words that come from Swahili. The questioner doesn't know.)

Grammar Application

A Julia and her classmates have some questions about loanwords. Complete their conversation with *some* or *any*.

Julia   We use ___*some*___ Japanese words in English, for example,
(1)
karaoke and *sushi*.

Simon   Yeah, that's true. Do we use _____ Indonesian words in
(2)
English? Do you know, Taufik?

Taufik   Yes, there are _____ food words, for example, *satay*.
(3)

Nick   Pilar told me _____ Spanish words, for example, *papaya*
(4)
and *Florida*. *Florida* means "a place with flowers."

Julia   What about Arabic?

Taufik   There aren't _____ Arabic students in the class, so
(5)
let's check online.

Nick   Miriam, you lived in Ghana. Tell us _____ words from
(6)
African languages that we use in English.

Miriam   Hmm. Yeah, sure. Well, *cola*, *jazz*, and *safari* are from African
languages. There are probably _____ more words, but
(7)
I don't know _____ others.
(8)

Julia   Thanks, everyone. Now we know _____ words in English
(9)
that come from other languages. Let's organize them.

B Over to You Do you know any other English words that come from other languages?
Tell the class.

A *I know some Italian words in English.*

B *Really? I don't know any Italian words. What words do you know?*

A *I know* pesto *and* pizza. *I don't know any others.*

Exercise 2.2 *Yes/No Questions with Some and Any*

A Complete the conversations. Write the questions. Use *some* or *any* and the words in parentheses.

Conversation 1

Samantha   So, Rafa, I know you're from Spain.

You're from Barcelona, right?

Do you have any friends from Madrid
                (1)
(have/friends/from Madrid)?

Rafa   Yes, I do. I have some friends who still live there.

And you were born in Canada, right?

_____
                (2)
(have/friends/from there)?

Samantha   Yes, I have some friends from Toronto and Montreal.

Conversation 2

Rafa   How's your English class, Tomoko?

_____
                (3)
(have/classmates/from Latin America)?

Tomoko   Yes, I do. I have some classmates from Peru, Mexico, and Argentina.

Rafa   _____
                (4)
(are there/students/from South Asia)?

Tomoko   I'm not sure, but I hope so! I want to meet people from all over the world.

Conversation 3

Tara   Hey, guys! I made chocolate chip cookies this morning.

_____
                (5)
(want/cookies)?

Rafa   Oh, yes! Thanks!

_____
                (6)
(have/milk)?

Tara   Yes, I do. It's in the refrigerator. Help yourself.

Conversation 4

Samantha   Rafa, I like your CD collection.

_____ (7)

(can/I/listen to/music)?

Rafa   Sure! Go ahead. I have a lot of salsa. It's fun to dance to!

Samantha   Oh, I don't know how to dance salsa.

_____ (8)

(are there/salsa clubs/around here)?

Rafa   Yes, there are some clubs downtown. They give dance lessons. Samantha,

_____ (9)

(want/to take/lessons)?

Samantha   Sure!

Rafa   Great! Let's go sometime!

B Pair Work Practice the conversations with a partner.

Exercise 2.3 Statements and Questions

A Write affirmative and negative statements using the verbs in parentheses. Make them true for you. Use *some* for affirmative statements and *any* for negative statements.

1 I _____*have some/don't have any*_____ books in English at home. (have)

2 I _____ recording equipment. (own)

3 I _____ friends at work. (have)

4 I _____ words in Italian. (know)

5 I _____ people from El Salvador. (know)

6 I _____ TV shows in English. (watch)

7 I _____ podcasts from news websites. (download)

8 I _____ knowledge of French. (have)

9 I _____ e-mails in Portuguese. (write)

10 I _____ online music stores. (use)

B Pair Work Ask and answer questions with a partner based on your sentences in A. Use *any* in your questions.

A *Do you have any books in English at home?*

B *Yes, I have some books in English at home.*

3 Quantifiers: *A Lot Of, A Little, A Few, Much, Many*

Grammar Presentation

Quantifiers can refer to large or small amounts.	*I know a lot of English words.* *I need a little extra information for my paper on loanwords.*

3.1 Affirmative Statements

	A Lot Of / A Little	Noncount Noun
I found	a lot of a little	information.

	A Lot Of / A Few / Many	Plural Noun
She has	a lot of a few many	friends in Indonesia.

3.2 Yes / No Questions

	A Lot Of / A Little / Much	Noncount Noun
Did you learn	a lot of	English?
Did you need	a little	help?
Do you have	much	homework?

	A Lot Of / A Few / Many	Plural Noun
Did you meet	a lot of	people?
Do you have	a few	minutes?
Can you speak	many	languages?

Is There	A Lot Of / A Little / Much	Noncount Noun	
Is there	a lot of a little much	information	in the article?

Are There	A Lot Of / A Few / Many	Plural Noun	
Are there	a lot of a few many	people	in your class?

3.3 Using Quantifiers

A In affirmative statements: Use *a lot of* for large quantities of plural nouns and noncount nouns.	I met *a lot of* Russian speakers in North Carolina. There is *a lot of* help available for students.
Use *a little* for small quantities of noncount nouns.	I understand *a little* Swedish.
Use *a few* for small quantities of plural nouns.	Dane has *a few* friends in Asia.
Use *many* for large quantities of plural nouns.	There are *many* people that speak Swahili in the neighborhood.
B In negative statements: Use *not a lot of* for small amounts of plural and noncount nouns.	There isn't *a lot of* information about some words. There aren't *a lot of* students from Denmark at the school.
Use *not much* for small amounts of noncount nouns.	Two months isn't *much* time to learn a new language.
Use *not many* for small amounts of plural nouns.	There aren't *many* people from Austria in my class.
C In questions: Use *a lot of* with plural and noncount nouns.	Do you have *a lot of* relatives in Ireland? Is there *a lot of* bad weather in Maine?
Use *much* in questions with noncount nouns.	Do you have *much* homework in Spanish class?
Use *many* with plural nouns.	Are there *many* Chinese restaurants in Boston?
D Don't use *much* in affirmative statements.	The website had *a lot of* information about Latin. NOT ~~The website had much information about Latin.~~
E Use short answers with *a lot, a few,* and *not many* to refer to plural nouns.	"How *many* students did a presentation on loanwords?" "*A lot. / A few. / Not many.*"
Use short answers with *a lot, a little,* and *not much* to refer to noncount nouns.	"How *much* work did you do on your paper?" "*A lot. / A little. / Not much.*"

Grammar Application

Write *C* for the count nouns and *NC* for the noncount nouns.

dictionary __C__   homework _____   student _____   song _____   furniture _____

time _____   music _____   knowledge _____   word _____   Korean (language) _____

Listen and complete the paragraph about an English class with *a lot of, a little, a few,* or *many.*

Karina's English class at Dixon College is very international. Her class has __*a few*__ Russians:
(1)
Karina and two others. There are _____
(2)
students from Brazil, perhaps 80 percent. There are

_____ students from Japan, but not many.
(3)
The rest are from other Asian countries like Malaysia, Thailand, and Vietnam.

They come from all over the world and bring interesting stories with them.
Rosa is from São Paulo, Brazil, and listens to _____ Brazilian music.
(4)
She loves it. She also has _____ songs from Puerto Rico on her
(5)
computer, but not many. Seri, from Penang, has _____ beautiful
(6)
furniture from Malaysia in her house. Keiko, from Japan, taught Karina and Rosa

_____ Japanese, but the words are difficult to remember. Noom, from
(7)
Bangkok, loves his country's food. Sometimes he makes _____ Thai
(8)
food for his classmates, but not much because it's very hot for them. Linh, who moved
from Vietnam, eats _____ spicy food. She loves it! Sometimes, Karina
(9)
brings in _____ *borscht,* a Russian soup. Only Keiko and Noom like it, so
(10)
she doesn't make a lot of it. The best part of Karina's diverse class is that she can hear

_____ languages besides English every day!
(11)

A Circle the correct words.

Dustin	Hi, Dr. Lanza. Thank you for doing this interview for *Student Voices*. First, are there **much / <u>many</u>** countries in Asia where (1) English is the official language?

Dr. Lanza	Well, there aren't **many / much**, but there are **a little / a few** – for example, (2) (3) Pakistan, Singapore, and the Philippines.
Dustin	How **many / much** words are there in English? (4)
Dr. Lanza	It's hard to say. Anywhere from 250,000 to 750,000, perhaps! Dictionaries have **much / a lot of** words, but they don't contain all of them. A big English (5) dictionary has hundreds of thousands of words.
Dustin	Really? That's **many / a lot**! How many words do native English speakers (6) know? Do they know **a lot of / many** vocabulary? (7)
Dr. Lanza	Yes, every native speaker knows **much / a lot of** words. Adults probably know (8) 20,000 to 30,000 words.
Dustin	Very interesting! Thanks for this interview, Dr. Lanza!

B Pair Work Tell a partner what you know about other cultures and languages. Use the conversation in A as a model. Remember to use *a lot of, a few, a little,* and *many.*

Answer the questions that students in an English class are asking each other before class. Use *a lot, a few, a little, not many,* and *not much.*

1 How much time did you work on your paper?

   A lot . I worked all day on it.

2 I wasn't in class yesterday. How much homework did we have for today?

   _____ . The teacher only assigned two online exercises.

3 How many classes do you have today?

   _____ . I only have two today. Tomorrow I have four!

4 How much time did you spend on homework last night?

   _____ . I was very busy, so I didn't have a lot of time.

5 How many minutes do we have before class starts?

   _____ . It's going to start in two minutes!

Exercise 3.5 *A Lot Of, Much, and Many*

📊 Data from the Real World

People often use *a lot of* in speaking. In writing, they often use *much* and *many*.	**Say**: *"There are a lot of different languages and cultures in South America."* **Write**: *There are many different languages and cultures in South America.* **Say**: *"Schools in poorer countries often don't have a lot of modern equipment."* **Write**: *Schools in poorer countries often do not have much modern equipment.*	**a lot of** *(bar chart: writing = low, speaking = high)*
Use *a lot of* in speaking and writing in affirmative statements with noncount nouns.	*The website has a lot of information about English as a global language.*	

A Change *a lot of* to *much* or *many* in the essay.

Communication Shortage

many

In the twentieth century, ~~a lot of~~ young people had pen pals[1] from other countries. They wrote letters to them and learned about other countries, cultures, and languages. Traveling was expensive, so they did not have **a lot of** opportunities to meet their pen pals. There was not **a lot of** direct contact between people from different countries, so letters were

5 a good way to communicate.

Now there are not **a lot of** traditional pen pals. Instead, there are **a lot of** social media sites on the Internet. People post photos, videos, and comments. People are busy and they don't have **a lot of** time, so now they use apps to send short messages around the world. Today apps such as Twitter® are popular. People typically send **a lot of** "tweets" every day. However, can

10 people exchange **a lot of** information in these very short messages? Can people learn **a lot of** interesting things about the other person's culture? These are good questions for discussion.

[1]**pen pal:** someone you exchange letters with as a hobby, especially someone from another country

B Pair Work Discuss the essay in A with a partner. Ask each other these questions.

1 What social media do you use to communicate with your friends? Why?

2 Do you think social media sites and apps are a good way to learn about other people and cultures?

3 What kinds of information do people exchange online?

4 Avoid Common Mistakes ⚠

1 Use *many* with plural nouns.

       many
Do you write ~~much~~ essays?

2 Use *much* with noncount nouns in <u>negative</u> statements and questions. In affirmative statements with noncount nouns, use *a lot of*, not *much*.

                 much
The students don't have ~~many~~ work in the lab today.

      a lot of
There is ~~much~~ information on loanwords online.

3 For quantities, use *some* with noncount nouns. Do not use *a / an* with noncount nouns.

     some
I need ~~an~~ information about Korea.

4 Use *any* with negative statements, and use *some* with affirmative statements.

        any   *some*
I don't have ~~some~~ dictionaries to use.   I learned ~~any~~ Japanese words from a Japanese friend.

Editing Task

Find and correct 11 more mistakes in this interview with Dr. Matthew Sutton, Director of the Language Center at Marsland College.

Roberto   Hello, Dr. Sutton. My name is Roberto Ferrer and I'm a student here at the
college. I'd like to ask you ~~any~~ *some* questions about the Language Center for our
college paper. How does the Language Center help language students?

Dr. Sutton   Thanks for asking, Roberto. The center is very important. We give students
5   much information about foreign languages and cultures, and we have much
learning material for 30 different languages.

Roberto   Wow, that sounds like much information on different languages that students
can find here.

Dr. Sutton   It is, Roberto. Much students find the center really helpful. You see, much
10   students work and do not have many time to study. They can come to the
center before or after class. They can spend a few minutes or one or two
hours here. They can use our computers and equipment for projects, or just
meet friends.

Roberto   That sounds great. Do much students use the center?

15   Dr. Sutton   Right now, about 100 students use the center every day.

Roberto   Does the center have modern equipment?

Dr. Sutton   Yes, it does. Every year, we buy a new equipment, for example, computers
and 3D printers. We also spend much money to make the center a
comfortable place. For example, we recently bought a new furniture.
20   Please come and visit! We are open every day.

Roberto   All right. Thanks for your time, Dr. Sutton!

Articles: *A / An* and *The*

Changes and Risks

1 Grammar in the Real World

A Do you like to take risks?[1] Read the magazine article about how people respond to risk. When you make a decision, what steps do you take?

B Comprehension Check Circle the correct answers from the magazine article.

1 Making decisions during difficult times is

   a different for everyone.   **b** always hard.   **c** easy for everyone.

2 If you are an *ostrich*, you

   a like to take risks.   **b** do not like to take risks.   **c** look at your choices before you make a decision.

3 If you are a *rock climber*, you

   a like to take risks.   **b** do not like to take risks.   **c** look at your choices before you make a decision.

4 If you are an *analyst*, you

   a like to take risks.   **b** do not like to take risks.   **c** look at your choices before you make a decision.

C Notice Which article (*a* or *an*) comes before these words the first time they appear?

	a	*an*
1 ostrich		
2 car		
3 new job		
4 important decision		
5 business		

Compare the words that come after *a* with the words that come after *an*. Look at the beginning sounds of the words. How are they different?

[1]**take a risk:** do something where there is a possibility of being hurt or of a loss or defeat

DECISIONS IN RISKY TIMES

In uncertain or difficult times, it's sometimes hard for people to make decisions. For example, when **the** economy is bad, people worry about money and their jobs. Some take risks to try to make things better. Others don't take any risks and hope to stay safe. Guy Burgess,
5 of **the** University of Colorado, says people deal with difficult times differently.

Some people become *ostriches*.[1] **An** ostrich does not like risks. For example, Connor is nervous about **the** economy. He doesn't buy anything expensive, like **a** car, since **the** car he has still works. He doesn't look for **a** new job even though he hates **the** job he has. He knows **the**
10 job he has now is stable.[2]

Others become *rock climbers*. They love taking risks. For example, Kala found a new job and makes a lot more money. But **the** job does not have good health insurance, and it's short-term.[3] She isn't worried because she enjoys taking risks.

15 Finally, some become *analysts*.[4] For example, Lorena looks carefully at her choices before she makes **an** important decision. She decides to sell her house and put **the** money into a business. She knows she can make a lot of money with **the** business.

Some risks are worth taking and others are dangerous. It's important
20 to know which type of risk taker you are before you make big decisions.

[1]**ostrich:** here, a person who ignores reality or does not accept the truth

[2]**stable:** safe, not likely to change

[3]**short-term:** not for a long time

[4]**analyst:** someone who studies or examines something in detail, such as finances, computer systems, or the economy

2 Articles: *A / An* and *The*

Grammar Presentation

<table>
<tr>
<td>Articles are used with nouns. *A / An* is the indefinite article. *The* is the definite article.</td>
<td>*Claire is an analyst. She thinks carefully before she makes a decision, especially when the decision is an important one.*</td>
</tr>
</table>

2.1 Indefinite Article: *A / An*

<table>
<tr>
<td>**A** Use *a / an* with singular count nouns.</td>
<td>*She made a decision about her job.*
An analyst examines something in detail.</td>
</tr>
<tr>
<td>**B** Use *a* when the noun begins with a consonant sound.</td>
<td>She made *a decision* about her job.</td>
</tr>
<tr>
<td>**C** Use *an* when the noun begins with a vowel sound.</td>
<td>*An analyst examines something in detail.*</td>
</tr>
<tr>
<td>**D** Use *a* before words such as adjectives or adverbs that begin with a consonant sound.</td>
<td>*Tony found a great apartment in Chicago.*</td>
</tr>
<tr>
<td>**E** Use *a* before words that begin with *u* when the *u* makes a "you" sound.</td>
<td>*James went to a university in Boston.*
The economy is a universal concern.</td>
</tr>
</table>

2.2 Definite Article: *The*

<table>
<tr>
<td>You can use *the* before singular or plural count nouns and before noncount nouns.</td>
<td>*The job is a good one.*
The choices were interesting.
The information is very useful.</td>
</tr>
</table>

▶▶ Indefinite and Definite Articles: See page A19.

2.3 Using *A / An* and *The*

<table>
<tr>
<td>**A** Use *a / an* to introduce a person or thing for the first time to a listener. When you mention the person or thing again, use *the*.</td>
<td>*Tom bought a car.*
(The listener does not know about this car.)
The car was not very expensive.
(Now the listener knows about this car.)</td>
</tr>
</table>

2.3 Using *A / An* and *The* (continued)

B Use *the* to talk about specific people or things that both the listener and speaker know about.

The president discussed the plan.
(Everyone knows the president and the plan.)
The moon and the stars were beautiful last night.
(Everyone knows the moon and the stars.)
"The game was interesting." "I agree."
(The speaker and listener are thinking of the same game.)

Grammar Application

Exercise 2.1 Sentences with *A / An*

A Complete the sentences with *a* or *an*.

1 A rock climber takes __*a*__ risk easily.

2 _____ analyst thinks about choices before he / she decides.

3 _____ ostrich doesn't like to take risks and wants to be safe.

4 Connor doesn't look for _____ job because he already has one.

5 Kala was glad she got _____ interview.

6 Lorena owns _____ business.

7 She made _____ decision about the business.

8 She decided to sell her house and rent _____ apartment.

9 I hope to go to _____ university in Europe.

10 I want to go to _____ information session and talk to _____ academic adviser.

B Over to You **Which kind of risk taker are you? Discuss with a partner and explain your choice.**

A *I'm a rock climber because I love to take risks. I left a good job to go back to college.*

B *Oh, I'm an ostrich. I don't like to take risks at all.*

We pronounce *a* and *an* with a weak sound, /ə/ or /ən/, because we don't stress the articles.	a decision a business a risk	an analyst an ostrich an opinion

A Listen and repeat the phrases in the chart above.

B Read the interview and complete the sentences with *a* or *an*.

Reporter Hi, my name is Steve. I'm a reporter with the *New Times*, and I have some questions for you about taking risks. Can you describe ___*a*___ decision that was really difficult for you?
(1)

Student Yes, I made _____ decision to leave my job.
(2)

Reporter Do you think there was _____ risk in that decision?
(3)

Student Yes, there was _____ risk because I left _____ good job, and I don't know about the new one yet.
(4)
(5)

Reporter Of the three types of risk takers – _____ "ostrich," _____ "rock climber," and _____ "analyst" – which type are you?
(6)
(7)
(8)

Student Oh, I'm _____ analyst!
(9)

Reporter Do you think analysts always make good decisions?

Student Yes, because _____ analyst looks at all of the choices carefully.
(10)

Reporter How do you think _____ ostrich manages stress?
(11)

Student Well, _____ ostrich makes sure everything in his or her life is stable.
(12)

Reporter Do you know someone who is _____ rock climber?
(13)

Student I do! My sister is _____ rock climber. She always takes risks!
(14)

C Pair Work Practice the interview with a partner.

Exercise 2.3 *A / An or The?*

A Complete the conversation with *a, an,* or *the.*

Emma	Guess what, Isabella? I want to start __*a*__ catering business![1]
	(1)

Isabella	That's great! I know you love to cook!

Emma I went to _____ exciting class for new female entrepreneurs. _____ teacher for the
(2)   (3)
class taught us a lot of things. For example, now I know how to get _____ loan[2]
(4)
from a bank. When I get it, _____ loan can help me buy the equipment I need to
(5)
start _____ business.
(6)

Isabella Are you nervous? Isn't it risky to start
your own business?

Emma Of course! There is definitely _____
(7)
risk in starting your own business.
When you know _____ risks, you can
(8)
plan well. _____ class also taught
(9)
me to write _____ marketing plan.
(10)
_____ plan can guide my sales[3] of my
(11)
catering services. I need to design
_____ menu and make _____ website
(12)   (13)
for my business. When _____ menu is ready and _____ website is up, I'll be ready
(14)   (15)
to go!

Isabella Wow, that all sounds great! Do you need my help? I'm in _____ web design
(16)
course right now. I can design something really great for your new business!

Emma Thanks! I'd like that.

---

[1]**catering business:** a business that provides and serves food and drinks for a particular event, such as a wedding or party
[2]**loan:** money that you can borrow but you have to pay back with interest (extra money)
[3]**sales:** the number of items sold

B Complete the story with *a*, *an*, or *the*.

Martin moved to New York City from Bogotá, Colombia, a year ago. He lives in __*a*__ neighborhood (1) on the Upper West Side. He was worried because _____ neighborhood is expensive. He found _____ (2) (3) entry-level[1] job at _____ bank, but he did not make (4) enough money. This made him uncomfortable because he does not like to take risks. His friends told him he could always get _____ second job. He took (5) their advice and got _____ interesting job as a server (6) at _____ coffee shop. _____ job is great! _____ coffee (7) (8) (9) shop is near his apartment, so he can walk to work.

_____ job is much more relaxing than _____ bank job. (10) (11) Martin gets to chat with _____ customers who come in (12) as he fills their orders. He makes a lot of new friends there, too. Also, _____ second job allows him to save (13) money. Now he feels much better and enjoys life in New York City!

[1]**entry-level:** starting level

C Pair Work Talk to a partner about Emma in A and Martin in B. Is one of them an ostrich? An analyst? A rock climber? Why?

3 Article or No Article?

Grammar Presentation

We sometimes do not use an article before plural count and noncount nouns.	*Rock climbers love taking risks.* *I have homework to do.*

3.1 No Article

Use no article before plural count and noncount nouns when the nouns have a general meaning.	*Analysts do not make quick decisions.* *I need money to buy that car!* *Insurance is very expensive.*

3.2 *The* and No Article with Geographical Places and Languages

A Use *the* before the names of:

• mountain ranges	*the Andes, the Himalayas, the Rocky Mountains*
• regions	*the Midwest, the Arctic, the Great Lakes*
• famous places and buildings	*the Grand Canyon, the Eiffel Tower, the White House*
• rivers	*the Amazon, the Nile, the Mississippi River*
• seas and oceans	*the Mediterranean, the Atlantic, the South China Sea*
• deserts	*the Sahara, the Mojave Desert*

B Use no article before the names of:

• most countries	*Canada, Colombia, Japan*
• continents	*Europe, Asia, Africa*
• individual mountains	*Mount Everest, Mount Kilimanjaro, Mount Fuji*
• individual lakes	*Lake Michigan, Lake Tahoe, Lake Victoria*

C Some countries have *the* in their names.

Some countries have *the* in their names.	*the United States, the United Kingdom, the United Arab Emirates, the Netherlands, the Philippines*

D Use no article before the name of a language.

Use no article before the name of a language.	*Can you speak Japanese?* *Chinese is a difficult language for English speakers.*

Grammar Application

A Complete the conversation with *the* or Ø for no article.

Mi-Young You know, life as an international student is very stressful. We took a big risk to come to this new country!

Adriana You think so? I like taking risks. I think it's exciting. I don't worry about things. What do you worry about?

Mi-Young Oh, everything! I worry about __the__ (1) future. I worry about _____ (2) money. I worry about _____ (3) life in general.

Adriana Yeah, I guess it is a little stressful. We work and we study long hours. We also have to use _____ (4) English all the time!

Mi-Young True. We're at work or in class all day, and we never see _____ (5) sun. _____ (6) teachers are good, and our classmates are fun, but _____ (7) courses are really difficult. All I think about is _____ (8) home – there was no risk there!

Adriana I think _____ (9) risks are important, though. They sometimes help you succeed. Right now, _____ (10) education is important. That's what I worry about.

Mi-Young Aha! So you worry about something! You're just the same as everyone else!

Adriana I guess so. Well, everybody worries – _____ (11) life is like that!

B Pair Work Practice the conversation with a partner.

Exercise 3.2 More Practice with *The* and No Article

A Complete the professor's welcome speech with *the* or Ø for no article.

Welcome, ___Ø___ international students! We're so excited to have you here.
(1)
Get ready for a fun and busy year! We at _____ university understand many of you
(2)
are far away from _____ home. We know that can be scary. You all took _____
(3)   (4)
risks in coming here, and you're all very brave.

In your packets, there's _____ information on housing. There are _____
(5)   (6)
maps of _____ entire campus and this part of _____ city. You're all invited to
(7)   (8)
_____ weekly socials[1] where you can
(9)
share _____ information about what
(10)
you learn. It's also a time to meet _____
(11)
friends, both old and new!

We also assigned _____
(12)
"language buddies." _____ buddies
(13)
are other students who help with _____
(14)
English practice every day. When you
need _____ help with anything, please
(15)
contact me! We want you to feel like this
is your home away from _____ home.
(16)
Once again, welcome!

[1]**socials:** get-togethers, or parties

B Over to You Talk to a partner about a time when you took a risk like the one in A.
Did other people help you? What was helpful for you?

A *I enrolled in night classes. The college helped me find a part-time job during
the day.*

B *How did the college help you do that?*

A *They gave me some information about local businesses. These companies
needed part-time workers.*

Complete the blog with *the* or ∅ for no article.

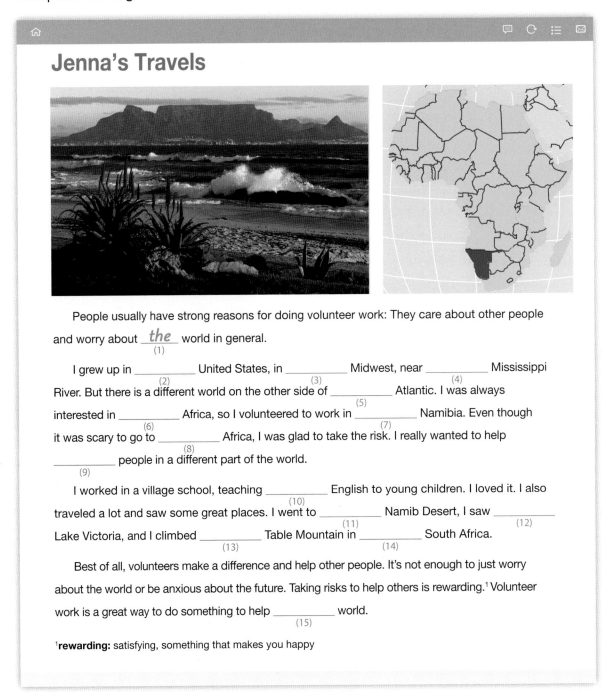

Jenna's Travels

People usually have strong reasons for doing volunteer work: They care about other people and worry about __*the*__ world in general.
(1)

I grew up in _____ United States, in _____ Midwest, near _____ Mississippi
(2)   (3)   (4)
River. But there is a different world on the other side of _____ Atlantic. I was always
(5)
interested in _____ Africa, so I volunteered to work in _____ Namibia. Even though
(6)   (7)
it was scary to go to _____ Africa, I was glad to take the risk. I really wanted to help
(8)
_____ people in a different part of the world.
(9)

I worked in a village school, teaching _____ English to young children. I loved it. I also
(10)
traveled a lot and saw some great places. I went to _____ Namib Desert, I saw _____
(11)   (12)
Lake Victoria, and I climbed _____ Table Mountain in _____ South Africa.
(13)   (14)

Best of all, volunteers make a difference and help other people. It's not enough to just worry about the world or be anxious about the future. Taking risks to help others is rewarding.[1] Volunteer work is a great way to do something to help _____ world.
(15)

[1]**rewarding:** satisfying, something that makes you happy

4 Avoid Common Mistakes ⚠

1   Do not use *a / an* with a noncount noun.

I'm making a̶ progress with my English.
I have a̶ homework tonight.

2   Do not use *the* to talk about things or people in general.

Life
T̶h̶e̶ life is often difficult for t̶h̶e̶ students.
Students get t̶h̶e̶ homework every night.

3   Do not use *the* with the names of languages, most countries, or continents.

T̶h̶e̶ Japanese is a beautiful language.
I want to go to t̶h̶e̶ Australia.

4   Use *a* before consonant sounds. Use *an* before vowel sounds.

a
I have to make a̶n̶ decision quickly!

an
There is a̶ online university in Caracas.

Editing Task

Find and correct 10 more mistakes in these sentences about risk taking.

1   I read an interesting article about how t̶h̶e̶ people manage risk.

2   The professor gave us an lecture on economics.

3   A ostrich worries about getting a good job when he or she finishes college.

4   Analysts hope they have an insurance at work, but will find an new job if they need to.

5   Some people feel a fear when they have to move to a new country.

6   I hope to become an volunteer in the South America after the college.

7   I don't speak the Spanish, so that's an risk. But maybe it can be fun!

Possessive Pronouns and Indefinite Pronouns

Meals Around the World

1 Grammar in the Real World

A What is your favorite breakfast food? Read the conversation between three college roommates as they discuss typical breakfasts in their countries. What do people in your country usually eat for breakfast?

B Comprehension Check **Complete the chart. Check (✓) the box next to the food people eat for breakfast in each place. Use the conversation in A to help you.**

United States	Hong Kong	Mexico
☐ cereal	☐ cereal	☐ cereal
☐ coffee	☐ coffee	☐ coffee
☐ dumplings	☐ dumplings	☐ dumplings
☐ tea	☐ tea	☐ tea
☐ French bread	☐ French bread	☐ French bread

C Notice **Circle the correct answer. Use the conversation to help you.**

1 We always drink coffee or hot chocolate. My father loves strong coffee, and **his** is very sweet!

   What noun does the pronoun **a** my father **b** my father's coffee
   his replace?

2 They put cheese in their eggs, but I don't put it in **mine**.

   What noun does the pronoun **a** cheese **b** eggs
   mine replace?

3 Your grandparents ate a large breakfast! I'd like to try **theirs**.

   What noun does the pronoun **a** breakfast **b** grandparents
   theirs replace?

WHAT'S FOR BREAKFAST?

Kyla - Is that all you eat for breakfast? It's so little!

Sara - Well, it's typical in Mexico to have coffee and a nice *bolillo*, or crusty French bread. It's all I want most days, but on weekends, I have a big breakfast with my family.

5 **Meil-li** - We do that in our family, too. In Hong Kong, we used to have *dim sum* every Saturday.

Sara - What's that?

Meil-li - It's a lot of small, light dishes: dumplings – steamed or fried dough filled with meat, seafood, or vegetables –
10 rice noodle rolls, *congee* – a sort of rice soup, thick like oatmeal – and tea, of course. What do you have at your family brunches?[1]

Sara - We have *huevos rancheros* – fried eggs with a spicy sauce and a *tortilla* – beans, a lot of fresh fruit,
15 sometimes fish that my father catches on his boat. We always drink coffee or hot chocolate. My father loves strong coffee, and **his** is very sweet!

Meil-li - Our breakfast is pretty good, Sara, but I want to try **yours**! How about breakfast in the United States, Kyla?

20 **Kyla** - Well, some people here say breakfast is the most important meal of their day. I have cereal, milk, fruit, yogurt, sometimes eggs – and always coffee. It's a lot of food, but it's not a heavy meal. It's not like the meals people had in the past. For example, my grandparents always had coffee, juice, potatoes, a big plate of
25 eggs with ham and cheese, and pancakes or donuts! They put cheese in their eggs, but I don't put it in **mine**.

Sara - Your grandparents ate a large breakfast! I'd like to try **theirs**. Did **everybody** eat like that?

Kyla - Many did, I think. People did hard physical work and
30 needed a big meal in the morning. Today, some people still eat like that, and some don't have time to eat **anything** at all!

[1]**brunch:** a meal you sometimes eat in the late morning that combines breakfast and lunch

2 Possessive Pronouns

Grammar Presentation

Possessive pronouns tell us who something belongs to.	*That coffee is* *mine*. *I think this one is* *yours*. *Hers* *is still in the kitchen.*

2.1 Possessive Pronouns

Personal Pronouns	Possessive Determiners	Possessive Pronouns
I	**my** + noun **My** *apples are sweet.*	**mine** *Mine are sweet.*
you	**your** + noun **Your** *apples are sweet.*	**yours** *Yours are sweet.*
he	**his** + noun **His** *apples are sweet.*	**his** *His are sweet.*
she	**her** + noun **Her** *apples are sweet.*	**hers** *Hers are sweet.*
it	**its** + noun **Its** *apples are sweet.*	**Its** cannot be a pronoun. ~~Its are sweet.~~
we	**our** + noun **Our** *apples are sweet.*	**ours** *Ours are sweet.*
they	**their** + noun **Their** *apples are sweet.*	**theirs** *Theirs are sweet.*

▶▶ Subject and Object Pronouns: See page A18.

2.2 Using Possessive Pronouns

A Possessive pronouns show who or what a noun belongs to.	*This is* <u>my sister's</u> *cereal. The cereal is* *hers*.
B When you use a possessive pronoun, don't repeat the noun or noun phrase.	*Those apples are* *mine*. NOT *Those are* ~~mine~~ *apples*.

2.2 Using Possessive Pronouns *(continued)*

C Possessive pronouns have one form. They do not change when the noun is plural.	*This apple isn't mine. Mine is on the table.* *These apples aren't mine. Mine are on the table.* NOT *These apples aren't ~~mines~~. ~~Mines~~ are on the table.*
The verb changes when the replaced noun is plural.	*My apples are on the table. Mine are on the table.* *Mine is replacing my apples, so we need to use a plural verb.*
D There is no possessive pronoun for *it*.	*That tree's apples are juicy. Its apples are juicy.* NOT *~~Its~~ are juicy.*

📊 Data from the Real World

Research shows that possessive determiners are much more common in writing.

I eat breakfast every day. My breakfast is always delicious!

Possessive pronouns are much more common in conversation.

"My breakfast is good. How is yours?"
"Mine is delicious!"

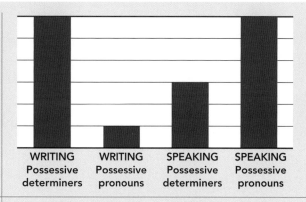

| WRITING Possessive determiners | WRITING Possessive pronouns | SPEAKING Possessive determiners | SPEAKING Possessive pronouns |

Use possessive pronouns to answer questions with *whose*.	*"Whose peaches are these?"* *"They're mine."* *"Whose apple is this?"* *"It's hers."*

🖥 Grammar Application

Exercise 2.1 Possessive Pronouns

Rewrite each sentence. Replace the possessive determiner and noun in bold with a possessive pronoun.

1 That is **my coffee**.   *That is mine.*

2 Did you finish **your breakfast**?   _____

3 **Their breakfast** tasted delicious.   _____

4 John didn't take **my donut**; he took **her donut**!   _____

5 Oh, you can have **our pancakes**.   _____

6 **His hot chocolate** is probably the best.   _____

7 I like fruit with **my breakfast**.   _____

A Complete the sentences with *theirs*, *yours*, *his*, or *hers*.

Meal Times Around the World

People from all around the world eat their main meal at different times. Mexicans eat ___*theirs*___ in the afternoon. They eat between 2:00 and 4:00 p.m.
(1)

People in Spain have their main meal in the afternoon, too. Dinner in Spain is late. They usually eat _____ at 10:00 p.m.! Some visitors don't like that
(2)
custom. While in Spain, you can eat _____ early because restaurants are
(3)
open for travelers like you!

In Thailand, dinner is the main meal. Thais usually eat _____ early in
(4)
the evening.

In the United States, dinner is also the main meal. You might notice that families don't eat together all the time. For example, sometimes the father works late and misses dinner. In cases like this, he has _____ when he gets
(5)
home. Sometimes the daughter has soccer practice in the evening. These evenings, her parents make her an early dinner. She often eats _____ at
(6)
5:00 p.m., before the rest of the family.

B Over to You Tell a partner about the eating habits in your country. What time do people eat their main meal? What do they eat?

Exercise 2.3 Possessive Pronouns, Possessive Determiners, and Verbs

A Complete the sentences with the correct words. Then listen and check your answers.

Sara	Kyla, let's cook dinner!

Kyla	Wow, your kitchen is complicated. Look at all the shelves!

Sara	Well, that's Franny's shelf. She eats a lot of junk food. Those bags of chips **is /~~are~~** (1) **her / hers**. (2) As you can see, **her / hers** (3) shelf is full of chips and candy.

Kyla	It looks like Su's shelf is full of healthy things.

Sara	Yes. Those vitamins **is / are** (4) **her / hers**. (5) **Her / Hers** (6) shelf is always very neat, too. Su and Mari share one shelf. That top shelf is **their / theirs**. (7) It always has baskets of fruit on it.

Kyla	Which shelf is **your / yours**? (8)

Sara	This one **is / are** (9) **my / mine**. (10)

Kyla	Oh, so are those your bowls?

Sara	Yes, those are **yours / mine**. (11) They're from Japan.

Kyla	They're very pretty. **Who's / Whose** (12) things are on this shelf?

Sara	Oh, those are **ours / our**. (13) We all share that shelf. OK. Well, let's start cooking.

Kyla	Right. So, **who's / whose** (14) coming for dinner tonight?

Sara	Our families. We have a lot of cooking to do.

B Pair Work Practice the conversation in A with a partner.

Theirs and *there's* (*there is*) sound the same but mean different things. Be careful with the spelling of these two words.

I ate my lunch in the office, but they ate theirs in the park.
NOT *I ate my lunch in the office, but they ate ~~there's~~ in the park.*

Near the café there's a park.
NOT *Near the café ~~theirs~~ a park.*

Read the blog. Choose the correct words.

>> **MY BLOG**

Olof's Year Abroad

Friday, September 17

Hi! I'm Olof. I'm Swedish, and I study English in the United States. My new college friends had a party to welcome me. It was a party like we have in Sweden. In Sweden this party is a smorgasbord. Americans call ___ there's /(theirs) ___ (1) a potluck. Both parties have a variety of food, but ___ there's / theirs ___ (2) a small difference. With ___ there's / theirs ___ (3), all the guests bring a different dish to share. Sometimes a potluck host asks people to say what specific dish they want to bring. This way, people don't bring the same things. In Sweden, however, the host usually provides most of the food. The food at a smorgasbord is all Swedish, but the food at a potluck often is all different. In fact, ___ there's / theirs ___ (4) often food from different countries, like at my friends' potluck. ___ There's / Theirs ___ (5) included Mexican tamales, Thai spring rolls, and even Swedish meatballs! I had a lot of fun at the party. I especially liked the Swedish meatballs that my friends made. ___ There's / Theirs ___ (6) were just like the meatballs in Sweden!

3 Indefinite Pronouns

Grammar Presentation

| Indefinite pronouns refer to people or things that are not specific, not known, or not the focus of the sentence. | *Everyone loved the food at the party.*
Somebody made dinner.
Does anyone want breakfast? |

3.1 Indefinite Pronouns

	-one	*-body*	*-thing*
some +	someone	somebody	something
any +	anyone	anybody	anything
every +	everyone	everybody	everything
no +	no one	nobody	nothing

3.2 Using Indefinite Pronouns

A Use an indefinite pronoun with *-one* or *-body* to refer to a person or a group of people.	*Everyone knows fruit is good for you.* *Somebody brought this delicious salad.*
B Use an indefinite pronoun with *-thing* to refer to things (not people).	*I know something about healthy food choices.* *Everything I eat is from my garden.*
C Use a third-person singular verb when the subject is an indefinite pronoun.	SUBJECT VERB *Something smells good!* SUBJECT VERB *Everyone eats food.*
D Use indefinite pronouns with *some +*, *every +*, and *no +* in affirmative statements.	*Someone ate all the apples.* *Everyone eats vegetables.* *No one eats junk food in my family.*
E Use indefinite pronouns with *any +* in negative statements.	*She doesn't eat lunch with anybody.* *I don't see anything healthy about junk food.* *He doesn't think anyone should eat fast food.*
Don't use indefinite pronouns with *no +* in negative sentences.	NOT *She doesn't eat lunch with nobody.* NOT *I don't want nothing for dessert.*

3.2 Using Indefinite Pronouns (continued)

F In *Yes/No* questions, use indefinite pronouns with *some +*, *any +*, or *every +*.	*Is* **someone** *home?* *Does* **anyone** *eat apples?* *Is* **everyone** *here?*
You can use indefinite pronouns with *no +* in *Yes/No* questions, but it's very formal.	*Is* **nobody** *home?*

3.3 Types of Statements That Use Indefinite Pronouns

	Affirmative Statements	Negative Statements	Yes/No Questions
anyone, anybody, anything	no	yes	yes
someone, somebody, something	yes	no	yes
everyone, everybody, everything	yes	no	yes
no one, nobody, nothing	yes	no	no

Grammar Application

Exercise 3.1 Indefinite Pronouns with *-one*, *-body*, or *-thing*

A Complete the words with *-one*, *-body*, or *-thing*. Sometimes there is more than one correct answer.

1 We sent **every** *one* in our class an invitation to our international dinner party last night.

2 Gladi wanted to bring dessert. She brought **some**_____ from Laos.

3 I didn't know **any**_____ about Laotian food before the party.

4 **Some**_____ brought some delicious Mexican *enchiladas*.

5 **No**_____ brought any Chinese food.

6 Maybe that's because our class doesn't have **any**_____ from China in it.

7 **Every**_____ was delicious, so people ate a lot.

8 By 10:00, there was **no**_____ left to eat, so we played games and danced instead!

B Pair Work Compare your answers with a partner. Which sentences can have more than one answer?

Exercise 3.2 *Yes / No Questions with Indefinite Pronouns*

A Complete the questions with an indefinite pronoun. Sometimes there is more than one correct answer.

1 Do you know ____*anyone / anybody*____ who eats rice for breakfast?

2 Does _____ eat dinner after 9:00 p.m.?

3 Do you know _____ in your neighborhood?

4 Do you know _____ about cooking?

5 Does _____ cook for you?

6 Can you tell me _____ about food in your country?

B Pair Work Ask and answer the questions in A with a partner.

A *Do you know anyone who eats rice for breakfast?*

B *Yes! I usually eat rice in the mornings.*

Exercise 3.3 Indefinite Pronouns

A Complete the sentences. Choose the correct indefinite pronoun.

Yuki Hello?

Lisa Yuki? Hi, it's Lisa. Did you get my message about coming over to my house for dinner?

Yuki Hi, Lisa. No, I didn't get your message. **Anybody / Nobody** told me you called! Sure,
(1)
I can come for dinner. What time?

Lisa Come at 7:00. What do you want to eat?

Yuki I don't know **anybody / anything** about cooking, and I like **everyone / everything**,
(2)   (3)
so you decide.

Lisa Well, OK. I don't really cook either. How about sushi from Matsuri Restaurant? I know
the owner. I can have **something / someone** there make us a special dinner.
(4)

Yuki That sounds great. So you don't mind calling? I don't know **no one / anyone** at
(5)
that restaurant.

Lisa Sure. Do you want me to call Roberto? **Something / Someone** told me he loves sushi.
(6)

Yuki Oh, yes, I know. I can call him. Do you want to invite **anybody / anything** else?
(7)

Lisa I'm not sure if **no one / anyone** else is around tonight, but that's OK. See you tonight!
(8)

B Pair Work Practice the conversation in A with a partner.

Data from the Real World

We use indefinite pronouns with *-one* more often in writing and formal speaking.	*If **anyone** likes pizza, it's college students.* ***Everyone** needs to eat the right foods.*	
We use indefinite pronouns with *-body* more often in informal speaking.	*Does **anybody** like pizza?* ***Everybody** should eat what they like!*	

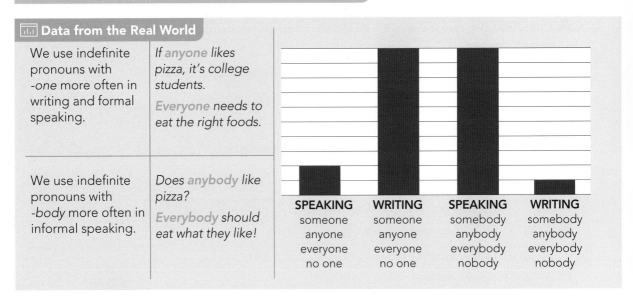

SPEAKING	WRITING	SPEAKING	WRITING
someone anyone everyone no one	someone anyone everyone no one	somebody anybody everybody nobody	somebody anybody everybody nobody

Check (✓) the box if the indefinite pronoun is more common in speaking or writing.

	Speaking	Writing
someone	☐	✓
everybody	☐	☐
anybody	☐	☐
anyone	☐	☐
no one	☐	☐
everyone	☐	☐
somebody	☐	☐
nobody	☐	☐

4 Avoid Common Mistakes ⚠

1 **Don't repeat the noun after the possessive pronoun.**

That's not your apple. It's mine ~~apple~~.

2 **Don't confuse theirs with *there's*.**

The apple is not mine. It's ~~there's~~. [theirs]

3 **Possessive pronouns have one form. They do not change when the noun is plural.**

The apples are ~~mines~~. [mine]

4 **In negative statements, use indefinite pronouns with *any*.**

I don't want to eat ~~nothing~~. [anything]

Editing Task

Find and correct six more errors in this blog about a favorite place to eat.

Jessie's Snack Blog
Tuesday, March 8

BEST SANDWICHES IN TOWN

Everyone has a favorite sandwich shop in town, and the Snack Stop is definitely mine ~~favorite~~. I eat sandwiches a lot, and there's are the best. What do you think? Please leave a comment and let me know!

5 **COMMENTS:**

Richard: I ate there once with my brother and sister, but I didn't like it. Everyone says the sandwiches are delicious, but ours sandwiches weren't good at all. Plus, my sister ordered dessert, but the server didn't bring her nothing. We had to remind him of our order. Then he charged my
10 brother for French fries, but the fries were mines.

Jeff: Wow. I remember the first time I ate at the Snack Stop. It was with my cousin. My sandwich was delicious, and so was hers sandwich. In fact, there wasn't nothing wrong with the whole meal.

Imperatives

1 Grammar in the Real World

A What do people do on the first day of a new job? Read part of a web article. What are two good things to do at a new job?

B Comprehension Check Complete the chart. Use the article to help you. Check (✓) *Yes* or *No*.

When you're at a new job, . . .	Yes	No
1 smile and introduce yourself to people.	✓	☐
2 interrupt people who are busy.	☐	✓
3 ask about your co-workers' families on your first day.	☐	✓
4 look down when you talk with people.	✓	✓
5 smile and be helpful.	✓	☐

C Notice Find these sentences in the article. Complete the sentences.

b **1** _____Say_____ "Good morning" or "Hi" and the person's name.

d **2** ___look___ at people when you talk to them.

a **3** _Don't interrupt_ people who are very busy.

c **4** ___Smile___ and be helpful.

What do the verbs in 1–4 do? Circle the correct answers.

a describe people's habits   c describe the past

b give advice   d tell you what to do

Dos and *Don'ts* at a New Job

It's easy to make mistakes when you go to work at a new job. There are unspoken[1] rules that people don't tell you. Here are some tips to help you avoid some common mistakes.

- **Be** friendly. When you arrive at your new job, **smile** and **introduce** yourself to people. **Say** "Good morning" or "Hi" and the person's name (if you know it).

- **Look** at people when you talk to them. It isn't polite to look down, but you shouldn't stare,[2] either.

- **Don't interrupt**[3] people who are very busy.

- When people at work know each other well, they sometimes talk about their families or their lives at home. **Don't do** this in the beginning. **Wait** until you know people a little. **Don't assume** that people want to talk about private things immediately, or at all.

In some workplaces, there are uniforms[4] or rules about clothes. If there are no rules, **notice** what other people wear. If they wear jeans or other casual clothes, then you can wear jeans, too.

Above all, **smile** and **be** helpful. **Show** that you want to learn and work hard.

---

¹**unspoken:** not said, even though somebody thinks or understands it

²**stare:** look directly at someone for a long time

³**interrupt:** stop something from happening for a short period, or start talking when someone else is already talking

⁴**uniform:** special clothing that shows you are part of an organization or job

2 Imperatives

Grammar Presentation

Imperatives tell people to do things. They can give instructions, directions, or advice.	*Be friendly.* *Don't interrupt people who are very busy.*

2.1 Statements

AFFIRMATIVE			NEGATIVE		
Base Form of Verb			*Do + Not*	**Base Form of Verb**	
Smile	and be helpful.		**Don't/ Do not**	**interrupt**	people who are very busy.
Look	at people when you talk to them.			**do**	this in the beginning.

2.2 Using Imperatives in Writing

Imperatives are common in texts that tell people what to do and what not to do. They appear: • on public signs and advertisements	*Do not enter.* *Stand behind the yellow line.* *Buy now and save $4.99.*
• on forms and websites	*Please write in CAPITAL LETTERS.* *Log in. Enter your password. Search.* *Restart your computer after you install a new program.*
• in texts with instructions (like manuals, recipes, and labels)	*Add hot water and stir.* *Lift here to open.*
• in texts with advice (e.g., magazine articles, leaflets)	*Wait until you know people a little.* *Show that you want to learn and work hard.*

2.3 Using Imperatives in Speaking

A Imperatives are common in classrooms and demonstrations.	*Listen to the conversation.* *Don't open your books.* *Turn on the computer and enter the password.*
B You can use imperatives to give directions.	*Make a left at the next traffic light.* *Don't turn right.*

2.3 Using Imperatives in Speaking (continued)

C You can use imperatives in common social expressions or offers.

Have a good day!
Take care.
Have a cookie.

D You can use imperatives to warn people about dangers.

Watch out!
Be careful! There's a step there.

E When you know people well, you can use imperatives in everyday situations to ask for things or to give instructions or advice.

Call me later.
Don't forget your keys.
Don't worry.

When you don't know people well, don't use imperatives to tell them to do something. Even if you say *please*, you can sound rude.

F *Do not* is very strong and is not common in conversation. It is common to write it in formal situations, but do not use it in informal conversation.

Grammar Application

Exercise 2.1 Imperatives: Advice

A Give some advice about work. Use the negative or affirmative forms of the verbs in parentheses.

1 _____**Don't ask**_____ (ask) about co-workers' lives at home when you are new.

2 _____Don't take_____ (take) a lunch break every day.

3 _____Don't enjoy_____ (enjoy) long coffee breaks in the morning and afternoon.

4 _____Eat_____ (eat) lunch with your co-workers.

5 _____Socialize_____ (socialize) with your co-workers after work if they invite you.

6 _____Don't talk_____ (talk) about vacations or your weekend plans at work.

7 _____Don't talk_____ (talk) about money or politics.

8 _____Learn_____ (learn) from your mistakes.

B Pair Work Compare your answers with a partner. Are your imperatives the same? Discuss which advice is different.

C Over to You Write six sentences about work in a culture you know well.
Use the imperative.

Don't ask about your co-workers' families.
Don't take too many breaks.
Have lunch with your boss when she invites you.

Exercise 2.2 Imperatives: Social Customs

A Jane is taking a work trip to Japan and India. Use the verbs in the box to give her some
advice. You need to make the verb negative two times.

~~eat~~	~~give~~	~~take~~	~~wear~~
~~forget~~	~~keep~~	~~take off~~	~~wrap~~

1 ___*Take off*___ your shoes.

2 ___Take___ a small gift.

3 ___Wrap___ your gift nicely.

4 ___Don't eat___ food with your left hand.

5 Also, ___don't give___ things to people
with your left hand.

6 ___Keep___ your feet on the ground
when you sit.

7 ___Wear___ nice clothes.

8 ___Don't forget___ to write a thank-you note later.

Do you take off your shoes?

Or wipe your feet?

B Over to You What are some social dinner customs you know? Write four imperatives
about social dinner customs in a country you know well.

In the United States, bring flowers to the host(ess). Don't take your shoes off.

1 ___Wash your hands first / pray___

2 ___In Cameroon, you bring desserts, fruit or more food.___

3 ___In China your bring something when you come___

4 _____

Exercise 2.3 Imperatives: Signs

A Look at the signs and complete the imperatives in the chart. Use the verbs from the box.
Sometimes you need to make the verb negative. Then compare your answers with a partner.

bring	drink	feed	ride	throw	turn	use	wear

Throw your trash here.
(1)

Don't feed the animals.
(2)

Don't ride your bicycle here.
(3)

Don't drink the water.
(4)

Don't bring food or drink into the museum.
(5)

Don't turn left here.
(6)

Don't use your cell phone.
(7)

Wear your helmet.
(8)

B Pair Work With a partner, write a list of six signs you see every day. How many use imperatives?

Do not use elevators in case of fire.

1 No right turn on RED

2 STOP

3 NO U-TURN

4 YIEL

5 SPEED LIMIT 45

6 ONE-WAY ST.

C Over to You Write six signs for doors in your home and one for your classroom door. Make them funny. Then read your signs to a partner.

refrigerator door	
bedroom door	
front door	
living room door	
closet door	
kitchen door	
classroom door	

My sign for the refrigerator says, "Do not drink my soda!" What does your sign say?

Exercise 2.4 Imperatives: Directions

A Look at the map. Write down directions from Rogers College to Bob's Cafe. Use some of the imperative directions in the box below.

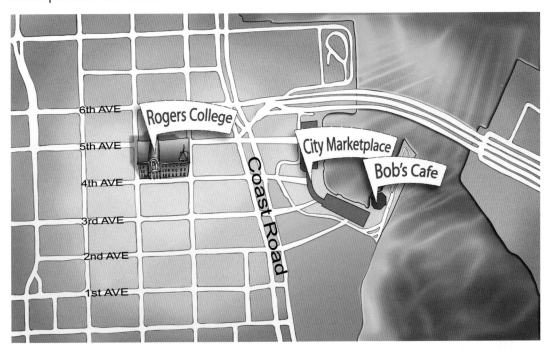

Common Directions				
Take a right on . . .	Go straight on . . .	Go around the corner.	Cross the street.	Walk up the street two blocks.
Go past City Marketplace.	Cross Second Avenue.	Cross Coast Road.	Be careful!	Watch for cars!

Go straight on 4th Avenue.

_____

_____

_____

_____

B Pair Work Write directions to a place in the neighborhood you are in. Read them to a partner. Switch roles. Guess your partner's place.

Data from the Real World

Research shows that people often use *always* and *never* in writing to make imperatives stronger.

This is not common in conversation.

Always shake hands when you meet someone new.
Never wear shoes in someone's house.
NOT ~~Never do not wear~~ shoes in someone's house.

A Complete the sentences from a brochure about visiting Brazil with *always* or *never*. Then listen to the student podcast.

WHEN YOU VISIT **BRAZIL**

1 _____Always_____ make eye contact when you speak with someone.

2 __Never__ arrive at a party early.

3 __Always__ bring your hostess a small gift.

4 __Never__ eat in class.

5 __Always__ ask your server for the check in a restaurant.

6 __Always__ tip your server.

B Over to You For each topic, write three pieces of advice for visitors to the country you are in now. Use *always* and *never* for strong advice. Read your sentences to a partner.

Advice for eating in restaurants:

1 Always ask about the menu.

2 Always tip the server.

3 Never get into a fight.

Advice for talking to people:

1 Always make eye contact.

2 Never be loud.

3 Listen to the other person. _Always_

Advice for going to a new college:

1 _____

2 _____

3 _____

3 Avoid Common Mistakes ⚠

1 **Use *don't* to form negative imperatives.**

Don't
~~No~~ forget to do your homework.

2 **Remember to write *do not* as two words.**

Do not   *Do not*
~~Donot~~ be late for class.   ~~Do n't~~ be late for class.

3 **Use an apostrophe to write *don't*. Put the apostrophe between the *n* and *t*.**

Don't   *Don't*
~~Dont~~ send text messages during class.   ~~Do'nt~~ eat in the computer lab.

Don't
~~D'ont~~ forget to save your work.

Editing Task

Find and correct nine more mistakes in these sentences about advice for college students in different countries.

Don't
1 ~~Dont~~ be late for class.

Don't
2 No stand up when the teacher walks into the classroom.

Do not
3 Donot use the teacher's first name.

Don't
4 No forget to write the date your assignment is due.

Don't
5 Dont forget your homework assignment.

Don't
6 Do'nt copy another student's homework.

Do not
7 Donot buy or download essays on the Internet.

Don't
8 D'ont listen to your MP3 player in class.

Don't
9 No answer your phone in class.

Don't
10 Do n't send or read text messages in class.

21 Ability and Possibility

Making Connections

1 Grammar in the Real World

A How do you stay in touch with friends and family? Read the article. Does technology help you stay in touch? *Yes, it does*

B Comprehension Check **Answer the questions. Use the article to help you.**

1 How does the Internet help people connect with each other?

2 Why is it easy to make a cat video?

3 Do you agree with the idea that people were lonely in the past? Why or why not?

C Notice **Find these sentences in the article. Complete the sentences with *can*, *could*, or *could not*.** *Kud not*

1 Fifty years ago, people *could not* go online and watch funny cat videos.
   Pueden Podria   No pude,

2 Anyone with a smartphone *can* make a video.

3 In the past, people *could not* share their lives in this way.

4 For example, a person from Morocco *can* team up with someone from Japan.

PRESENT   PAST
A-   Can   Could
      Can not   Could not
      Can't   Couldn't
      Could = Kud you
B-   I can drive   = I am able to drive *Poder*
SAME   Junping can read = Junping is able to read
       We can speak well = We are able to speak well

218 C - I KNOW HOW TO... Cook, dance, use the computer
       = Only THINGS WE LEARN = play the piano

TECHNOLOGY FOR MAKING CONNECTIONS

Fifty years ago, people **could not** go online and watch funny cat videos. However, today they **can**, and they do! There are more than 12,000 cat videos on YouTube, and a lot of people watch them. This happens because
5   people **are able to** connect with strangers. Anyone with a smartphone **can** make a video. Anyone who sees it **can** share it.

In the past, people **could not** share their lives in this way. People **could** share ideas and information with
10   friends, neighbors, and coworkers, but they **were not able to** connect with the rest of the world. Also, they **could not** make and post videos so easily.

Another way people connect with strangers is through computer games.
15   In online games, players **can** be from different countries, but they **can** meet in the game. For example, a person from Mexico **can** team up with someone from Japan. They do not share
20   personal information, but they **are able to** communicate like friends.

Cat videos and computer games are just two ways technology is changing friendship and community.
25   Some people miss the face-to-face contact that they **were able to** have in the past. Others like the changes because they are never lonely.

2 Can and Could for Ability and Possibility

Grammar Presentation

Can and could express ability or possibility.	*Anyone who sees it can share it.* *People could share ideas and information with friends, neighbors, and coworkers.*

2.1 Statements

AFFIRMATIVE

Subject	Can / Could	Base Form of Verb	
I You We They He / She / It	**can** **could** ~~kud~~	**use**	e-mail.

NEGATIVE

Subject	Can / Could + Not	Base Form of Verb	
I You We They He / She / It	**cannot** **can't** **could not** ~~kud not~~ **couldn't**	**use**	e-mail.

2.2 Yes/No Questions and Answers

Can / Could	Subject	Base Form of Verb	
Can **Could**	I you we they he / she / it	**use**	the computer?

2.2 | Yes / No Questions and Answers *(continued)*

AFFIRMATIVE ANSWERS

Yes	Subject	Can / Could
Yes,	I you we they he / she / it	can. could.

NEGATIVE ANSWERS

No	Subject	Can / Could + Not
No,	I you we theys he / she / it	cannot. can't. could not. couldn't.

2.3 | Information Questions

Wh- Word	Can / Could	Subject	Base Form of Verb	
Who			**ask**	about the program?
What	can	I you we they he / she / it	**do**	on that website?
When	could		**share**	a video?
Where			**use**	our cell phones?
How			**communicate**	with each other?

2.4 | Using *Can* and *Could*

A	Use *can* to talk about ability or possibility in the present.	*I can use the Internet at the school library.* *Friends can post comments to each other.*
B	Use *could* to talk about ability or possibility in the past.	*I could use the Internet at my old school.* *My grandparents could only get the news through radio and television when they were young.*
C	You can spell *cannot* as one word or as two words (*can not*), but it is usually spelled as one word (*cannot*). Spell *could not* as two words.	*I cannot remember my password.* *I can not remember my password.* *We could not share with the public.* NOT ~~We couldnot share with the public.~~ NOT ~~I couldnot~~ read the e-mail.
D	Use the contractions *can't* or *couldn't* in speaking, e-mails, and conversations but not in formal writing.	*They can't remember the password.* *I couldn't read your e-mail.* *In the past, people could not share experiences in this way.*

▶▶ Modal Verbs and Modal-like Expressions: See page A25.

Exercise 2.1 *Can* and *Could* for Ability and Possibility

A Complete the sentences in the blog. Circle the correct words.

>> **Serena's Blog**

My New Life in the United States

When I was a student in Chile, I **can / (could)** do everything easily. However, now I am a student at a community college in San Diego. When I first came here, I **cannot / (could not)** do many things without help. In this post, I want to share my experience so other new students **(can) / could** learn from it.

A few months ago, I **can't / (couldn't)** find places. I got lost many times. Then I started using my GPS. Now I **(can) / could** find everything on campus. Last week, I went to the computer center because I **cannot / (could not)** login into my computer class. They told me to change my password. Now I always go there when I have a problem. I also like the student services building. Students **(can) / could** play games and relax. They **(can) / could** meet new people. Right now, I **(cannot) / could not** speak English very well, so I want to join the International Club. Then I **(can) / could** practice.

Food was another problem for me. I wanted food from my country, but I **cannot / (could not)** find it in the cafeteria. Then my American roommate took me to a Chilean restaurant. It's not far, so I **(can) / could** eat there a couple of times a week. I **(can) / could** usually meet other Chilean people, so I feel happy.

Now, I **(can) / could** say that I like my new life on campus!

B Unscramble the words to make *Yes/No* questions and information questions with *can* and *could*.

1 Can / fit / your / phone / in your pocket / ?

Can you fit your phone in your pocket?

2 Can / with your eyes closed / you / text / ?

Can you text with your eyes closed?

3 check / your e-mail / can / When / you / ?

When can you check your e-mail?

4 can / buy / I / a good computer / Where / ?

Where can buy I a good computer?

5 How / learn / I / to design websites / can / ?

How can I learn to design websites?

6 five years ago / you / send / an e-mail / Could / ?

Could you send an e-mail five years ago?

7 your parents / their passwords / remember / Can / ?

Can your parents remember their passwords?

8 online / 50 years ago / Could / shop / people / ?

Could people shop online 50 years ago?

9 text messages / Who / 10 years ago / could / send / ?

Who could send text messages 10 years ago?

10 make / you / Could / with your phone / a video / in 2005 / ?

Could you make a video with your phone in 2005?

11 you / Can / text / quickly / ?

Can you text quickly?

12 How / communicate / could / people / 20 years ago / ?

How could people communicate 20 years ago?

C Pair Work Ask and answer the questions in B with a partner.

Sometimes it's hard to hear the difference between *can* and *can't*.	
People usually do not pronounce the *a* in *can* very clearly.	*I can use a laptop* usually sounds like *I c'n use a laptop.* *Can I use your phone?* usually sounds like *C'n I use your phone?*
People always say the *a* in *can't* very clearly.	*I can't use a tablet.*[1] *He can't find his phone.*
In short answers, people always say the *a* in *can* and *can't* clearly.	*Yes, I can.* *No, I can't.*

[1]**tablet:** electronic reading device

A Listen and repeat the sentences.

1 I **can** use a laptop.

2 I **can't** use a laptop.

3 I **can** design a blog.

4 I **can't** design a blog.

5 He **can** find his phone.

6 He **can't** find his phone.

B Listen. Complete the chart. Check (✓) all the things you can do on the *Gen 5* and *Linkage* websites. Write an ✗ for everything you can't do.

	Gen 5 website	Linkage website
1 chat	✓	✗
2 join interest groups	✓	✓
3 download songs	✓	✓
4 send songs to friends	✗	✓
5 find a job	✗	✓
6 post pictures	✓	✗

C Pair Work Look at the chart in B. Choose the website that is best for you. Share your reasons with a partner.

I like Gen 5. You can chat with Gen 5, but you can't chat with Linkage.

3 Be Able To and Know How To for Ability

Poder (handwritten above "Able")

Capacidad (handwritten below "Ability")

Grammar Presentation

Can (handwritten)

Be able to expresses ability. *Know how to* expresses things we learned to do in the past.

Warren *is able to* edit movies on his phone.
I *know how to* post videos on the Internet. Someone taught me.

3.1 Be Able To: Affirmative Statements

Subject	Be	Able To	Base Form of Verb	
I	am / was			
You We They	are / were	able to	send	text messages.
He She It	is / was			

3.2 Be Able To: Negative Statements

Subject	Be + Not	Able To	Base Form of Verb	
I	am not / 'm not was not / wasn't			
You We They	are not / aren't were not / weren't	able to	send	text messages.
He She It	is not / isn't was not / wasn't			

3.3 Be Able To: Yes/No Questions

Be	Subject	Able To	Base Form of Verb	
Am / Was	I			
Are / Were	you we they	able to	send	text messages?
Is / Was	he / she / it			

3.4 *Know How To*: Affirmative Statements

Subject	*Know*	*How To*	Base Form of Verb	
I You We They	**know**	**how to**	design	a website.
He / She / It	**knows**			

3.5 *Know How To*: Negative Statements

Subject	*Do + Not*	*Know How To*	Base Form of Verb	
I You We They	**do not / don't**	**know how to**	design	a website.
He / She / It	**does not / doesn't**			

3.6 *Know How To*: Yes / No Questions

Do	Subject	*Know How To*	Base Form of Verb	
QUESTIONS **Do**	I you we they	**know how to**	design	a website?
Does	he / she / it			

3.7 Using *Be Able To* and *Know How To*

A You use *be able to* to express ability. It has the same meaning as *can / could*.		*They are able to translate the menu with their phones.* *Mariko wasn't able to find the file.*	
B You use *know how to* to talk about things you learned to do.		*Suri knows how to create a web page.* *My grandmother didn't know how to send e-mail until I taught her.*	

▸▸Modal Verbs and Modal-like Expressions: See page A25.

Grammar Application

Exercise 3.1 Expressing Ability with *Be Able To* and *Know How To*

Complete the questions and answers about a class survey. Circle the correct words.

A Class Survey On Technology Know-How!

By Ian Wright

use = yus

Do my classmates and teacher know how to use different types of technology? I wanted to know, so I surveyed them to find out. Here are the questions I asked and the answers I got!

Q Mike, **do / (does)** Juan know how to use photo editing software?
(1)

A Yes, Juan **know / (knows)** how to use photo editing software.
(2)

Q **(Do) / Does** our classmates know how to use business networking sites?
(3)

A No, they **(don't) / doesn't** know how to use business networking sites.
(4)

Q Sam, **is / (are)** you able to design online games?
(5)

A No, I **(am) / are** not able to design online games.
(6)

Q Tony and Tara, **(do) / does** you know how to post a review?
(7)

A Yes, we **(know) / knows** how to post a review.
(8)

Q Sarah, **(is) / are** our teacher able to put tests online?
(9)

A No, our teacher **(isn't) / aren't** able to put tests online.
(10)

Q **(Do) / Does** our classmates **(know) / knows** how to create a group on social media?
(11)   (12)

A Yes, they **is / (are)** able to create a group on social media.
(13)

Exercise 3.2 Expressing Ability with *Be Able To* and *Know How To*

A Complete the sentences with the correct form of *be able to* or *know how to*. Use the words in parentheses.

Queta and her husband, Marco, live in Texas, but right now Marco has a new job in Nigeria. For Marco, flights to visit Queta and their daughter, Daniela, are very expensive. He _does not know_
(1)
how he can find cheaper flights. Of course, Queta and Marco
Know how to use video calling, but Marco _is able to talk_ to Daniela
(2)   (3)
and Queta at night only because he is at work all day. However, Queta and Daniela
are not able to talk at that time. That's because Marco's nighttime is their
(4)
daytime. They _are no able_ to leave work or school at that time. Unfortunately,
(5)
Marco _is not able_ to change the hours he works, so the family does not use
(6)
video calling except on the weekends. Queta and Marco _don't know_ how to
(7)
solve this problem. Living so far apart is difficult! But they _Know how to_ send
(8)
instant messages, and they can text or email photos, so for now this is an easy solution.

B Complete the conversation with the correct form of *can (not)*, *be (not) able to,* or *(not) know how to*. Sometimes there is more than one correct answer.

Jerry   My phone bill is so expensive!

Mark   That's because you still _____*don't know how*_____ to use an app for phone calls.
(1)

Jerry   No, I hate technology. Don't you?

Mark   I like it when I __am able to / can__ save money.
(2)

Jerry   Hmm. What is this app?

Mark   I use TalkNow. I __am able to / can__ call anyone in the world for free!
(3)

Jerry   OK, TalkNow, you say?

Mark   Yes.

Jerry   OK, but I __don't know how to__ download the app.
(4)

Mark   Really? I __cannot__ believe that!
(5)
Everyone __can / is able to__ download an
(6)
app, even my six-year-old grandson.

Jerry   Well, I __don't know how to__ do it.
(7)

Mark   I'm sure your wife _____*can*_____ do it.
(8)

Jerry   Probably, but I __cannot / am to able to__ ask her for
(9)
help. She's at work.

Mark   OK, when _____*can*_____ I come over?
(10)

Jerry   How about right now?

C Pair Work Work with a partner. Ask each other about some popular technology.
Use *Yes/No* questions with *can, could, be able to,* and *know how to.*

A *Do you know how to upload videos from your phone?*

B *Yes, I do.*

A *Are you able to edit videos on your phone?*

4 Avoid Common Mistakes ⚠

1 **There is only one form of *can* and *could*.**

can
He ~~cans~~ send e-mail.

could
Ten years ago, she ~~coulds~~ only use a computer for typing reports.

2 **Use the base form of the verb with *can* and *could*.**

listen
Sue can ~~listens~~ to audio books on the bus.

listen
Yesterday Sue could ~~listened~~ to music all day.

3 **Do not use *to* with the base form of the verb.**

I can ~~to~~ schedule a video conference.

4 **Use *could* to talk about ability in the past.**

could not
Yesterday I ~~cannot~~ send an attachment.

Editing Task

Find and correct six more mistakes on Jenny's *Connected* page.

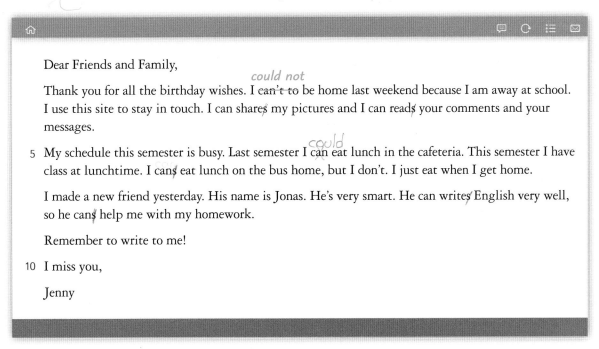

Dear Friends and Family,

could not
Thank you for all the birthday wishes. I ~~can't to~~ be home last weekend because I am away at school. I use this site to stay in touch. I can ~~shares~~ my pictures and I can ~~reads~~ your comments and your messages.

5 My schedule this semester is busy. Last semester I *could* ~~can~~ eat lunch in the cafeteria. This semester I have class at lunchtime. I ~~cans~~ eat lunch on the bus home, but I don't. I just eat when I get home.

I made a new friend yesterday. His name is Jonas. He's very smart. He can ~~writes~~ English very well, so he ~~cans~~ help me with my homework.

Remember to write to me!

10 I miss you,

Jenny

Requests and Permission

College Life

1 Grammar in the Real World

A Do you have an academic adviser? Read the academic adviser's web page. What are some things an academic adviser can help you with?

B Comprehension Check **Answer the questions. Circle *Yes* or *No*.** Use the article to help you.

1 Do students ask Henry different kinds of questions? (Yes) No

2 Does Henry discuss very personal problems? Yes (No)

3 Does Henry go to students' classes to talk about his work? (Yes) No

4 Can students find more common questions on the school's home page? (Yes) No

C Notice **Find the student questions in the article. Complete the sentences.**

1 _____Can_____ you help me choose the right classes for my major?

2 _____Could_____ you give me some advice, please?

3 _____Can_____ you give me information about tutors, please?

4 _____Would_____ you come to our class and talk about your work as an academic adviser, please?

What is the purpose of all these questions?

DEPARTMENT OF LANGUAGES

Hello,

My name is Henry Driscoll, and I am one of the academic advisers for the Department of Languages. My job is to help you with your educational and career goals. Students often come to my office to ask
5   questions. Here are some typical questions:

- **Can** you help me choose the right classes for my major?

- I want to take some courses in another department. **Could** you give me some advice, please?

- I need a tutor to help me with my English. **Can** you give me
10   information about tutors, please?

- **May** I come to your office to talk with you about a problem I have?

- I have a financial problem. **Can** you help me?

- I have a problem with my classes. **Can** you help me with it?

Often my answer is, "Sure! No problem. Of course I can help."
15 But sometimes I have to say, "Sorry, I **can't** help you with that" or "I'm sorry, I **can't** discuss that." For example, I **cannot** discuss questions about very personal issues, such as health or family problems. However, I **can** always refer[1] you to a person who can help you.

Here is my favorite question: "**Would** you come to our class and talk
20 about your work as an academic adviser, please?" To that question, the answer is always YES!

For more information and FAQs,[2] go to the school's home page at www.DCweb.cambridge.org.

[1]**refer:** send you to a different place or to a person who knows more about or can help more with a subject

[2]**FAQs:** frequently asked questions

2 *Can*, *Could*, and *Would* for Requests

Grammar Presentation

We use *can*, *could*, and *would* to ask people to do things.	*Can you help me, please?* *Could you give me some advice?* *Would you please help me with my paper?*

2.1 *Can*, *Could*, and *Would* for Requests

Can / Could / Would	Subject	Base Form of Verb	
Can ᴄᴜᴅ **Could** ᴡᴜᴅ **Would**	you	advise	me about the program?
		open	the door for me, please?
		come	to our class and talk about your work, please?

2.2 Using *Can*, *Could*, and *Would* to Make Requests

A Use *can*, *could*, and *would* to ask people to do something.	*Can you meet me at 2:00 p.m. today?* *Could you give me some advice?* *Would you reserve a seat for me, please?*
B *Could* and *would* are more polite than *can*. Use *could* and *would* in formal situations.	*Can you give me a call tonight?* *Could you advise me about my project, please?* *Would you help me write my résumé, please?*
C Use *please* when you ask a person you do not know well to do something.	*Excuse me. Can you tell me the way to Mason Street, please?*
Use *please* in formal situations.	*Would you please come this way?*
You can use *please* at the end of the sentence or after the subject.	*Could you sign this document, please?* *Could you please sign this document?*

▸▸ Modal Verbs and Modal-like Expressions: See page A25.

2.3 Answering Requests

A When you agree to a request, you can give a short answer.	*Can you come tonight?"* *"Yes." / "Yes, I can."*
You can include the request in your answer.	*"Can you help me?"* *"Yes, I can help you."*
Often we say other words of agreement instead of *yes*. Informal Responses: *OK, sure, no problem* Formal Responses: *of course, certainly*	*"Could you please help me find the career adviser's office?"* *"Sure I can."* *"Certainly. Just follow that corridor. First door on the left."*
B We use *cannot* or *can't* in negative answers to requests, even when the request uses *could* or *would*.	*"Could you please give me your book?"* *"No, I can't. I don't have it with me."* *"Would you come to the meeting with us?"* *"No, I can't. Sorry, I'm busy."*
Can't is informal.	*"Can you help me with this vocabulary word?"* *"No, I can't. I don't know what it means."*
Cannot is more formal.	*"Could you help me with my health issues, please?"* *"No, I cannot discuss health problems with you."*
We often use *sorry* instead of *no*.	*"Would you like to go out tonight?"* *"Sorry, I can't. I have a lot of homework."* *"Can you pass the dictionary?"* *"Sorry, I can't reach it."*
I'm sorry is more formal than *sorry*.	*"Could you please tell me the time?"* *"I'm sorry. I can't. I don't have a watch."*
We often give a reason when we give a negative response to a request.	*"Would you speak to our class tomorrow?"* *"No, I'm sorry. I can't. I'm in a conference all day."* *"Can you help me tonight?"* *"Sorry, I can't. I have to work."*

Grammar Application

 A Complete the sentences with *can*, *could*, *would*, or *can't*. Then listen to the conversations. Check your answers.

Elena I need to talk to Professor Baker.
_____*Can*_____ you tell me what building
(1)
he's in?

Freda Yeah, sure. He's in the Ross Building.
I'm going there now. Come on! So,
what's up?

Elena Oh, it's just a problem about the
exams. __*Can*__ you come with me to
(2)
Professor Baker's office? Do you know
where it is?

Freda Yeah, sure. I met with him last semester.

Elena When I finish with the professor,
__*Can*__ we meet up again later?
(3)

Freda Yeah, good idea!

Elena Just one problem. I don't know what
time the meeting finishes. __*Can*__
(4)
you wait for me in the cafeteria?

Freda No problem. I can do my homework.

Elena Hello, Professor Baker. Do you
have a minute?

Prof. Baker Certainly. __*Would*__ you close
(5)
the door, please?

Elena Of course. __*Could*__ you help
(6)
me, please? I have an exam next
Tuesday, and I have a family
wedding on that day. __*Would*__
(7)
you write a letter to the exam
professor about this?

Prof. Baker Oh, I'm sorry. I __*can't*__.
(8)
A family wedding is not an
excuse to miss an exam.
That's the college's policy.

Elena Oh! Really?

Prof. Baker I'm very sorry. Those are
the rules.

Elena Oh, well, OK. Thank you for
your time.

B Pair Work Practice the conversations in A with a partner.

Exercise 2.2 Making and Answering Requests

A Change the imperatives to questions. Use *can*, *could*, or *would*. Sometimes there is more than one correct answer.

1 Help me write my résumé.

Can you help me write my résumé?

2 Meet me at the cafeteria after class today.

Can you meet me at the cafeteria?/ friend

3 Tell me the things that I need to put in the résumé.

Could you tell me the things that I need to put./advisor

4 Show me your résumé.

Can you show me your resume? classmate and friend

5 Advise me on the correct style for a résumé.

Could you advise me on the correct style / teacher /mentor

6 Correct my mistakes.

Could you correct my mistakes / teacher, classmate

7 Help me arrange my résumé so it looks good.

Can you help me arrange my resume.

8 Read my résumé and make sure it's OK.

Can you read my resume and make sure / classmate

B Pair Work Work with a partner. Ask and answer the questions in A. First, agree to the requests. Use *sure*, *no problem*, and *of course*. Then give negative answers. Use *sorry* and *I'm sorry*. Give a good reason for your negative answers. Take turns.

A *Can you help me write my résumé?*   **A** *Can you help me write my résumé?*

B *Sure!*   **B** *Sorry, I can't help you. I'm really busy today.*

3 Can, Could, and May for Permission

Grammar Presentation

<table>
<tr>
<td>We use *can*, *could*, and *may* to ask for permission to do things.</td>
<td>*Can* I make an appointment for tomorrow?
May I please come in?
Could I ask you a question?</td>
</tr>
</table>

3.1 Can, Could, and May for Permission

Can / Could / May	Subject	Base Form of Verb	
Can **Could** **May**	I	use	this pencil?
		leave	early today?
		ask	a question?

3.2 Using Can, Could, and May for Permission

A Use *can* in most situations.	*Can* I borrow your pen? *Can* I take a picture with your camera?
B *Could* is more polite than *can*.	*Could* we use Room 208 for our student meeting?
Use *could* with strangers and people you do not know well.	*Could* I study with you for the exam?
Use *could* in formal situations.	*Could* I talk to you for a moment?
C *May* is very polite.	Professor Wodak, *may* I interview you for the student newspaper, please?
Use *may* with people you do not know well in very formal situations.	*May* I use your pen for a moment?
D *Please* can make a request for permission more polite. Use *please* when you ask a person you do not know well for permission.	Can I use this telephone, *please*? May I use your pen for a moment, *please*?
Use *please* in formal situations. Use *please* at the end of the request or after the subject.	Doctor Takano, may I *please* ask a question about my project? May I ask a question about my project, *please*?

▸ Modal Verbs and Modal-like Expressions: See page A25.

3.3 Answering Requests for Permission

A When you agree to a request for permission, you can give a short answer.	*"Can I sit in this chair?"* *"Yes."*
You can include the request in your answer.	*"Could I work in your group?"* *"Sure, you can work in our group!"*
Often we say other words of agreement instead of *yes*. Informal responses: *sure, no problem, go ahead* Formal responses: *of course, certainly*	*"Can I see your homework?"* *"No problem!"* *"May I contact you by e-mail?"* *"Of course."*
B We often use *sorry* when we give a negative answer to a request for permission. People do not usually say *no*. They say *sorry* and give a reason.	*"Could I see that?"* *"Sorry. It's not mine."*
I'm sorry is more formal than *sorry*.	*"Can I speak to you for a moment?"* *"I'm sorry. I'm very busy. Maybe after class?"*

Grammar Application

Exercise 3.1 Requests for Permission with *Can, Could,* and *May*

A Complete the requests. Circle the best answer.

1 To a friend: **Can** / **May** I call you later?

2 To a professor: **May** / **Could** I leave early today?

3 To a stranger: **Can** / **May** I look at your bus schedule for a moment?

4 To a friend: **Could** / **May** I see your phone?

5 To a boss: **May** / **Could** I speak to you for a moment?

6 To a friend: **May** / **Can** we finish this tomorrow?

B Pair Work Practice saying and answering the requests in A with a partner. Give some affirmative answers and some negative answers.

A *Can I call you later?*
B *Sure. Call me anytime.*

A *Can I call you later?*
B *Sorry, I'm busy tonight. I can call you tomorrow.*

A Complete the chart. Who is the speaker? Where does the request take place? Use your own ideas.

A student	A professor	A boss	A co-worker	Who?	Where?
1 Can I sit next to you, Joanna?				*student*	*in class / in a café*
2 Could I please leave early today, Professor?				student	in class
3 May I have next Monday off, please? It's my birthday.				boss	office
4 Could I use your office for an hour today?				co-worker	At work
5 May I use your telephone, please?				professor boss	At school At work
6 Could I please make two copies of my report?				boss co-worker	At work
7 Can I have one of your French fries?				student	in a cafe
8 May I please talk to you about my schedule?				2, 3	At work
9 Can I look at your project? There are problems with mine.				1, 4	At work in class

B Pair Work With a partner, write answers to the requests in A. Practice saying and answering the requests.

A *Can I sit next to you, Joanna?* **A** *Could I leave early today, Professor?*
B *Sure!* **B** *I'm sorry. You left early yesterday.*

Exercise 3.3 Formal Requests for Permission

Complete the sentences with the words in parentheses. Reorder the words to make requests for permission.

Dear Professor Machado,

My name is Ricardo Yaka. I am the editor of the *English Now* newsletter. _May I interview you_
(1)
(I/interview/may/you) for about 15 minutes for this month's newsletter? _____
(2)
(come/could/I/to your office/please) for the interview?

The newsletter often has articles about the lives of faculty members. We know that students like to read about their professors' college experiences.
May I ask you
(3)
(ask/I/may/you) about your college days? To make it easy for you,
Can I please send you (can/you/I/please/send) a list of
(4)
my questions?

The articles in our newsletters are informal, and many have photographs.
Could I please take (please/I/could/take)
(5)
your picture? You can see a copy of the newsletter before the interview.
May I e-mail (e-mail/I/may) it to you?
(6)
The newsletter is very popular. About 200 students read the interviews every month, and more students read the newsletter on the Internet.
May I please put (I/may/please/put) your interview
(7)
on our website, too?

After you have read the questions, _could I please visit_
(8)
(visit/I/could/please) you at your office sometime this week?

Thank you very much. I look forward to your reply.

Kind regards,

Ricardo Yaka

Write a request for permission based on each situation.

1 You want to come in late for work tomorrow. Ask your boss.

Could I come in late tomorrow, please? / May I
please come in late tomorrow?

2 You want to use your best friend's pen. Ask him/her.

Can I use

3 You want to change the channel on the TV at home. Ask a family member.

Can I change

4 You want to hand in your homework one day late. Ask your teacher.

Could I hand in

5 You want to speak to your boss after work today. Ask him/her.

My I speak to you

6 You want to borrow your classmate's electronic dictionary. Ask him/her.

Can I borrow

7 You want to charge your phone in the school office. Ask the secretary.

Could I change me

8 You want to use the atlas behind the reference desk in the library. Ask the librarian.

May I you the atlas

9 You want to borrow your roommate's bicycle. Ask him/her.

Can I borrow yr bicycle

10 You want to get your professor's e-mail address. Ask him/her.

May I get yr e-mail

4 Avoid Common Mistakes ⚠

1 **Use the correct word order for making requests.**

Can you
~~You can~~ help me?

2 **Use the base form of the verb after *can, could, may,* or *would.***

help
Can you ~~to help~~ me?

3 **Use *can, could,* or *would* to ask people to do something. Do not use *do.***

Would
~~Do~~ you come to my office, please?

4 **Use *can, could,* or *would* to ask people to do something. Do not use *may.***

Could
~~May~~ you reserve a place for me, please?

Editing Task

Find and correct eight more mistakes in this e-mail about a college music show.

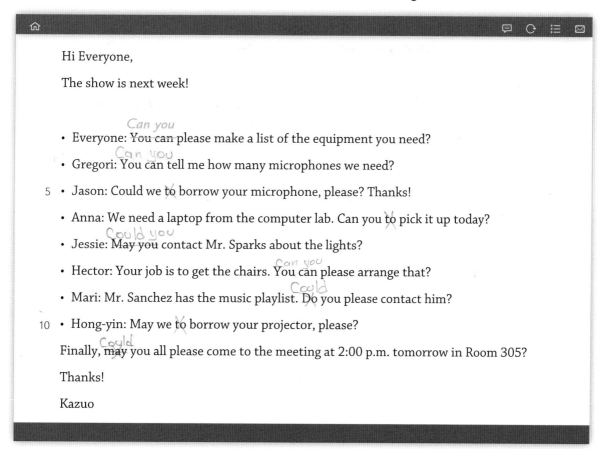

Hi Everyone,

The show is next week!

- Everyone: ~~You can~~ *Can you* please make a list of the equipment you need?
- Gregori: ~~You can~~ *Can you* tell me how many microphones we need?
5 - Jason: Could we ~~to~~ borrow your microphone, please? Thanks!
- Anna: We need a laptop from the computer lab. Can you ~~to~~ pick it up today?
- Jessie: ~~May you~~ *Could you* contact Mr. Sparks about the lights?
- Hector: Your job is to get the chairs. ~~You can~~ *Can you* please arrange that?
- Mari: Mr. Sanchez has the music playlist. ~~Do~~ *Could* you please contact him?
10 - Hong-yin: May we ~~to~~ borrow your projector, please?

Finally, ~~may~~ *Could* you all please come to the meeting at 2:00 p.m. tomorrow in Room 305?

Thanks!

Kazuo

Present Progressive

Body Language

1 Grammar in the Real World

A What do you do during a conversation? Do you smile? Do you cross your arms? Do you nod your head? Do you make eye contact? Read the article about body language. Why is it important?

B Comprehension Check **What can these gestures mean? Use the article to help you. Circle *a* or *b*.**

1 A person is leaning toward you in a conversation.

   a He doesn't like what you are saying.   **(b)** He is interested.

2 Your friend is crossing her arms during an argument.

   (a) She doesn't agree with you.   **b** She is thinking about something else.

3 A person is touching her chin a lot during a discussion.

   (a) She is thinking.   **b** Maybe she's lying.

C Notice **Complete these sentences. Use the forms of the verbs from the article.**

1 Nod to show you ___are listening___ (listen).

2 Some experts say that when you keep your hands under the table, it can mean you ___are___ not ___telling___ (tell) the truth.

3 However, a hand on the chin can just mean you ___are thinking___ (think).

Look at the verb forms. How many parts does each verb have? What do they have in common?

BE + VERB - ING

UNDERSTANDING BODY LANGUAGE

Body language is a crucial[1] part of face-to-face communication. Some experts[2] say that 93 percent of communication is nonverbal.[3] Of course, the meaning of body language varies from culture to
5 culture. Even in one culture, experts do not always agree on the meaning of every gesture.[4] However, here are some things to remember for your next conversation, meeting, or interview. They apply mostly to communication in North America.

10 ### How **Are You Sitting**?

Lean[5] toward the other person to show you are interested in what he or she **is saying**. Nod to show **you are listening**.

Are You **Crossing** Your Arms?

15 Crossing your arms can seem defensive.[6] In an argument, it can mean you don't agree.

What **Are** Your Hands **Doing**?

Keep your hands out and open. Some experts say that when you keep your hands
20 under the table, it can mean you **are not telling** the truth. However, a hand on the chin can just mean you **are thinking**.

Where **Are** You **Looking**?

Make eye contact. When you **are talking**
25 to someone face-to-face, it is important to look at them. This shows that you **are listening** to them.

Learn to use positive body language. After all, what you *do* may communicate
30 more than 90 percent of your message.

---

[1]**crucial:** extremely important
[2]**expert:** a person with a high level of knowledge or skill about a subject
[3]**nonverbal:** not spoken
[4]**gesture:** a movement of the body, hands, arms, or head to express an idea or feeling
[5]**lean:** move your body so it's bent forward
[6]**defensive:** wanting to protect or defend oneself

2 Present Progressive Statements

Grammar Presentation

The present progressive describes actions and events that are in progress now and around the present time. "In progress" means the action started before now but is not finished or complete.

He is not listening to the professor.

We are studying body language in my psychology class.

2.1 Affirmative Statements

Subject	Be	Verb + -ing
I	**am**	
You We They	**are**	talking.
He She It	**is**	

Contractions

I am → I**'m**
You are → You**'re**
We are → We**'re**
They are → They**'re**
He is → He**'s**
She is → She**'s**
It is → It**'s**

2.2 Negative Statements

Subject	Be + Not	Verb + -ing
I	**am not**	
You We They	**are not**	talking.
He She It	**is not**	

Contractions

I am not	→	I**'m not**	
You are not	→	You**'re not**	You **aren't**
We are not	→	We**'re not**	We **aren't**
They are not	→	They**'re not**	They **aren't**
He is not	→	He**'s not**	He **isn't**
She is not	→	She**'s not**	She **isn't**
It is not	→	It**'s not**	It **isn't**

2.3 Spelling -ing Forms

A For most verbs, add -ing.	talk → talk**ing** say → say**ing** go → go**ing**
B If the verb ends in a silent -e, delete e and add -ing.	live → liv**ing** make → mak**ing** write → writ**ing**

2.3 Spelling -ing Forms (continued)

C For *be* and *see*, don't <u>drop</u> the e because it is not silent.	be → being see → seeing
D If the verb ends in *-ie*, change the *ie* to y and add *-ing*.	lie → lying
E If the verb has one syllable and follows the pattern consonant – vowel – consonant (CVC), double the last letter and add *-ing*.	sit → sitting put → putting get → getting
F Do not double the consonant if the verb ends in *-w, -x,* or *-y*.	grow → growing fix → fixing say → saying
G If the verb has two syllables, ends in the pattern CVC, and is stressed on the last syllable, double the last letter and add *-ing*.	begin → beginning
H If the verb has two syllables and is stressed on the first syllable, do not double the last letter before adding *-ing*.	listen → listening travel → traveling visit → visiting

▸▸ Spelling Rules for Verbs Ending in *-ing*. See page A20.

2.4 Using Present Progressive

A Use the present progressive for actions in progress as you write or speak. The action is not finished.	*I am writing for information about . . . (in a letter)* *Look at that man. He's talking to that woman, but he's not smiling.*
B You can also use the present progressive for actions in progress "around now," at the present time.	*I am studying psychology this semester.* *This week we're looking at body language.*
C Use contractions in speaking. Do not use contractions in very formal writing.	*He's taking psychology this semester.* *I am writing to express my interest in this job. (in a letter)*
D You can use the present progressive with present time expressions like *now, right now, at the moment, this week/month, these days.*	*Sorry, I can't talk. I'm going into class right now.* *I'm working two jobs at the moment.*

Grammar Application

A Complete the sentences below using the present progressive. Use contractions when possible.

Couple = kopol

1 The woman _is talking_ (talk).
2 She _is leaning_ (lean) toward the man.
3 He _is smiling_ (smile).
4 The man _is listening_ (listen) to her.
5 They _are making_ (make) eye contact.
6 They _are geting_ (get) along.
7 The man and woman _are not getting_ (not get along).
8 They _are not smiling_ (not smile).
9 The woman _is not looking_ (not look) at the man.
10 She _is leaning_ (lean) away from him.
11 She _is not talking_ (not talk).
12 Maybe they _are having_ (have) an argument.

B Pair Work With a partner, describe some more things the people in A are doing. Use these verbs or your own ideas. Write affirmative and negative sentences for each picture.

drink	eat	laugh	look	sit	talk

A What are the people doing before class? Use the words to write sentences about them. Use the present progressive.

1 Fatima / text her friend _Fatima is texting her friend._
2 Pedro / chew his pen _Pedro is chewing his pen_
3 Carlos and Eun / not sit up straight _Carlos and Eun are not siting up_
4 Ana and Kerry / talk _Ana and Kerry are talking_
5 Lee and Tyler / not look each other in the eye _Lee and Tyler are not looking_
6 Yumi / not smile _Yumi is not smiling_
7 Maria / stare at the door _Maria is staring at the door_
8 The teacher / write on the board _The teacher is writing on the board._

B Over to You Look around your classroom. What are people doing? Write three affirmative sentences and three negative sentences about your classmates. Then compare your sentences with a partner.

There are many time expressions you can use with the present progressive. These are some:

(right) now	*at the moment*	*tonight*	*today*	*this morning/afternoon/evening*
this week	*this semester*	*this month*	*this year*	

You can put a time expression at the beginning or at the end of a sentence. You usually put a comma after the time expression if it is at the beginning of a sentence. If the time expression is just one word, you don't have to use a comma.	*Right now, I'm typing a letter.* *Julia is listening to her professor at the moment.* *Today I'm studying for an exam.*

Complete the e-mail. Use the present progressive form of the verbs in parentheses and an appropriate time expression (TE) from the box. More than one time expression can be correct.

Hi Josh,

How are you? How's college? I'm fine. I **'m sitting** (sit) in a classroom **right now** (TE).
(1) ____(2)____
I **'m waiting** (wait) for class to start. **This semester** (TE), we **are studying**
___(3)___ ____(4)____ ___(5)___
(study) communication. I **'m enjoying** (enjoy) it. **This week** (TE), I
____(6)____ ___(7)___
'm writing (write) a paper on nonverbal communication. I **'m taking** (take) a
___(8)___ ___(9)___
marketing class **this semester** (TE), too.
___(10)___

I **'m not playing** (not play) a lot of sports **this week** (TE). I'm too busy!
___(11)___ ___(12)___
I **'m working** (work) in a grocery store. My parents **are planing** (plan) a trip to
___(13)___ ___(14)___
Mexico in the summer, and I **'m saving** (save) some money to go with them.
___(15)___

What else is new? Oh, my cousin **is staying** (stay) with us.
___(16)___
I think he **is enjoying** (enjoy) his time with us.
___(17)___

OK. That's all for now. Class **is starting** (start).
___(18)___
Write to me soon,

Alex

📊 Data from the Real World

Research shows that in speaking, people usually use the negative forms *'s not* and *'re not*, especially after pronouns.

He / She / It's not . . . ing
You / We / They're not . . . ing

He / She / It isn't . . . ing
You / We / They aren't . . . ing

People often say *isn't* and *aren't* with names and nouns when it is difficult to add *'s not* and *'re not*.

Marcos **isn't** working. *(names and nouns)*

He**'s not** working. *(pronouns)*

Complete the conversation with negative contractions. Then listen and check your answers.

Carla   Hey, Rod. You_**'re not studying**_ (study) today?
(1)

Rod   No, Chris _isn't coming_ (come) to class today.
(2)

Carla   You're doing a project together, right?

Rod   Yes, with Jon, Lisa, and Cristina . . . but it _isn't going_ (go) well.
(3)
We _aren't getting_ (get) along well, either.
(4)

Carla   Really? Why not?

Rod   Well, Chris _isn't doing_ (do) his share of the work. He _isn't reading_
(5)   (6)
(read) the books, and he _isn't coming_ (come) to meetings with the group.
(7)

Carla   What do the others in the group think?

Rod   They _aren't feeling_ (feel) too happy with him. In fact, they
(8)
aren't speaking (speak) to him. We wrote a letter to the teacher about him.
(9)

Carla   Maybe it's time to talk to him about it. I know he _isn't doing_ (do)
(10)
a good job, but maybe there's a reason for it.

Rod   I guess we _aren't giving_ (give) him a chance to explain.
(11)

3 Present Progressive Questions

Grammar Presentation

Present progressive questions ask about actions and events that are in progress now and around the present time.	*Are you crossing your arms?* *What are your hands doing?* *What are you studying?*

3.1 Yes/No Questions

Be	Subject	Verb + -ing
Am	I	
Are	you we they	**working?**
Is	he/she/it	

3.2 Short Answers

AFFIRMATIVE	NEGATIVE	
Yes, I **am**.	No, I**'m not**.	
Yes, you **are**.	No, you**'re not**.	No, you **aren't**.
Yes, we **are**.	No, we**'re not**.	No, we **aren't**.
Yes, they **are**.	No, they**'re not**.	No, they **aren't**.
Yes, he/she/it **is**.	No, he/she/it**'s not**.	No, he/she/it **isn't**.

3.3 Information Questions

Wh- Word	Be	Subject	Verb + -ing
Who	am	I	hearing?
What			feeling?
When		you we they	leaving?
Where	are		studying?
Why			laughing?
How	is	he/she/it	going?

Wh- Word as Subject	Be	Verb + -ing
Who	is	talking?
What		happening?

3.4 Using Present Progressive Questions

A	Use the present progressive to ask questions about actions in progress as you write or speak. The action is not finished.	*Look at that man. Is he talking to that woman?*
B	Use the present progressive to ask questions about actions in progress at the present time (now) or "around now."	*"Are you studying for an exam?"* *"Yes."* *"What are you doing?"* *"I'm studying."*
C	The *Wh-* word is sometimes the subject.	*"Who's studying in the library now?"* *"Jo and Marta."* *"What's going on?"* *"We're studying."*
D	You can use the present progressive with present time expressions like *now, right now, at the moment, this week/month,* and *these days* to ask questions.	*Are you going into class right now?* *Are you working two jobs at the moment?*
E	Time expressions always come at the end of the question, not at the beginning.	*What are they talking about right now?* *Is she crossing her arms at the moment?*

Grammar Application

Exercise 3.1 *Yes/No Questions and Answers*

Write the questions and answers. Use the correct form of the verbs in parentheses.

Ashley Hi, Jack. __*Am*__ I __*disturbing*__ (disturb) you?

            (1)   (1)

Jack No, __I'm not__. Not at all.

        (2)

Ashley __Are__ you __studing__ (study)?

       (3)   (3)

Jack Yes, __I I am__. Well, kind of.

         (4)

Ashley Oh, _____ you __watching__ (watch)

          (5)   (5)

 a movie?

Jack No, __they're not__. It's a video for my French class.

        (6)

Ashley __Are__ the actors __speaking__ (speak) French?

       (7)   (7)

Jack Yes, __the are__. I think that guy __saying__ (say), "I love you."

        (8)   (9)

Ashley __Is__ you __telling__ (tell) me you can't understand it?

      (10)   (10)

Jack Well, yes. I only started my French class last week!

Exercise 3.2 Forming Questions and Answers

A Unscramble the words to make present progressive questions.

1 notes? / you / are / taking

   Are you taking notes?

2 doing / what / your classmates / are / right now?

   What are your classmates doing right now?

3 is / your teacher / what / saying?

   What is your teacher saying?

4 to the teacher? / listening / who / is

   Who is the teacher listening to?

5 right now? / happening / is / what / in class

   What is happening in class right now?

6 are / up straight? / you / sitting

   Are you sitting up straight?

B Pair Work Ask and answer the questions in A with a partner.

4 Present Progressive and Simple Present

Grammar Presentation

The present progressive describes actions and events that are in progress now and around the present time. The simple present describes things that happen repeatedly or all the time.	*I'm studying psychology right now.* *I take four classes every semester.*

4.1 Present Progressive and Simple Present

A Use the present progressive for actions and events in progress now.	*I'm writing an essay about body language.* *Sorry, I can't talk. I'm going into class.*
Use the simple present for repeated actions and events.	*I write one essay every month.* *I go to school on Mondays and Wednesdays.*

B Use the present progressive for temporary events.	*A friend is visiting this week. She's staying with me.*
Use the simple present for permanent situations.	*I come from Ohio, but my family lives in Texas.*
C Use the present progressive with present time expressions like *right now*, *at the moment*, and *today*.	*I'm riding the train at the moment.* (on the phone) *Right now, I'm going to work.*
Use the simple present with frequency adverbs like *often*, *never*, *every week*, etc.	*I often look at people on the subway and watch their behavior.* *Do you usually smile when you meet new people?*

4.2 Non-active or Stative Verbs

A Stative verbs describe states, not actions.	*I don't like rude people.* NOT *I'm not liking rude people.*
These are some stative verbs: *love, know, want, need, seem, mean,* and *agree.* Use the simple present with stative verbs, not the present progressive.	*What do you know about this?* NOT *What are you knowing?* *They seem upset.* NOT *They are seeming upset.* *Experts don't agree on the meaning of some gestures.* NOT *Experts are not agreeing on the meaning of some gestures.*
B Some verbs have a stative meaning and an action meaning.	STATIVE *I think grammar is fun.* (= an opinion) ACTION *I'm thinking about my homework.* (= using my mind) STATIVE *The book looks interesting.* (= appears) ACTION *We're looking at the book right now.* (= using our eyes) STATIVE *Do you have a dog?* (= own) ACTION *Are you having a good time?* (= experiencing)
C You can use *feel* with the same meaning in the simple present and the present progressive.	*I feel tired today.* OR *I'm feeling tired today.* *How do you feel?* OR *How are you feeling?*

▸▸ Stative (Non-Action) Verbs: See page A26.

Grammar Application

Exercise 4.1 Statements

Complete the sentences about students in an English class with the present progressive or the simple present. Use the verbs in parentheses.

1 In our English class, I normally _sit_ (sit) up straight.

2 Right now, my friend José _is relaxing_ (relax) in a comfortable chair.

3 Our classmate Maria _crosses_ (cross) her arms a lot when she listens.

4 In conversations, I usually _make_ (make) eye contact with my partner, Sara.

5 Sara often _chews_ (chew) on her pens and pencils when she's nervous.

6 Three other students _are chewing_ (chew) gum at the moment.

7 No one _is sitting_ (sit) quietly in class right now!

8 Our teacher usually _stands_ (stand) in class when she lectures.

Exercise 4.2 Vocabulary Focus: Some Common Stative Verbs

Possession	have, own
Feelings, wants, and needs	be, feel, hate, like, love, mind, need, want
Senses	hear, look (= seem), seem, sound, feel
Thought	agree, believe, know, mean, remember, think, understand

A Complete the questions with the present progressive or the simple present.

1 _Do_ you _own_ (own) a car?

2 _Are_ you _looking_ (look) for a new car right now?

3 _Does_ your voice _sound_ (sound) soft or loud?

4 _Does_ your last name _mean_ (mean) anything?

5 _Do_ you usually _understand_ (understand) movies in English?

6 _Are_ you _reading_ (read) anything interesting at the moment?

7 _Do_ you _like_ (like) English grammar?

8 _Do_ you _mind_ (mind) working late on weekends?

9 _Do_ you _feel_ (feel) tired after school?

B Pair Work Ask and answer the questions in A with a partner.

A professor is showing a video to the class. Complete the sentences using the present progressive or the simple present form of the verbs. Some sentences are negative.

Children and Body Language

The children in this animated video _are playing_ (1) (play). They _do not know_ (2) (not know) that we _film_ (3) (film) them. They _____ (4) (look) busy, don't they?

These little girls _do not sit_ (5) (not sit) on the floor. They _____ (6) (look) at each other. They _____ (7) (make) eye contact. They _____ (8) (talk) about their friends. They _____ (9) (seem) very happy together. _____ (10) you _____ (10) (agree)?

It _____ (11) (seem) that little girls often _____ (12) (talk) about their friends. They often _____ (13) (tell) secrets, too. When little girls talk, they _____ (14) (like) to look at their friends. On the other hand, little boys usually _____ (15) (play) games. In general, they _do not look_ (16) (not look) at their friends. They often _____ (17) (sit) side by side.

5 Avoid Common Mistakes ⚠

1 To form the present progressive, use *be* and verb + *-ing*.

   am   *studying*
I living in a dorm this semester.   I am study business administration.

2 Check the spelling of the *-ing* verb form.

        writing
I'm writeing a paper on psychology.

3 Use present progressive for temporary and ongoing activities at the present time.

      am writing
Right now, I write an essay on reality shows.

Editing Task

Find and correct nine more mistakes in this student's essay and progress report.

Talent Shows

        are
Talent shows becoming a very popular form of entertainment these days.
                      are
The contestants[1] in the shows trying to be famous. They sing every week. Millions
of people watch these shows every week.

    People like the shows for a number of reasons. First, the shows have good music.
For example, this season they are including a woman who sings opera. Second,
viewers can vote for the winners every week. Third, the contestants in the shows come
from ordinary backgrounds.

[1]**contestant:** someone who competes in a game show

Progress Report – Psychology 111

                    are studying
      In my group, we study one talent show this semester called *Do You*
       looking   *ing*
Get It? We are look at the body language of the contestants. We are try to
                         am
see how it changes. I looking at hand gestures, and I am writeing a paper
                             is going   *am*
about the hand gestures of the losers. The paper goes well. I finding some
interesting things to write about.

UNIT 24 Past Progressive and Simple Past

Inventions and Discoveries

1 Grammar in the Real World

A Can you think of an accidental invention or discovery? Read the magazine article about the invention of Post-its. Who had the idea of using glue with bookmarks?

B Comprehension Check **Answer the questions. Use the article to help you.**

1 In 1968, what was Spencer Silver's job?

2 What did he make?

3 What did Arthur Fry use Silver's invention for?

4 What product did the company make based on Silver's and Fry's ideas?

C Notice **Find the sentences in the article. Write the missing verbs. Notice that there are two lines for the verbs.**

1 In 1968, Spencer Silver, a researcher for the company 3M, _____ _____ to make a strong glue.

2 Five years later, Arthur Fry, one of Silver's coworkers, _____ _____ in a choir.

3 He _____ _____ about the problem.

4 Silver and Fry _____ _____ to solve two different problems.

What are the first words in each verb? What ending is on the second word in each verb?

256

A Great Invention

In 1968, Spencer Silver, a researcher[1] for the company 3M, **was trying** to make a strong glue, but he actually invented a very weak glue. The glue stuck[2] things together, but they could

5 separate easily. Silver showed the invention to his company's management, but they weren't interested. They didn't see a use for it.

Five years later, Arthur Fry, one of Silver's co-workers, **was singing** in a choir. The bookmarks[3]

10 that he put in his songbook **were** always **falling** out whenever he opened the book. He **was thinking** about the problem, remembered Silver's glue, and had the idea to use it on his bookmark. The weak glue worked. Fry could stick the notes

15 on the page and easily take them off again. He gave his co-workers samples of the notes, and they were very popular. So finally Fry's company decided to make the new product.

In 1980, Post-its were in stores nationwide.

20 Marketing of the invention was easy. Everyone wanted to buy the small sticky notes. Today the whole world uses Post-it notes. Most people do not realize that this invention was just a lucky accident: Silver and Fry **were trying** to solve two

25 different problems, and Fry saw the connection. Thanks to Fry, we now have a product that we can't live without!

---

[1]**researcher:** a person who studies a subject in order to discover new information about it

[2]**stuck:** simple past of stick

[3]**bookmark:** something you can put between pages in a book to show where you stopped reading

2 Past Progressive

Grammar Presentation

The past progressive describes things that were in progress at a specific time in the past.	*Arthur Fry was singing in a choir.* *I was studying psychology last semester.*

2.1 Statements

AFFIRMATIVE

Subject	Past of *Be*	Verb + *-ing*
I He She It	was	working.
You We They	were	

NEGATIVE

Subject	Past of *Be* + Not	Verb + *-ing*
I He She It	was not wasn't	working.
You We They	were not weren't	

2.2 *Yes / No* Questions   Short Answers

Past of *Be*	Subject	Verb + *-ing*
Was	I he she it	working?
Were	you we they	

AFFIRMATIVE

	Subject	Past of *Be*
Yes,	I he she it	was.
	you we they	were.

NEGATIVE

	Subject	Past of *Be + Not*
No,	I he she it	was not. wasn't.
	you we they	were not. weren't.

2.3 Information Questions

Wh- Word	Past of Be	Subject	Verb + -ing
Who		I	**studying**?
What	**was**	he she	**doing**?
When		it	**researching**?
Where		you	**working**?
Why	**were**	we they	**experimenting**?
How			**feeling**?

Wh- Word as Subject	Past of Be	Verb + -ing
Who	**was**	**talking**?
What	**was**	**happening**?

▶▶ Spelling Rules for Verbs Ending in *-ing*: See page A20.

2.4 Using Past Progressive

A Use the past progressive to talk about an event in progress at a specific time in the past.	*In 2010, I was working in a science lab.* *"Were you studying in the cafeteria at lunchtime?"* *"No. I was studying in the library."*
B Use information questions to ask about events in progress at a specific time in the past.	*Why were the researchers working all night?* *What was Lucy wearing at the party?* *Who were you talking to this morning?*
C Use the full negative forms when writing in class.	*The machine was not working.*
Use negative contractions in everyday speaking.	*I wasn't working yesterday afternoon.*

Grammar Application

Exercise 2.1 Past Progressive Statements

A Complete the sentences with the past progressive form of the verb in parentheses.

1 I ___*was looking*___ (look) the Web the other day, and I found out some interesting information about inventions.

2 In 1968, another scientist, Spencer Silver, _____ (try) to make a strong glue, but he made a very good weak glue. Arthur Fry, a co-worker, put the glue on small pieces of paper and used the sticky papers at work. Soon the other co-workers _____ (use) the sticky papers, too. The sticky papers became Post-its.

3 In 1945, a scientist named Percy Spencer _____ (experiment) with microwave energy. He _____ (stand) too close to a machine when it melted a peanut candy bar in his pocket. The machine became the first microwave oven.

4 In 1930, Ruth Wakefield _____ (make) cookies for customers at her restaurant. She put small pieces of chocolate in the cookies and called them chocolate chip cookies. Soon Wakefield's customers _____ (ask) her for the cookie recipe, and it is now on bags of chocolate chips.

5 In 1853, George Crum, a chef at a New York restaurant, _____ (feel) unhappy with a customer. The customer _____ (refuse) to eat his potatoes because they were too thick. So Crum cut the potatoes into thin slices and fried them, and they became the first potato chips.

B Pair Work **Ask and answer *Wh-* questions with *Who* as the subject about the inventors in A. Use the past progressive.**

A *Who was feeling unhappy with a customer?*

B *George Crum was feeling unhappy because a customer wasn't eating his food.*

📊 **Data from the Real World**	
The past progressive is used most commonly with verbs of speaking and thinking, such as *talk, think, say, wonder,* and *ask.*	*What were you talking about at breakfast?* *Fry was thinking about bookmarks.* *He was wondering how to keep them inside his songbook.* *They were asking about the accident last night.*
The past progressive is also used with verbs that describe everyday actions, such as *do, try, look, get, come, work, sit, walk, take, watch, read, make, drive,* and *wear.*	*Silver was trying to invent a strong glue.* *He was working all day Thursday, so he missed class.* *Were you watching TV at 8 o'clock last night?* *Ruth Wakefield was making cookies.*

Exercise 2.2 Commonly Used Verbs

Write sentences with the commonly used verbs to describe what the people were doing at 7:15 p.m. yesterday evening.

1 José *was driving home from school.*
(drive / home from school)

2 Thomas was thinking about his children
(think / about his children)

3 Lorna was watching
(watch / TV)

4 Gabi and Jim were
(sit / in a restaurant)

5 Liz was to parking
(try / to park her car)

6 Kevin and Selena were looking
(look / at some photos)

7 Peter was working
(work / at his computer)

8 Clara was talking
(talk / to a friend on the phone)

A Read Joe's schedule for yesterday. Write questions about him. Use the words in parentheses with the verbs in the past progressive.

> 9:00 a.m.: in class — take notes!
> 11:30 a.m.: study English in the library
> 12:30 p.m.: have lunch at Chinese restaurant
> 1:30 p.m.: meet classmates at park to practice English
> 3:00 p.m.: work at computer store
> 7:00 p.m.: call Mom about Dad's birthday
> 11:00 p.m.: work on business project

1 (what/Joe/do/at 9:00 a.m.?) *What was Joe doing at 9:00 a.m.?*

2 (he/eat/lunch at 11:30 a.m.?) *Was he eating lunch at 11:30 a.m.?*

3 (what/he/study?) _____

4 (his friends/meet/him at 12:30 p.m. for lunch?) _____

_____

5 (where/his classmates/meet/him?) _____

6 (what/he/do/at 3:00 p.m.?) _____

7 (what/he/do/at 7:00 p.m.?) _____

8 (who/he/talk/to last night?) _____

9 (he/work/on his project/at 11:00 p.m.?) _____

_____

B Pair Work With a partner, practice asking and answering the questions in A. Then write and ask two more questions.

A *What was Joe doing at 9:00 a.m.?*   **A** *Where was Joe having lunch?*

B *He was taking notes in class.*   **B** *He was having lunch at a Chinese restaurant.*

C Pair Work Create your own schedules for a day last week. Do not show your partner. Ask and answer questions to find out what your partner was doing.

A *Were you working in the afternoon?*   **A** *What were you doing at 7:00 p.m.?*

B *Yes, I was.*   **B** *I was doing my homework.*

3 Time Clauses with Past Progressive and Simple Past

Grammar Presentation

A time clause tells when the main clause happened.	MAIN CLAUSE TIME CLAUSE *He called me on his phone* while he was walking home yesterday.

3.1 *When or While* + Event in Progress

A *When* refers to a particular time or period that something was in progress.

I met Joanna.
↓
——— *I was living in Houston.* ———→
I met Joanna when I was living in Houston.

B *While* means at the same time, or during the time that an event was in progress.

The phone rang three times.
↓ ↓ ↓
——— *We were having dinner.* ———→
The phone rang three times while we were having dinner.

3.2 Time Clauses with Past Progressive

	Time Clause (with Past Progressive)	Main Clause (Simple Past)
When **While**	**he was working,**	he discovered the cure.

Main Clause (Simple Past)		Time Clause (with Past Progressive)
He discovered the cure	**when** **while**	**he was working.**

3.3 Time Clauses with Simple Past

Time Clause (with Simple Past)	Main Clause (Past Progressive)
When he discovered the cure,	he was working.

	Main Clause (Past Progressive)	Time Clause (with Simple Past)
	He was working	**when he discovered the cure.**

3.4 Using Time Clauses with Past Progressive or Simple Past

A You can use a time clause with *when* or *while* and the past progressive to talk about an event that was in progress when a second event happened.

EVENT IN PROGRESS   *SECOND EVENT*
While Tim was thinking about the problem, he had an idea.

SECOND EVENT   *EVENT IN PROGRESS*
Mr. Crum invented chips **while he was working in a restaurant**.

Use the simple past for the second event in the main clause.

EVENT IN PROGRESS   *SECOND EVENT*
When we were sitting in the library, **the alarm went off**.

SECOND EVENT   *EVENT IN PROGRESS*
I met an old friend when I was walking home.

B You can also use a time clause with *when* and the simple past to talk about a second event that happened while another event was already in progress.

EVENT IN PROGRESS   *SECOND EVENT*
She was driving home **when she saw the accident**.

Use the past progressive for the event that was already in progress (in the main clause).

SECOND EVENT   *EVENT IN PROGRESS*
When my friend arrived, **I was watching TV**.

C Don't forget to use a pronoun in the second clause if the subject is the same in both clauses.

Marie was talking about her problem when she thought of a solution.

When Marie thought of a solution, she was talking about her problem.

D Remember that a time clause can come before or after the main clause.

MAIN CLAUSE   *TIME CLAUSE*
It started to rain while we were walking in the park.

MAIN CLAUSE   *TIME CLAUSE*
José was taking a test when his cell phone rang.

Use a comma when the time clause comes first.

TIME CLAUSE   *MAIN CLAUSE*
While we were walking in the park, it started to rain.

TIME CLAUSE   *MAIN CLAUSE*
When his phone rang, José was taking a test.

Grammar Application

Exercise 3.1 Past Progressive and Simple Past

Complete the sentences in the article. Use the past progressive or the simple past form of the verbs in parentheses.

Sometimes unexpected things happen, and someone invents or discovers something. The discovery of gravity – the force that pulls all the stars and planets to each other in the universe – is an example of this. In 1666, Isaac Newton, an English scientist, **was sitting** (sit) (1) in his garden when an apple _was falling_ (fall) from an apple (2) tree. Newton got the idea of gravity from that one moment.

Another story is about James Watt, who was born in 1736. Some people say that while James Watt _was looking_ (look) at a (3) boiling tea kettle, he _was getting_ (get) the idea for a (4) steam engine.[1]

In 1799, French soldiers _were working_ (work) in Egypt (5) when they _____ (find) a stone with writing on it. (6) This was the famous Rosetta Stone. The stone helped people learn how to read Egyptian writing.

In 1908, while a German woman _____ (make) a (7) cup of coffee, she _____ (discover) that paper worked (8) as an excellent filter for coffee and water. She invented coffee filters.

In 1895, a German scientist _____ (experiment) (9) with electricity when he _____ (notice) that one piece (10) of equipment _____ (create) some strange green (11) light around some objects. While he _____ (work), he (12) noticed that the stripes of light – or rays – _____ (go) (13) through paper but not thicker objects, and through humans but not through bones. By 1900, scientists everywhere _____ (14) (work) with the new rays, and doctors _____ (use) X-rays (15) to take pictures of people's bones.

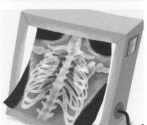

It's amazing that all these inventions and discoveries _____ (happen) by accident! (16)

[1] **steam engine:** an engine that makes something move because steam goes through it

B Now listen and check your answers.

C Pair Work Ask three questions using *What was/were . . . doing?* about the events in A. Ask and answer the questions with a partner.

    A *What was the German woman doing?*
    B *She was making a cup of coffee.*

Exercise 3.2 Past Progressive and Simple Past with *When* and *While*

A Combine the ideas in the stories about unexpected events using the past progressive and simple past. Circle *when* or *while*.

      Alice needed some money. She didn't know where she could get some. One day, she __was walking__ (1) (walk) down the street ___when/while___ (2) she _____ (3) (find) a $100 bill. She was able to pay her phone bill and buy groceries at the supermarket.

    ___When/While___ (4) Eric _____ (5) (write) a paper for school, he _____ (6) (receive) an e-mail from a stranger in France with the same last name. ___When/While___ (7) Eric _____ (8) (read) the e-mail and _____ (9) (learn) about the man's family history, he _____ (10) (realize) that they were cousins.

      Julia and Susan went to a party. They _____ (11) (look around) to see who they knew ___when/while___ (12) they _____ (13) (see) their co-worker John. They _____ (14) (smile) and _____ (15) (wave) at him, but he _____ (16) (not wave) back. The next day, ___when/while___ (17) they _____ (18) (work), they _____ (19) (see) him walk into the office. He said he wasn't at the party. It was his twin brother!

B Pair Work With a partner, tell stories about unexpected events. Take turns. Use *when* and *while* with the simple past and past progressive.

    A *What were you doing when it started to rain yesterday?*
    B *I was waiting for the bus.*

4 Avoid Common Mistakes ⚠

1 **Form the past progressive by using *was / were* + verb + *-ing*.**

    were
Some strange things happening in the laboratory.   We were ~~study~~ *studying* in the library.

2 **With the subjects *I, he, she, it*, or a singular noun, use *was* in the past progressive.**

    was
The professor ~~were~~ asking some questions about the experiment.

3 **With the subjects *you, we, they*, a plural noun, or a compound subject, use *were* in the past progressive.**

    were
The scientists ~~was~~ trying to find a solution to the problem.   Diana and I ~~was~~ *were* working in the library.

4 **In information questions, use question word order after the *Wh-* word in the past progressive.**

    were you
What ~~you were~~ doing at 5 o'clock yesterday?

Editing Task

What were you doing when . . . ? We asked some people to remember what they were doing on special days. Find and correct ten more mistakes in the questions and answers.

Person	Question	Answer
Juno (30 years old)	What ~~you were~~ *were you* doing when Barack Obama became president?	I watching TV all day.
Elsa (71 years old)	What was you doing when the first men landed on the moon?	I was listen to the radio, and I talking to a friend on the phone.
Pamela (18 years old)	What you doing at 2:00 p.m. on your birthday?	I were having lunch with some friends.
Andrea (37 years old)	What was you and your husband doing at midnight last New Year's Eve?	We dancing at a party at a friend's house.
Helen (52 years old)	What you were doing at 4:00 p.m. last 4th of July?	My family and I was having a picnic.

Subject and Object Pronouns; Questions About Subjects and Objects

Fast Food or Slow Food

1 Grammar in the Real World

A How many times a week do you eat dinner at home? Read the article. What do you eat when you are in a hurry?

B Comprehension Check Answer the questions. Use the article to help you.

1 What is different about American eating habits today?
2 Why are Americans cooking less at home?
3 What changes is one chef making to recipes?
4 Why is another chef visiting American towns?

C Notice Read the sentences from the article. Answer the questions about the words in bold.

1 "Nowadays, Americans are eating more unhealthy food, and **they** are getting heavier because of **it**."
   Who does *they* refer to? What does *it* refer to?

2 "For example, one chef recently wrote a new healthy-eating cookbook. **He** adapted the recipes for popular high-calorie dishes and made **them** healthier."
   Who does *he* refer to? What does *them* refer to?

3 "Another chef is visiting towns in the United States to help people think about their diets. **She** wants the people in these towns to change the way **they** eat."
   Who does *she* refer to? Who does *they* refer to?

SHOULD YOU CHANGE THE WAY YOU EAT?

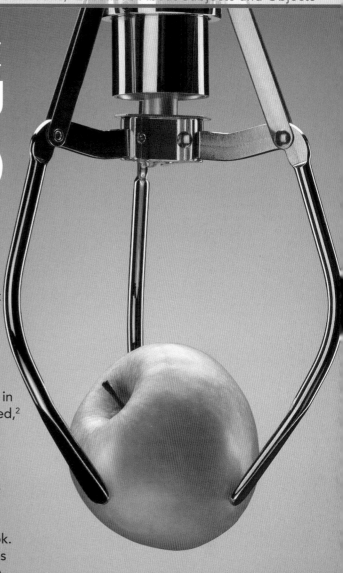

Eating habits in the United States are now different from what **they** were 40 years ago. Nowadays, Americans are eating more unhealthy food, and **they** are getting heavier because of **it**. Also, because
5 their schedules are busy, Americans do less cooking at home, and many of **them** often eat at fast-food restaurants. The food at these restaurants can be high in fat and calories,[1] and some of **it** is made from processed,[2] or pre-cooked, ingredients.[3] This means that many
10 Americans are eating less natural, less healthy food.

Some chefs are not happy about these new eating habits, and **they're** working to change **them**. **They** are promoting healthy food and encouraging Americans to be more careful about what **they** eat. For example,
15 one chef recently wrote a new healthy-eating cookbook. **He** adapted the recipes[4] for popular high-calorie dishes and made **them** healthier. This means that now people can cook their favorite meals and **they** get only half the calories. Another chef is visiting towns in the
20 United States to help people think about their diets.[5] **She** wants the people in these towns to change the way **they** eat. **She** also wants children to eat healthy food, so **she** is encouraging schools to create healthy lunch plans for **them**.

[1]**calorie:** a unit for measuring the amount of energy food provides

[2]**processed:** treated with chemicals that preserve or give food extra taste or color

[3]**ingredient:** one part of a mixture

[4]**recipe:** a set of instructions for how to prepare and cook a kind of food

[5]**diet:** the food and drink a person has every day

2 Subject and Object Pronouns

Grammar Presentation

Pronouns refer to nouns. There are different pronouns for subjects and objects.	*Rachel usually makes lunch for Diego.* (= RACHEL) (= DIEGO) *However, yesterday she decided to take him to a restaurant.*

2.1 Subject and Object Pronouns

Subject Pronouns	Object Pronouns
I	me
you	you
he	him
she	her
it	it
we	us
they	them

▶▶ Subject and Object Pronouns: See page A18.

2.2 Using Subject and Object Pronouns

A The subject in a sentence is the person or thing doing the action. Subject pronouns replace nouns that are the subject of a sentence.

SUBJECT   SUBJECT PRONOUN
Our chef wrote a cookbook. He included many new recipes.

SUBJECT   SUBJECT PRONOUN
Americans cook less at home. They often eat at restaurants.

B The object in a sentence is the person or thing receiving the action. Object pronouns replace nouns that are the object in a sentence or the object of a prepositional phrase.

OBJECT   OBJECT PRONOUN
I remember James. I met him in the cafeteria.

OBJECT   OBJECT PRONOUN
My sister loves hamburgers. My mom often makes them. She wants children to eat healthy food. She is making healthy lunch plans for them.

C A pronoun can refer to one or more noun phrases.

I grow carrots and tomatoes.

They taste good.

2.2 Using Subject and Object Pronouns (continued)

D When talking about yourself and another person, put yourself last. Use the correct pronoun. (SUBJECT = *I*; OBJECT = *me*)	*Eric and I* eat vegetables. *Martha told Eric and me about the new store.*
E Use a pronoun <u>after</u> the noun is introduced.	*My brother* eats fast food. *He* likes fries. NOT *He* eats fast food. ~~My brother~~ likes fries.

Grammar Application

Exercise 2.1 Choosing Pronouns

A Complete the sentences with the correct subject or object pronoun for the underlined words.

1 These days, many <u>people</u> are eating better. **(They)/ Them** are choosing healthy foods.

2 For example, instead of ice cream, some people order frozen <u>yogurt</u>. **It / He** doesn't have as many calories.

3 <u>My friends and I</u> love hamburgers, but **we / us** make <u>turkey burgers</u> because **they / them** are healthier!

4 I really don't like <u>vegetables</u>, but **they / them** are good for **I / me**.

5 My friend <u>Marco</u> loves pizza. I made one for **he / him** with just a little cheese and a lot of vegetables. **He / Him** loved it!

6 Marco and I ate vegetable pizza twice last week. **It / They** tasted great and made **we / us** happy!

B Pair Work Discuss these questions with a partner.

1 What food do you like to eat?
2 What food is good for you?
3 What food isn't good for you?

A *I love to eat pasta. How about you?*
B *I love it, too, but I need to eat more vegetables.*

A Complete the sentences using the correct subject pronoun or object pronoun for the underlined words. Use some of the pronouns in the chart.

Subject	I	you	he	she	it	we	they
Object	me	you	him	her	it	us	them

COLLEGE NEWS

Cobalt University Cafeteria: Now Serving . . . Vegetables!

By Yuki Tanaka

The university cafeteria is offering a new menu to give students healthy options for their meals. Students often eat unhealthy food. _**They**_ don't usually have time to
(1)
cook, so _____ eat in either fast-food
(2)
restaurants or in the cafeteria. To help _____ eat healthier food, the school asked
(3)
nutritionists[1] to create a healthy menu for the cafeteria. Nutritionists found that if _____ can offer quick food that is both healthy and tasty, students will enjoy
(4)
eating _____. Nutritionists also know that students perform better if _____ eat
(5)   (6)
healthy food because _____ gives _____ energy and nutrients[2] – two things
(7)   (8)
that are very important to a busy student.

I surveyed some students about the new menu yesterday. One student said, "My roommates and I just had breakfast here, and _____ loved _____." Another
(9)   (10)
student reported, "We asked for better food in the cafeteria, and the school listened
to _____. This is great news for everyone."
(11)
Check out the new menu as soon as you can! It's long, and you can order many
things from _____. For example, there are all kinds of salads, sandwiches, vegetarian
(12)
choices, and smoothies. Students can even order sushi. _____ is delicious!
(13)

[1]**nutritionist:** an expert on the subject of how the body uses food
[2]**nutrient:** something that plants, animals, and people need to grow

B Pair Work Compare your answers with a partner. Discuss any differences in the pronouns you chose.

3 Questions About the Subject and the Object

Grammar Presentation

Subjects are the people or things that do the action in a sentence. Objects receive the action in a sentence. *Wh-* questions with *who* or *what* can ask about the subject or the object.

"*Who* made this sandwich?"
SUBJECT
"*Rachel* made it."
"*What* did you eat?"
OBJECT
"I ate *a salad*."

3.1 Questions and Answers About the Subject

QUESTIONS		
Who / What	Verb	
Who	eats ate	fast food?
What	makes made	the food good?

ANSWERS		
Subject	Verb	
My sister	eats ate	fast food.
The spices	make made	it good.

SHORT ANSWERS	
Subject	Form of *Do*
My sister	does. did.
The spices	do. did.

3.2 Questions and Answers About the Object

Who / What	Form of *Do*	Subject	Verb	
Who	does did	James	see	in the cafeteria?
What	do did	the students	eat	for lunch?

Subject	Verb	Object
He	sees saw	Rachel.
They	eat ate	tacos.

3.3 Asking and Answering Questions About Subjects and Objects

A	Use *who* to ask about people.	"*Who* ate lunch with you?" "Kevin did."
		"*Who* did you take to lunch?" "I took Kevin."

B	Use *what* to ask about things.	"*What* smells good?" "The food does."
		"*What* did you eat for lunch?" "I ate a sandwich."

C Answer questions about the subject with the subject and *do / does / did.*	"Who wants dessert?" "I *do.*" "Who likes sushi?" "Carla *does.*" "Who went with you?" "Su-bin *did.*"
D You can answer questions about the object with just the object.	"Who did you see in the cafeteria?" "*Carla.*" "What did you eat for lunch?" "*A sandwich.*"
E Use *who* in object questions.	"*Who* did you eat with?" "I ate with my mom."
Whom is rarely used nowadays and is very formal.	~~With whom~~ did you eat?

F In conversation, subject questions are four times more common than object questions.	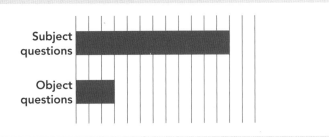

Grammar Application

Exercise 3.1 Using *Who* and *What*

A Complete the questions using *Who* or *What*.

Ana Maria is a writer for the university e-newsletter. She is curious about the eating habits of students. She interviewed several students on campus.

Ana Maria	Hi! My name is Ana Maria. __*What*__ did you eat (1) for lunch today?
Philip	I ate a garden salad.
Ana Maria	_____ did you eat with? (2)
Philip	I ate with my roommate here, Mike.
Ana Maria	Hi! _____ did you have for lunch? (3)
Mike	I had a chicken sandwich and fresh tomato soup.
Ana Maria	Thanks! Excuse me, can I ask you some questions? _____ usually cooks your dinner? (4)
Maya	My mom usually does.
Ana Maria	_____ is your favorite dish? (5)
Maya	It's definitely my mom's orange chicken. It's great.
Ana Maria	Thanks so much!

B Listen to the interviews in A. In each answer, underline the subject or object that Ana Maria's question asks about. Some questions may ask about more than one subject or object.

Ana Maria   *Hi! My name is Ana Maria. What did you eat for lunch today?*

Philip   *I ate a garden salad.*

Exercise 3.2 Forming Questions About Subjects and Objects

A Look at the restaurant receipts below for these students' lunches. Write questions about them. Use the underlined words in the answers to help you.

Ricardo's Lunch

BILL'S BURGER BAR

1 cola	$2.50
1 large fries	$4.25
1 double cheeseburger with tomatoes and mushrooms	$14.00
1 large chocolate milkshake	$6.99
Subtotal	$27.74
Tax	$2.13
Total	**$29.87**

Kai Lin and Clara's Lunch

The Garden Room

1 hot tea	$4.00
1 bottle of water	$4.50
2 large garden salads	$24.00
1 baked potato	$8.00
Subtotal	$40.50
Tax	$3.24
Total	**$43.74**

1 *Who ate fast food?* _____   Ricardo ate fast food.

2 _____   He ate a double cheeseburger.

3 _____   Kai Lin ate with Clara.

4 _____   He drank a milkshake.

5 _____   Clara had a baked potato.

6 _____   Kai Lin had a bottle of water.

7 _____   Kai Lin and Clara had a healthier lunch.

8 _____   Ricardo spent less money.

B Pair Work   Write three more questions about the receipts. Then ask and answer the questions with a partner.

A *Who drank a cola?*
B *Ricardo did.*

C Group Work Think about your last meal. Ask four classmates about their last meals, and tell them about your meal. Then enter their information in the chart and report to the class.

A *What did you have for lunch, Paulo?*

B *I had a chicken sandwich and some chips.*

A *Who did you eat with?*

B *I ate lunch alone.*

Who	What
1 *Paulo*	1 *chicken sandwich and chips*
2	2
3	3
4	4
5	5

Paulo had a chicken sandwich and chips. He ate alone. He said his lunch was great!

4 Avoid Common Mistakes ⚠

1	**Do not confuse subject and object pronouns.**
	I My friends and ~~me~~ eat together at school. *She* ~~Her~~ never eats breakfast.

2	**Use the correct gender in pronouns:** *he / him* **for males and** *she / her* **for females.**
	He Mr. Jack eats salad for lunch. ~~She~~ is concerned about his health.

3	**Use a pronoun after the noun is introduced.**
	Henry *He* ~~He~~ makes a tasty vegetable pot pie. ~~Henry~~ uses sweet potato, mushrooms, carrots, and cheese.

Editing Task

Find and correct the mistakes in Nicole and Alison's blog about fast food.

Fast Food Blog

Hi! Welcome to our Fast Food Blog!

Who eats fast food? So many of ~~we~~ _us_ do.

My sister and me started this blog because
a lot of our friends and family members had
unhealthy diets. We wanted to help they make

5   healthier choices. We also wanted to give other
people information to help they make better
choices about their diet.

Alison had the idea to start a blog. He
told me about her idea, and I liked it. Then my

10 friend James helped Alison and I design the site.
Thanks, James!

If you have questions about fast food or about
healthy eating, just post your question or e-mail it
to we. Alison and me read the questions every day

15 and try to answer them.

He sent us our first question. John wrote this:

"Why do so many Americans eat fast food?" Well, John, some people eat it because them have
very busy schedules. Other people eat it because it's affordable. But, of course, lots of people
just eat fast food because them like it! We do, too! Alison and me just want to remind people that

20 TOO MUCH fast food is not a good idea!

We hope that helps.

Infinitives and Gerunds

Do What You Enjoy Doing

1 Grammar in the Real World

A Can a teenager change the world? Read this article from a magazine for teens. How did Tavi's interest in fashion change her life?

B Comprehension Check Match Tavi's age with the event that took place in her life.

1 Tavi started writing a blog. _____   **a** age 11
2 She tried acting for the first time. _____   **b** age 15
3 She decided to turn her blog into a magazine. _____   **c** age 18

C Notice Find similar sentences in the article. Complete the sentences with the verb in parentheses. Use the article to help you with the form of the verb.

1 Like most young women, Tavi enjoyed _____ (learn) about style and fashion.
2 At the age of 12, Tavi decided _____ (start) an online blog.
3 Fashion editors discovered the blog, and invited Tavi _____ (go) to fashion shows.
4 Tavi did not expect _____ (become) a celebrity.
5 Tavi tried _____ (act) a few years later.

WRITER, EDITOR, AND ACTRESS — All Before Age 20

A lot of teenagers **like to share** their pictures and opinions online. A lot of young women **like to experiment** with fashion. Tavi Gevinson **loved to do** both. She also **enjoyed shopping** for unusual clothes. Her interests in social media and fashion went beyond a free-time
5 activity. Her interests helped her become a famous fashion blogger by the time she was only 11 years old!

Tavi began her career as a writer and editor in 2008 with her fashion blog *Style Rookie*. She **enjoyed posting pictures** of unusual outfits and writing about fashion trends. She **wanted to post online** for fun, and
10 she **did not expect to become** famous.

Soon her blog became very popular, and people **began to read** her opinions. Editors from international fashion magazines discovered her blog. They **started to invite** Tavi to fashion shows.

At 15 Tavi **decided to change** her blog. She started a magazine for
15 teens called *Rookie* about pop culture, fashion, and social issues. Soon it **began to get attention** and many girls wrote to Tavi about their hopes and dreams. *Rookie* **continues to publish** art and writing from celebrities, journalists, and the magazine's online readers.

At 18 Tavi **wanted to do** something different. She was interested in
20 theater, so she got a part in a New York play. Again she was successful. Tavi **continues to act** and she continues to run her magazine. What's next? Someday she **hopes to write** a book.

2 Infinitives

Grammar Presentation

An infinitive is *to* + the base form of the verb: *to design, to play, to do, to be.* Infinitives follow some verbs.

She *liked* *to share* pictures and opinions online.
She *wanted* *to do* it for fun.

2.1 Verb + Infinitive

Subject	Verb	Infinitive	
Teenagers	**like**	**to share**	online.
Tavi	**loved**	**to experiment**	with fashion.
People	**started**	**to read**	her blog.
Tavi	**wanted**	**to do**	something different.
She	**continues**	**to write and act.**	

2.2 Using Infinitives

A You can use an infinitive after these verbs: *want, need, like, love, hate, prefer.*

Tavi *wanted to start* a magazine.
She *needed to learn* about style.
Young people *like to share* pictures online.
Tavi *loves to write* articles.
Some people *hate to post* online.
I *prefer to take* photographs.

B You can use an infinitive after these verbs: *plan, decide, expect, hope.*

How does she *plan to develop* her magazine?
She *decided to act* in plays.
She never *expected to become* famous.
She *hopes to help* teenagers.

C You can use an infinitive after these verbs: *begin, start, continue.*

She *began to get* letters from young women.
People *started to invite* Tavi to fashion shows.
Her business *continues to grow*.

2.2 Using Infinitives (continued)

| **D** You can use an infinitive after these verbs: *learn, refuse, try.* | *She learned to create layouts.*
She refused to sell her business.
Someone tried to buy her company in 2006. |

▸▸ Verbs + Gerunds and Infinitives: See page A26.

2.3 Using Infinitives with *Would Like*

A *Would like* is a polite way to say *want.*	*Tavi would like to write a book someday.* (= She wants to . . .)
Use an infinitive after *would like.*	*They would like to design a website.*
B People usually use *I'd like, she'd like,* or *they'd like* in speaking.	*I'd like to learn more about business, too.*
C Notice the difference between *I'd like to* and *I like to.*	*I'd like to play chess online. (Person doesn't play yet.)* *Sometimes I like to play chess online. (Person plays sometimes.)*
D To ask someone if they would like to do something, say or write, "*Would you like* + infinitive . . . ?"	"*Would you like to read more about Tavi?*" "*Yes, I'd like to know more.*"

Grammar Application

Exercise 2.1 Infinitives

A It's the first day of computer class, and Professor Sullivan asked how his students and their friends use technology. Complete the sentences with infinitives from the boxes.

| buy | chat | ~~check~~ | reply | spend | write |

Jaime   I like __*to check*__ my e-mail before class.
(1)

Ana   My friend Paulo refuses _____
(2)
clothes in stores. He only shops online.

Rosa   My friends and I don't like _____
(3)
to e-mail. We prefer _____ on
(4)
social networking sites.

Clarissa   I love _____ time on the Internet.
(5)

Alejandro   I recently started _____ a blog.
(6)

do	miss	send	explore	watch

Sam   I love _____ text messages to friends.
(7)

Rafael   I watch TV on my cell phone on the bus. I don't want _____ my
(8)

favorite shows. I can watch them online anytime.

Sun-mil   I like _____ the Web. I bookmark all my favorite sites.
(9)

Susan   I try _____ the latest videos on YouTube when I have time.
(10)

Hiroshi   I like _____ everything my classmates said. I'm on my computer 24/7!
(11)

B Over to You **Make the sentences in A true for you. Then compare with a partner.**

A *I like to check my e-mail before class. How about you?*
B *Well, I like to check my e-mail in the evenings.*

Exercise 2.2 Pronunciation Focus: Saying *To: Want To, Would Like To*

In natural speech, people say *to* quickly. It can sound like /tə/ or /tə/.	*Children like to play on computers.* *She wanted to share her pictures.*
Want to often sounds like "wanna."	CONVERSATION *What do you want to do?* *Do you want to go?*
Do not use "wanna" in writing and formal speaking.	FORMAL SPEAKING *In this presentation, I want to talk about three problems.*
People say *'d* softly in *I'd like to.*	*I'd like to join that new social networking site.*

A Listen and repeat the sentences in the chart above.

B Listen to the conversation. Check (✓) the topics they talk about.

☐ careers   ☐ family

☐ computers   ☐ friends

☐ hobbies   ☐ teaching

☐ school   ☐ working with children

C Complete the conversation with the verbs + infinitives from the box. Then listen to the conversation and check your answers.

'd like to be	hope to have	like to work	need to stay	want to have
'd like to work	like to spend	need to do	~~want to do~~	want to teach

Vic   What do you __*want to do*__ as a career?
(1)

Bryan   I _____ a teacher. You know, I really _____ elementary
(2)   (3)
school. I _____ with children. How about you?
(4)

Vic   Well, I _____ my own business one day.
(5)

Bryan   Really? So, what kind of business do you _____?
(6)

Vic   Well, I _____ with computers somehow. Computers are my hobby
(7)
right now. I actually _____ time in front of a screen.
(8)

Bryan   So, how do you do that? I mean, what do you _____?
(9)

Vic   I guess I _____ in college another year and develop my computer skills.
(10)

D Pair Work With a partner, talk about what you would like to do or want to do on the Internet this week. Use these verbs: *chat, download, listen to, look for, read, reply, send, watch, write.* Say *to* quickly.

3 Gerunds

Grammar Presentation

A gerund is the base form of the verb + *-ing*: *going, watching, working.*

Gerunds follow some verbs.

She enjoyed writing about fashion.
She keeps working her magazine.

3.1 Verb + Gerund

Subject	Verb	Gerund	
I	stopped	taking	a web design course.
They	finished	reading	the new blog posts.
Tavi	enjoyed	shopping	with her friends.
She	continues	writing	for the magazine.

3.2 Using Gerunds

A You can use a gerund after these verbs: *enjoy, stop, avoid, miss, finish, keep, imagine.*

Tavi enjoyed working with teenagers.
She stopped going to school.
Sal avoided taking computer classes because he was afraid of computers!
I miss listening to music on my MP3 player.
They finished working on the new design yesterday.
She kept developing her website every day.
Can you imagine being famous at 15?

B Don't confuse the present progressive with verb + gerund. The present progressive uses the verb *be* + base form of verb + *-ing.*

VERB + GERUND
She enjoys developing the website.

PRESENT PROGRESSIVE
She is developing a website right now.

3.3 Verbs + Gerund or Infinitive

A You can use either a gerund or an infinitive after these verbs: *like, love, hate, prefer, begin, continue, start.*

The meaning is exactly the same.

She started to play with web designs.
She started playing with web designs.

▶▮ Verbs + Gerunds and Infinitives: See page A26.

📊 Data from the Real World

You can use some verbs with gerunds or infinitives. Research shows that some verbs use gerunds more often and some verbs use infinitives more often.

People use an infinitive more often with *like, love, hate, prefer,* and *continue.*	
People use a gerund more with *start.* They use an infinitive or a gerund equally with *begin.*	

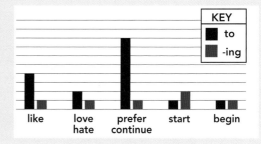

Grammar Application

Exercise 3.1 Gerunds

A Complete the questions with gerunds. Use the verbs in the box. Sometimes more than one answer is correct.

| do | e-mail | learn | play | read | use | visit | write |

Chad is writing an essay on students and their computer use. He created this online survey for students around campus to complete. He hopes to get some useful information.

My Own Survey

☐ **1** When did you start ___using___ a computer?
☐ **2** Do you enjoy _____ new computer programs?
☐ **3** Do you like _____ games online?
☐ **4** Do you like _____ social media?
☐ **5** Do you enjoy _____ your friends?
☐ **6** Do you prefer _____ the news online or in a newspaper?
☐ **7** Do you always back up your files when you finish _____ a report or an essay?
☐ **8** What do you dislike _____ on your computer?

B Pair Work With a partner, ask and answer the questions from Chad's survey. You can add extra information.

A *When did you start using the software?*
B *Only about two years ago.*

A *What did you start using it for?*
B *I needed to write papers for school.*

Exercise 3.2 Gerunds or Infinitives

A Circle the correct form of the verbs in this article. Sometimes both are correct.

Sarah Amari never expected **to make / making** money from her hobby, but now she
(1)
runs a successful business. Sarah always enjoyed **to take / taking** photographs. She also liked
(2)
to edit / editing them on her computer. She continued **to work / working** on her photographs
(3)   (4)
until she liked the result. She never expected **to give / giving** them to people. Then one day a
(5)
friend said she wanted **to use / using** one of Sarah's photographs. She planned **to put / putting**
(6)   (7)
it on a birthday card. This gave Sarah an idea. She decided **to make / making** greeting cards
(8)
with her photographs. She learned **to design / designing** her own website, and then she started
(9)
to sell / selling her cards online. She kept **to add / adding** new cards for different holidays and
(10)   (11)
celebrations. The business continues **to grow / growing**. Sarah is doing something she loves.
(12)

B Complete the sentences with a gerund or an infinitive. Sometimes both are possible.

Monica and Jenna are new community college friends and are getting to know each other.

Monica Jenna, how do you stay in touch with your friends?

Do you like _**to text**_ (text) them?
(1)

Jenna Not really. I prefer _____ (chat) on a social
(2)

networking site. I like _____ (read) their news
(3)

and I enjoy _____ (check) out all their photos.
(4)

Monica I like that, too. I also enjoy _____ (read) my
(5)

friends' updates on my phone. I have a great cell phone

plan, so I can text as much as I want.

Jenna Cool. But can you imagine _____ (live) without computers?
(6)

Monica No! I love the Internet, too. I miss _____ (check) messages when
(7)

I'm in class or at work.

Jenna Hey, I hear there's a new social networking site called *Hands Around the World*.

Do you want _____ (join) it?
(8)

Monica Not really. I can't continue _____ (check) all those sites.
(9)

I have too many friends online already.

Jenna I do, too. But I love _____ (meet) new people. There's a big world
(10)

out there, and you never know what interesting people you can meet.

Monica Be careful, Jenna. Don't start _____ (give) people too much
(11)

information about yourself.

Jenna Don't worry. I avoid _____ (say) too much about myself online.
(12)

Monica Good. You have to be careful these days. Let's meet again after class so we can

start _____ (study).
(13)

Jenna OK. See you then.

C Pair Work Ask and answer these questions with a partner.

1 *What Internet sites do you like visiting?*

2 *What social media do you prefer to use? Why?*

3 *Do you enjoy texting? How often do you text?*

4 *Do you like meeting new friends online?*

Exercise 3.3 Vocabulary Focus: *Go + Gerund*

You can use *go* + a gerund for some sports and leisure activities.	I **go dancing** every weekend. I **went dancing** last week. I would like to **go swimming** soon.

go bowling	go fishing	go running	go skating
go camping	go hiking	go shopping	go skiing
go dancing	go jogging	~~go sightseeing~~	go swimming

Pair Work **Complete the questions with the verbs + gerunds from the box above. (You do not need to use all the verbs + gerunds above.) Then ask and answer the questions with a partner. Make the questions true for you.**

1 Do you usually __*go sightseeing*__ on vacation?

2 Do you and your friends ever _____ ?

3 Do you like to _____ on the weekend?

4 How often do you and your friends _____ ?

5 Did your family _____ last year?

6 Do you or your friends _____ every week?

7 Would you like to _____ with your friends or family?

8 Would you like to _____ ?

4 Avoid Common Mistakes ⚠

1 **Don't use a base form when you need an infinitive or gerund.**

to
Eliza hopes ˄finish college soon.

meeting
I enjoyed ~~meet~~ you.

2 **Learn which verbs take an infinitive.**

to take
I want ~~having~~ my own business.

to have
Joe needs ~~taking~~ one more computer class.

3 **Learn which verbs take a gerund.**

learning
I enjoyed ~~to learn~~ about website design.

working
Ashley keeps ~~to work~~ hard on her business.

4 ***I would like to / I'd like to* means "I want to do this." *I like to* means "I do this now and I enjoy it."**

I'd like to
~~I like to~~ go to college next year.

5 **In writing, use want to. Never write wanna.**

want to
I ~~wanna~~ work in the summer.

Editing Task

Find and correct six more mistakes in this student's e-mail to her professor.

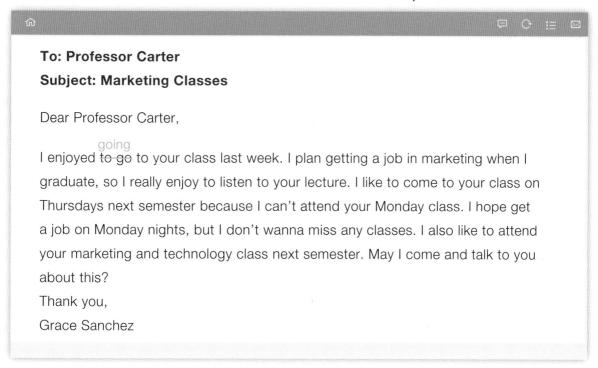

To: Professor Carter

Subject: Marketing Classes

Dear Professor Carter,

I enjoyed ~~to go~~ going to your class last week. I plan getting a job in marketing when I graduate, so I really enjoy to listen to your lecture. I like to come to your class on Thursdays next semester because I can't attend your Monday class. I hope get a job on Monday nights, but I don't wanna miss any classes. I also like to attend your marketing and technology class next semester. May I come and talk to you about this?

Thank you,

Grace Sanchez

Future with *Be Going To,* Present Progressive, and *Will*

The Years Ahead

1 Grammar in the Real World

A What are your plans after graduation? Read this article from a college newsletter. Are any of these students doing something you would like to do?

B Comprehension Check **Answer the questions. Use the newsletter to help you.**

1 What are three different things the students at Greenlough College plan to do after graduation?

2 What is one reason Sarah Woodley is going to Chile to teach English?

3 What does the Teach for America program do?

4 How did José Marquez get his new job?

C Notice **Read the sentences. Look at the underlined verb in each sentence. Is the sentence about something now or in the future? Check (✓) the correct box.**

	Now	Future
1 Sarah Woodley is moving to Chile to teach English.	☐	☐
2 George Guzmán is going to take a special course.	☐	☐
3 I will be nervous teaching kids for the first time.	☐	☐

What's Next?

Every June, thousands of students graduate from college. What are these new graduates' plans and hopes for their future? Several graduates recently shared their plans with us.

Sarah Woodley, who is getting a degree in English, **is moving** to
5   Chile to teach English. "I really want to experience living in a different culture. I**'m going to enjoy** learning Spanish while I teach English. I'm also **going to enjoy** helping people!"

Tara Stout **is joining** the Teach for America program. It's a program that places new college graduates in city schools across the country to
10   teach for two years. Tara says, "I know I **will be** nervous teaching kids for the first time, but teaching is my dream. This is a perfect way to begin!"

José Marquez **is graduating** with an associate's degree in graphic design.[1] "I used the career center here at Greenlough, and I found a job at an advertising company as a junior designer. I**'m starting** right after
15   graduation. I **will certainly put** all of my training in this field to good use! I'm expecting terrific results."

Finally, George Guzmán, also an English major, **is going to take** a special course in publishing[2] this summer. "I really want to become an editor.[3] Meeting people in publishing **will help** a lot. I'm sure I**'ll find** a
20   good job."

We are so excited for all of these graduates and their classmates. Congratulations and good luck, graduates!

[1]**graphic design:** using pictures and diagrams, especially made by a computer, to make advertisements, posters, logos, etc.
[2]**publishing:** the business of making books, magazines, and newspapers
[3]**editor:** a person who corrects and makes changes to texts such as books and magazines

2 Future with *Be Going To* or Present Progressive

Grammar Presentation

We can talk about the future using *be going to* or the present progressive.	*Sarah is going to enjoy learning Spanish.* *José is starting his new job right after graduation.*

2.1 Statements with *Be Going To*

AFFIRMATIVE

Subject	Be	Going To	Base Form of Verb	
I	am			
You We They	are	going to	get	a job.
He She It	is			

NEGATIVE

Subject	Be + Not	Going To	Base Form of Verb	
I	am not			
You We They	are not	going to	get	a job.
He She It	is not			

2.2 *Yes/No* Questions with *Be Going To*

Be	Subject	Going To	Base Form of Verb	
Am	I			
Are	you /we / they	going to	get	a job?
Is	he / she / it			

▸▸ Short Answers with *Be Going To*: See page A13.

2.3 Information Questions with *Be Going To*

Wh- Word	Be	Subject	Going To	Base Form of Verb	
Who	am	I		interview	tomorrow?
What		you we they		do	after graduation?
When	are		going to	leave	for New York?
Where				work	after college?
Why	is	he she it		move	to Canada?
How				pay	his loans?

3.4 Using *Will* to Talk About the Future (*continued*)

Wh- Word as Subject	Be	Going To	Base Form of Verb	
Who	is	going to	get	a job after college?
What			happen	after school?

2.4 Statements with Present Progressive

AFFIRMATIVE

Subject	Be	Verb + -ing	
I	am		
You We They	are	moving	next week.
He / She / It	is		

NEGATIVE

Subject	Be + Not	Verb + -ing	
I	am not		
You We They	are not	moving	next week.
He / She / It	is not		

▸▸ Spelling Rules for Verbs Ending in -ing: See page A20.
▸▸ Present Progressive (Contractions): See page A8.

2.5 *Yes/No* Questions with Present Progressive

Be	Subject	Verb + -ing	
Am	I		
Are	you we they	moving	tomorrow?
Is	he/she/it		

Short Answers

Yes, you **are**.	No, you**'re** not.
Yes, we **are**. Yes, they **are**.	No, we**'re** not. No, they**'re** not.
Yes, he / she / it **is**.	No, he**'s** / she**'s** / it**'s** not.

2.6 Information Questions with Present Progressive

Wh- Word	Be	Subject	Verb + -ing	
Who	am	I	interviewing	tomorrow?
What	are	you we they	doing	after graduation?
When			leaving	for New York?
Where			working	after college?
Why	is	he she it	moving	to Canada?
How			paying	his loans?

Wh- Word as Subject	Be	Verb + -ing	
Who	is	getting	a job after college?
What		happening	after school?

2.7 Using *Be Going To* and Present Progressive

A Use *be going to* when you talk about plans or intentions for the future.	*She's going to* apply for a job in a software company. *(intention)*
B Use the present progressive for arrangements already made for the near future.	*She's applying* for a job in a software company tomorrow. *(arrangement already made)*
C Use *be going to* when you feel certain about something in the future based on evidence in the present.	*The sky is very dark. It's going to rain.* *I love my classmates. I'm going to miss them.*
D Use full forms when writing in class.	*They are graduating next week.*
E Use contracted forms in everyday speaking and informal writing.	*I'm going to rewrite my résumé.*

Grammar Application

Exercise 2.1 *Be Going To*

A A group of college students is talking about summer plans. Complete the conversation with *be going to* + the verb in parentheses. Use contractions when possible.

Laurie I _**'m going to travel**_ (travel) around Europe with
        (1)
my backpack for the summer!

Daniela Great! My sister and I _____ (join) a
                        (2)
volunteer group to help city kids. What about
you, Luke?

Luke I _____ (look) for a job right away.
        (3)

Imelda Laurie, you _____ (do) the same thing as
                    (4)
me! I _____ (go) to Europe, too.
        (5)

Matthew It sounds like all of you _____ (do) some
                            (6)
fun things. Not me. I _____ (work) at the
                        (7)
bakery all summer. How about you, Fiona?

Fiona	My mother _____ (be) here from Ireland

My mother _____ (be) here from Ireland
(8)

next month. She _____ (take) me to San
(9)

Francisco! I can't wait.

Ruth Hey, maybe we can see you in San Francisco,

Fiona. My friend Anna and I _____ (rent)
(10)

a camper and drive across the United States.

Yolanda I wish I could join you! I _____ (not go)
(11)

anywhere! I _____ (stay) home and relax!
(12)

It all sounds great!

B Pair Work Write information questions about the friends in A. Then ask a partner for the answers. Write the answers.

A *Where's Laurie going to travel this summer?* **B** *She's going to go to Europe.*

1 _____ _____

2 _____ _____

3 _____ _____

Exercise 2.2 Future Use of Present Progressive

A Complete the sentences using the present progressive form of the verbs.

Ruth and Anna are in Arizona. Fiona is in New York waiting for her mother to arrive. Ruth and Fiona are texting each other. They want to meet up in San Francisco.

Ruth How are you? __*Is*__ your mom __*coming*__ (come) today?
(1)   (1)

Fiona I'm fine. She _____ (arrive) this evening.
(2)

Ruth We're in Arizona. We _____ (go) to the Grand
(3)

Canyon tomorrow. The weather is going to be beautiful,

so we _____ (meet) the tour group at 7:00 a.m.
(4)

Fiona Have a great time! Mom and I _____ (5) (leave) for San Francisco on Friday. When

_____ (6) you _____ (6) (get) there?

Ruth Probably by Saturday afternoon. Where

_____ (7) you _____ (7) (stay)?

Fiona At the Golden Gate Bridge Hotel. Call us when you arrive. We _____ (8) (go) to the aquarium early on Sunday. I hope you can join us.

B Pair Work Ask *Yes/No* and information questions to find out your partner's plans for the next few weeks. Use the time expressions in the box. Use the present progressive in your questions.

| at (5:00 p.m.) | at lunchtime | next (Monday) | this weekend | tomorrow | tonight |

A Are you staying in town this weekend?
B No, I'm going to New Jersey.

A What are you doing tonight?
B I'm playing basketball with some friends.

Exercise 2.3 *Be Going To* or Present Progressive

A Listen to the speech and complete the sentences with *be going to* or the present progressive form of the verb in parentheses.

Welcome, students, and thank you for coming today!

As you know, we're all here because of your efforts to help Redview Community College become a better place of learning! With your help, we now have enough money to begin improvements.

First, we *'re replacing* (1) (replace) all the old computers in the library with new ones. The technician _____ (2) (come) in on Monday to begin work. The librarian _____ (3) (order) new reference materials. They _____ (4) (be) here by next semester.

We _____ (expand) our recycling program. I _____ (meet)
(5)   (6)
with some people from the environmental studies program this afternoon to finalize the details.

The biggest news is that we _____ (build) a new student center.
(7)
It _____ (have) a food court, a large bookstore, and conference rooms for
(8)
student groups to meet in. We think that the builders _____ (start) next week.
(9)
Unfortunately, it _____ (not be) ready until next year.
(10)

I hope you're looking forward to the great new services on campus! Thank you, once again,
for all of your help!

B Pair Work **Look at the speech again with a partner. Discuss which items in the speech are
(a) plans or intentions for the future, or (b) definite plans already made for the near future.**

A *I think that replacing the old computers is a definite plan.*
B *I agree. It says, "The technician is coming on Monday." That's also definite.*

C Group Work **Write three information questions about the speech. Use present
progressive and *be going to* + verb. Ask your group. Write the answers.**

A *What is the librarian ordering for the library?*   **B** *She's ordering new reference materials.*

1 _____   _____

2 _____   _____

3 _____   _____

3 Future with *Will*

Grammar Presentation

We can use *will* to talk about facts in the future or to make predictions.	*I will be 25 next year.* *The economy will grow next year.*

3.1 Statements

AFFIRMATIVE

Subject	Will	Base Form of Verb	
I You We They He / She / It	**will** **'ll**	**have**	a healthy life.

NEGATIVE

Subject	Will + Not	Base Form of Verb	
I You We They He / She / It	**will not** **won't**	**have**	a healthy life.

3.2 Yes/No Questions

Will	Subject	Base Form of Verb	
Will	I you we they he / she / it	**have**	a healthy life?

Short Answers			
Yes, I Yes, you Yes, we Yes, they Yes, he / she / it	**will.**	No, I No, you No, we No, they No, he / she / it	**won't.**

3.3 Information Questions

Wh- Word	Will	Subject	Base Form of Verb	
Who			**meet**	at the interview tomorrow?
What		I you we they he she it	**do**	in your training program?
When	**will**		**return**	your documents?
Where			**find**	information about careers?
Why			**travel**	to South America?
How			**build**	new apartments?

3.4 Using *Will* to Talk About the Future

A	Use *will* for predictions and expectations about the future.	*The economy will grow next year.*
B	Use *will* for things that are certain in the future. You could also use *be going to*, but *will* is more common in academic writing.	*Next year will be the city's 150th anniversary.* *Next year is going to be the city's 150th anniversary.*
C	Use *will* for an immediate decision about a future action, often with *I'll* or *we'll*.	*(to a server in a restaurant) I'll have the chicken salad, please.* *I have to go. I'll call you this evening. Bye.*
D	Do not use *will* for arrangements already made in the near future. Use the present progressive.	*I'm sorry, I'm busy this evening. I'm meeting Andrea.* NOT ~~I'll meet Andrea.~~
E	Do not use *will* for plans and intentions. Use *be going to*.	*I'm going to buy a new laptop, so I'm looking at prices on the Web.* NOT ~~I'll buy a new laptop.~~

3.4 Using *Will* to Talk About the Future (*continued*)

F We often use *I think, I suppose,* and *I guess* before statements with *will. I guess* is informal.	*I think it will cost* about $250. *I guess it won't happen* until next year.
G Use full forms when writing in class.	*The building will not be ready until 2028.*
H Use contracted forms in everyday speaking and informal writing.	*She'll be 28 on her next birthday.*

Grammar Application

Exercise 3.1 *Will* and *Will Not* for Predictions

A Complete the sentences about life in 2030 using *will* or *will not* and the verb in parentheses.

Science Tomorrow
By Scott Lupine

One of my favorite things to do is to think about how life will be in the future. Here are some of my ideas about a "green" future in the year 2030.

1 Cars and trucks __*will run*__ (run) on clean hydrogen[1] power.
2 All used products _____ (be) recycled.
3 People _____ (make) energy in their homes.
4 People _____ (grow) their own fruit and vegetables.
5 We _____ (not use) oil for energy.
6 We _____ (store) body heat to warm a building.
7 We _____ (get) all our power from the sun, wind, and water.
8 We _____ (change) garbage into energy.
9 We _____ (not pay) high prices for alternative energy.[2]

[1]**hydrogen:** a very light gas that is one of the chemical elements
[2]**alternative energy:** energy from a natural source, like wind, water, and the sun, that doesn't hurt the environment

B Over to You How many of the predictions in A do you think will be true? If you think the statements will *not* be true, change them. Explain your answers.

I think we will continue to use oil. There will still be some in the world.

A Write sentences with *be going to* or *will*. In one sentence, either one is possible.

Mia   I / move to a new apartment. (going to)

    1 *I'm going to move to a new apartment.*

Debra   When / that be? (will)

    2 _____

Mia   Next week. The landlady / give me the key soon. (going to)

    3 _____

Debra   I / help you move. (will)

    4 _____

Mia   Great. I / need all the help I can get. (will / be going to)

    5 _____

Debra   Then I think I / call Roberto and Ivan to help you, too. (will)

    6 _____

Mia   That / make it much easier for me. Thanks. (will)

    7 _____

Debra   Let's celebrate, then. You / love having your own place! (going to)

    8 _____

B Over to You Moving is a big change in life. Are you going to make any changes in the near future? Write sentences about the change. Then tell a partner about it.

I'm going to quit my job soon. Then I'll look for another one.

When people speak quickly and informally, they often use the contraction *'ll* instead of *will* after a *Wh-* word.	*Who'll* turn garbage into energy? *What'll* we do without oil? *How'll* we use body heat to warm a building? *When'll* we have cleaner cars and trucks?

Listen and repeat the questions in the chart above.

4 Avoid Common Mistakes ⚠

1 **Use the present progressive for arrangements already made for the near future. Do not use *will*.**

is meeting
Trudy is busy this evening. She ~~will meet~~ Alex.

2 **Use *be going to* for plans and intentions. Do not use *will*.**

am going to
I ~~will~~ apply to graduate school. Can you give me any advice?

3 **The form in *be going to* statements is *am / is / are* and the *-ing* form of the verb *go*.**

is
She ˄ going to do volunteer work.

4 **Use *will*, not the simple present, for predictions.**

will
Many more countries ˄ have a female president in the next 10 years.

will become
The earth ~~becomes~~ warmer over the next 30 years.

5 **Use question word order in information questions about the object.**

are you
What ~~you are~~ going to do during the vacation?

Editing Task

Find and correct eight more mistakes in this e-mail.

Hi Nuala,

am meeting
I ~~will meet~~ with a career adviser next week, and I going to discuss my future. What can I tell him? My dream is to work in television or the movies. I think I going to apply to a media studies program. I going to take a special course or something. I going to talk to some people who know about careers in TV soon. I think they give me some good advice.

Can we talk about this? What you are doing on Monday? I go away on the weekend, but I be back Monday morning. I'll call you then.

Thanks,

Fandi

Will, May, and Might for Future Possibility; Will for Offers and Promises

Will We Need Teachers?

1 Grammar in the Real World

A How do you think schools will be different in 2050? Read this article from an education magazine. How many changes did you predict?

B Comprehension Check **Answer the questions about the article.**

1 What is a virtual classroom?

2 Why can students in virtual classrooms live in different countries?

3 How will the teacher's job probably change?

4 In your opinion, will the combination of humans and technology make learning more or less enjoyable?

C Notice **Find these sentences in the article. Complete the missing part of the verbs.**

1 Professional workers _____ to update career skills.

2 They _____ be able to attend a traditional university.

3 Your teacher _____ human.

4 You _____ a talk by a famous human professor and then interact with the bot for your assignments.

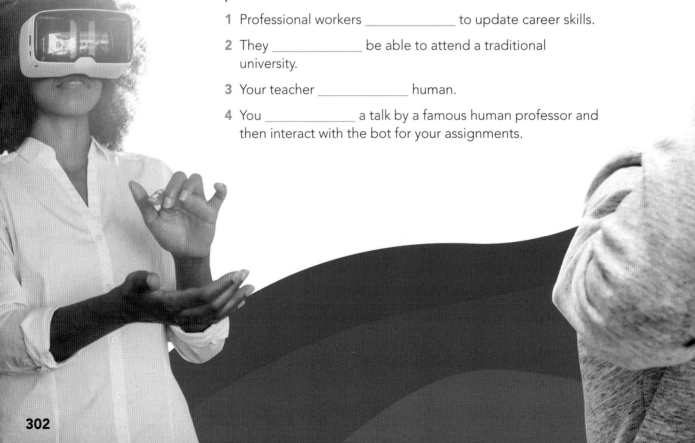

Virtual[1] Education

The year is 2050. As a 21st century worker, you **will need** to update your skills, so you take a class. What can you expect?

First, tomorrow's students **will be** different.
5   Professional workers **will need** to update career skills. More students **may have** jobs and families.

Second, education **will change**. People **won't attend** a traditional university. Universities and private companies **will offer** online courses to
10   students from all over the world. You **might be** in a class with ten thousand other students.

Third, your teacher **might not be** human. A teacher bot[2] **will type** and talk like a person. It **may even have** a name, but it **will be** an intelligent
15   machine communicating through the Internet. You **may watch** a talk by a famous human professor and then send the bot your assignments.

Finally, the learning environment will change. You **will put on** a headset to "go to class." In this virtual
20   classroom, you **will see**, hear, and **feel** like you are at a museum or maybe a traveler inside a human body.

One thing **may not** change. You **will probably still enjoy** the company of human classmates. Research shows that the best education still happens
25   in a social environment.

---

[1]**virtual:** through the use of a computer
[2]**bot:** An automated computer program

2 *May* and *Might*; Adverbs with *Will*

Grammar Presentation

<table>
<tr>
<td>You can use *may* or *might* and a base form of a verb to talk and write about what is possible in the future.</td>
<td>Students **may** not need to buy books.
Everyone **might** take classes online.</td>
</tr>
</table>

2.1 Statements with *May* and *Might*

Subject	May / Might	Not	Base Form of Verb	
I You We They He She	**may** **might**	(not)	go talk	to a different kind of school in the future. to classmates all over the world.
It			be	the future of education.

2.2 Using *Will*, *May*, and *Might*

A You can use *will* when you are 100 percent certain about something.	By 2050, there **will** be new ways to learn.
B Use *may* or *might* when you are less than 100 percent certain.	Students **may** do all of their work online.
They have a similar meaning, but *may* sounds a little more certain than *might*.	Your teachers **might be** bots.
C You can use *may* or *might* to answer questions with *be going to* or *will*.	"Are you going to enroll in an online course?" "I **might**. I **might not**. I'm not sure yet."
D You can use *might*, but not *may*, with *Wh-* words to ask questions about possibility. These questions are not very common.	What **might** machines be able to do in 2050?
E Use the full negative forms *might not* and *may not*. Don't use contractions.	Students **may not** have to sit in classrooms at all. Teachers **might not** be human.

2.2 Using Will, May, and Might *(continued)*

| **F** Don't confuse the adverb *maybe* and *may be*. | *I may be in college this time next year.* |
| Maybe usually comes before the subject. | *Maybe I'll go to college next year.* |

▶▶ Modal Verbs and Modal-like Expressions: See page A25.

📊 Data from the Real World

You can use *may* and *might* in speaking and writing. *Might* is more common in conversation.

May is more common in writing. *May* sounds more formal.

2.3 Using Adverbs with *Will* for Levels of Certainty

A You can use these adverbs *after* will, *between* will and *not*, or *before* won't.	*Online learning certainly won't replace the classroom.*
100% certain certainly, definitely, surely	*They will surely do all of their work online for most classes.*
less than 100% certain likely, probably, possibly	*Class materials will likely be online.* *Students will probably not use books.* *Some teachers will possibly be robots.*
B 📊 *Probably* is the most frequent of these adverbs. You can also use it in writing, but it is more common in speaking.	*I'll probably take the online course next term.* *Jake probably won't because his computer broke.*

🖥 Grammar Application

Exercise 2.1 *Will, May, and Might*

A Listen to the conversation. Complete the text with *will (not/won't)*, *may (not)*, or *might (not)*. Use contractions when possible.

Carla So what are your plans for the fall? Are you going to college?

Sharon Actually, I ___*might not*___ go to a college. But I think I _____
            (1)   (2)
            probably enroll in an online program.

Carla Oh, really? Like a degree online?

Sharon Yeah, or maybe just a few courses. The thing is that my family is definitely going to move this year. So with an online program, I probably _____ need to
                                                                                (3)
            change schools.

Carla	That's smart. You can study from anywhere. Do you know what you're going to take?
Sharon	I think so. I like chemistry, so I _____ definitely take chemistry. (4)
Carla	Oh, so you're interested in science?
Sharon	Yeah. And I _____ take biology, too. I _____ definitely take Spanish. (5) (6)
Carla	Awesome! But why Spanish?
Sharon	Well, my family's going to move to California, so I thought Spanish _____ be useful. (7)
Carla	Well, let me know how it goes.
Sharon	Sure. I _____ definitely keep in touch. I _____ be online all the time! (8) (9)

B Pair Work **Answer the questions. Compare your answers with a partner.**

1 What are Sharon's plans?

_____

2 Why is she making these plans?

_____

3 What is she going to study?

_____

4 How certain or sure is Sharon about her plans? Write her plans in the correct section of the chart.

SHARON'S PLANS	
Certain	**Not Sure**
	attend a college

Exercise 2.2 More *Will, May,* and *Might*

A Complete the sentences with *will (not)/won't, may (not),* or *might (not).* Give your own opinion. Sometimes there is more than one correct answer.

Classrooms of the Future

What do you think classrooms of the future will look like?

1 Many students _____*may not*_____ go to traditional universities.

2 They _____ not meet in classrooms.

3 Students _____ have classmates at different ages.

4 Classrooms _____ have equipment for experiments.

5 Some classrooms _____ be virtual.

6 Students _____ use classrooms to make things.

7 Students _____ collaborate with classmates.

8 Classes _____ be more interesting.

B Pair Work **Discuss your sentences about classrooms of the future with a partner. Do you agree?**

A *I wrote, "Students may go to class one or two days a week."*

B *I don't agree. I think we won't go to class at all.*

C Over to You **Complete the sentences with *will (not)/won't, may (not),* or *might (not).* Give your own opinion. Then discuss with a partner.**

Schoolwork and Exams

What do you think schoolwork and exams will be like in the future?

1 Students _____*will not*_____ need to take handwritten notes in lectures.

2 Students _____ do more activities online.

3 They _____ write in books.

4 They _____ go to libraries.

5 Exams _____ be different.

6 Students _____ need to memorize facts for exams.

7 People _____ need a keyboard because they will be able to talk to their computers.

8 Computers _____ teach and grade students' work.

9 Teachers _____ be in the same classroom as the students.

10 Students _____ have paper books.

11 Computers _____ be very small and light.

12 Students _____ only speak with other students online.

A Write sentences about your opinion with the words below. Use *will* or *will not/won't* and an adverb of certainty from the box.

certainly	definitely	likely
certainly not	definitely not	likely not
possibly	probably	surely
possibly not	probably not	surely not

1 Teachers / give all their classes from home.

Teachers will probably not give all their classes from home. / Teachers probably
won't give all their classes from home.

2 Teachers / be bots.

_____

3 Teachers / need to prepare for their classes.

_____

4 They / check exercises.

_____

5 Computer software / check students' work.

_____

6 Teachers / spend more time with each student.

_____

7 They / need to speak English.

_____

8 Computer software / translate from any language.

_____

B Pair Work Compare your sentences with a partner. Do you have the same ideas? What other ideas do you have about teachers in the future? Think of three more ideas.

A *I think teachers probably won't teach all their classes from home.*
B *Well, I think some teachers will. Some teachers will probably give classes in classrooms, too.*

C Over to You **Write sentences about your future. Use** *may, will,* **or** *might* **with an adverb** (*certainly, definitely, surely, likely, probably, possibly*). **Use the topics below.**

1 school plans *I'll probably enroll in an online degree program.*

2 place to live _____

3 subject of study _____

4 learn another language _____

5 start a business or find a job _____

6 your own idea _____

D Pair Work **Ask and answer questions with a partner about your plans.**

A *Are you going to go to a four-year college next year?*

B *I might. I'll definitely study somewhere.*

3 Offers and Promises

Grammar Presentation

This is an offer:	This is a promise:
I'll help you with your homework tonight.	*I'll call you. I won't forget.*

3.1 Making Offers

A You can use *I'll* to make an offer.	*"Where is the cafeteria?"* *"I'll show you. I'll take you there."*
B You can also offer other people's help using *will*.	*"My computer's not working."* *"My sister will help you. She knows all about computers."*

3.2 Making Promises

You can use *I'll*, *I will*, or *I won't* to make promises.	*I'll* send my comments on your assignment today. I **won't** forget. "Will you marry me?" "Yes, **I will!**"

Grammar Application

Exercise 3.1 Offers and Promises

A Complete the conversation. Use Pat's offers of help and Chris's promises. Add *I'll*.

PAT'S OFFERS	CHRIS'S PROMISES
~~lend you $10~~ look at the homework with you drive you home show you	help you with your math homework pay you back make you dinner

Chris I don't have any money for lunch.

Pat *I'll lend you $10.* (1)

Chris Thanks! _____ tomorrow. (2)

Chris Where's the computer room? I'm lost.

Pat _____ (3)

Chris I can't carry all my books home. They're so heavy.

Pat _____ (4)

Chris Great! Are you hungry? It's already 6:00 p.m.

_____ (5)

Chris I'm having trouble with my English homework.

Pat _____ (6)

Chris How can I thank you? I know. _____ (7)

B Pair Work Practice the conversation in A with a partner. Add more details.

A *I don't have any money for lunch. I left my wallet at home. I was in a hurry this morning.*

B *I'll lend you $10 for lunch. Would you like to have lunch together?*

A *Sure, thanks. I'll pay you back tomorrow.*

4 Avoid Common Mistakes ⚠

1 *Maybe* and *may be* have different meanings.
May be is the verb *may* + base form of the verb *be*. *Maybe* is an adverb. Use it before the subject.

~~may be~~
Books maybe rare in the future.

~~Maybe~~
May be people will stop using books.

2 Use *might* or *may* to talk about possibility in the future. Avoid using *can* for predictions about the future.

~~may / might~~
Some students can prefer to go to a regular class.

3 Use *will* to talk about certainty in the future. Avoid using *can*.

~~will~~
Everyone can study in a virtual classroom in the future.

Editing Task

Find and correct 10 more mistakes in this education article.

The Future of Education

     The Internet ~~can~~ *will* change education completely in the future. May be colleges will not be buildings with people and furniture, but complex websites. Teachers maybe characters in virtual worlds like *Second Life*. In the future, students can "travel" to different countries using their computers. They can walk around the world's famous museums without leaving home. May be students will go back in time. They can possibly "talk to" famous people from the past, like George Washington. History students can watch or be part of historic events. We can buy artificial brains so we won't have to go to school at all! There maybe many changes to education, but learning can definitely never stop.

29

Suggestions and Advice

Sugerencios y consejos

Study Habits

1 Grammar in the Real World

A What are two ways that you study? Read the web article about study tips. How many different suggestions does the writer give?

B Comprehension Check **Answer the questions.**

1 What should you do if you live in a noisy place and need to study?

2 Why might you want to eat a snack before you study?

3 How do you set a study goal?

4 Should you check your e-mail while you study? Why or why not?

5 How could you ask a friend to study with you?

C Notice **Answer the questions. Use the article to help you.**

1 Write the two verbs that come after the bold words in the third paragraph.

   a ___make___   b ___eat___

2 What verb form are the words in item 1? _____

3 Which is used most in the text: *should*, *might*, or *ought to*?
   ___should___

4 Find the form *"why don't you ... "* in the last paragraph. Is it asking for a reason or making a suggestion? ___Suggestions.___

Study to Learn, Learn to Study

By Amy Chin, Communications Major

By the time we get to college, we think we know how to study. Then the first time we get a test back with a low grade, we wonder what happened. Research shows that many students study ineffectively.[1] Here are a few suggestions about how to study more effectively.

5   First, it's important to find the right place to study. You **ought to** study in a quiet place. If you live with other people, you **should** probably try to study when no one else is at home. If your roommates are noisy, you **might want to** go to the library to study. If you have to study in a noisy place, try listening to soft music with earphones.

10   Once you find a quiet place, you **should** make sure you're not hungry. You **might want to** eat a small snack before you study so you can concentrate better.

Next, set a study goal. Look at your task and decide how much you want to accomplish[2] during this study session. For example, **should** you
15 read all four chapters now? Maybe you **ought to** read two now and the other two later. You **should** set a realistic goal and work to reach it. Setting a study goal will help you focus on the task you need to do, but it's easy to get distracted.[3] You **should** not check e-mail, text, or surf the Web while you study.

20   If you have to learn a lot of facts or study for a math test, you **might want to** study with a friend. Just say, "**Let's** meet after class and review our notes."

Why don't you try these suggestions for a month? You will definitely see results!

[1]**ineffectively:** in a way that doesn't get the results you want; not effectively

[2]**accomplish:** do or finish something successfully

[3]**distracted:** when someone's attention is taken away from what they are doing or should be doing

2 Suggestions and Advice

Grammar Presentation

You can make suggestions or give advice with *should, ought to, might want to, why don't,* and *let's.*	You *should* probably write new words in a vocabulary journal. You *ought to* listen to these suggestions! You *might want to* write sentences with each new word. *"Why don't we* study together?" *"Yes! Let's* study math first."

2.1 Statements with *Should, Ought To, Might Want To,* and *Let's*

AFFIRMATIVE

Subject	Modal / *Might Want To*	Base Form of Verb	
I You We They It He She	**should** **ought to** **might want to**	stay	inside in this weather.
			late.

NEGATIVE

Subject	Modal / *Might Want To*	Base Form of Verb	
I You We They It He She	**should not** **ought not** **might not want to**	stay	outside in this weather.
			late.

LET'S

Let's (Let + us)	*(Not)*	Base Form of Verb	
Let's	not	read	the chapter together.
		study	alone tonight.

2.2 Questions with *Why Don't You / We*

Why Don't	Subject	Base Form of Verb	
Why don't	you / we	study	in your room?
		go	to the library now?

Answers

OK. That's a good idea.

I can't.

2.3 Using *Should, Ought To, Might Want To, Why Don't You / We,* and *Let's*

A *Might want to* is softer and more polite than *should* or *ought to*.	You **might want to** take Ms. Novak's writing class.
B Use *maybe, probably,* or *I think* with *should* and *ought to* to soften the suggestion or advice.	**Maybe** we **should not** listen to loud music while we study.
In affirmative statements, *probably* can come before or after *should*.	We **should probably** study together. We **probably should** study together.
In negative statements, *probably* comes before *should not*.	We **probably should not** study together.
Maybe and *probably* always come before *ought to*.	We **probably ought to** go to the movies later. **Maybe** we **ought to** go to the movies later.
C Use the expression *Why don't you / we …* to make suggestions or give advice in a soft, polite way.	(SUGGESTION) **Why don't we** study together on Tuesday night? (ADVICE) **Why don't you** keep a vocabulary journal?
D Use the expression *Let's …* to make suggestions that include you and the listener. *Let's = Let us*	**Let's** study at the library. **Let's** not stay up late the night before our test.

▶▶ Modal Verbs and Modal-like Expressions: See page A25.

📊 Data from the Real World

We and *you* are the most common subjects for suggestions and advice.	**We** should keep a vocabulary journal. **You** ought to study for the test.
Should is the most common form used for suggestions and advice. *Ought to* is very rare. *Ought not to* is also very rare.	You **should** learn a new word every day.
Might is usually followed by *want to* when making suggestions or giving advice.	You **might want to** review for the vocabulary test.

Grammar Application

A The students in an English class are having some vocabulary problems. Give advice for each student. Use the words in parentheses and *should* (*not*), *might want to*, or *ought to*. Sometimes there is more than one correct answer.

Problem

1 Marissa doesn't read well because she doesn't know a lot of words.

2 Veronica wants to learn a lot of new words quickly.

3 Petra wants to remember how to use new words.

4 Ricardo is afraid to try new words.

5 Eniko and Irina want a fun way to practice vocabulary.

6 The whole class wants a good way to learn new words.

Advice

She ought to read more.
(she / read more)

She might want to
(she / practice new words every day)

She ought to
(she / write sentences with the new words)

He should
(he / practice using the words with a friend)

They should do
(they / do crossword puzzles)

They ought to
(they / create a picture in their minds that shows the meaning of each word)

B Pair Work With a partner, write three suggestions for learning new words. Use your own experience or ideas from the unit. Then share your ideas with the class.

A *Let's write new words on cards and practice them.*
B *We might want to tape the cards on a wall to practice.*

A Listen. Complete the class discussion with the missing words.

Professor Taking good notes is an important part of being a successful student. Let's hear some advice from students about how they take notes.

Teresa Some teachers speak very quickly. You __should__ ask these teachers if you
(1)
can record the class. Then you can listen to the notes again in your home. You
__shouldn't__ record the class without the teacher's permission.
(2)

Amadou You __might want to__ attend a workshop on note taking. That can be very
(3)
helpful. I know it helped me.

Alex   Find a student with good notes, and ask him or her if you can copy the

notes. You ___should probably___ offer to buy that student coffee or a snack.
(4)

___maybe___ you ___should___ suggest a time to meet once a
(5)   (5)

week to trade notes. If you aren't sure how to suggest this, here are some ways:

"___Why don't___ we get together on Thursdays to trade notes?" or "
(6)

___let's___ meet in the student union."
(7)

Professor   Thank you for your suggestions. I ___ought to___ add here that you
(8)

___shouldn't___ just copy the notes. You ___should___ compare
(9)   (10)

their notes with yours. Try to figure out what's different.

B Pair Work **Use the information in A to give your partner suggestions or advice about taking notes. Take turns.**

A *Why don't you ask the teacher's permission to record the class?*

B *That's a good idea.*

A *You should attend a workshop on note taking.*

B *I'll look for one.*

C Over to You **Many people give us advice and suggestions. What is some advice that you received recently? Was it helpful?**

3 Asking for and Responding to Suggestions and Advice

Grammar Presentation

Use *Yes/No* and information questions to ask for suggestions and advice.	*"Should I register for a writing class?"* *"That's a good idea."* *"When should I register for class?"* *"Why don't you register next week?"*

3.1 Yes/No Questions to Ask for Suggestions and Advice

Should	Subject	Base Form of Verb		Answers
Should	I	take	a math class?	That's a good idea.
	we	meet	you in the student union?	I think it's closed.

Wh- Word	Should	Subject	Base Form of Verb		Answers
What			bring	to class?	I don't know.
Where			meet	you?	Let's meet at the library.
Who		I you we they he she it	ask	for help?	Ask Professor Li.
When	should		tell	the boss?	As soon as possible.
How			study	for the test?	She ought to study one chapter at a time.
Why			be	difficult?	Because the teacher gives hard tests.

3.3 Responding to Questions for Suggestions and Advice

A For a strong, <u>positive</u> response to a Yes/No question for suggestions or advice, use:
Yes./That sounds great./Definitely./Absolutely.

"*Should we eat lunch before our class?*"
  "Yes. *That sounds great!*"
  "*Definitely!*"
  "Oh, *absolutely!*"

B If you are <u>uncertain</u> about the answer to a Yes/No question, use:
Maybe./Probably./I'm not sure.

"*Should we eat lunch before our class?*"
  "*Maybe.*"
  "*Probably. Let's check my schedule.*"
  "Oh. *I'm not sure.*"

C For a strong, <u>negative</u> response to a Yes/No question for suggestions or advice, use:
That's not a good idea.

Why don't we + different idea

I'd like to, but + reason

"*Should we eat lunch before our class?*"
  "*That's not a good idea. We don't have enough time.*"
  "*Why don't we eat after class?*"
  "*I'd like to, but I have to study.*"

D Respond to information questions with: probably/maybe/why don't you

Using should alone is stronger.

"*What class should I take next semester?*"
  "*You should probably take a writing class.*"
  "*Maybe you should take a writing class.*"
  "*Why don't you take a writing class?*"

Data from the Real World

What should I/we . . . ? and *Where should we . . . ?* are the most common information questions used to ask for suggestions/advice.

What should I / we ... ?	
Where should I / we ... ?	

Grammar Application

Exercise 3.1 Responding to Questions for Advice

A Complete the conversation. Use the cues to help you.

Jill Hi, Sandra! I'm so glad to see you! Could you help me with something? I need to find an apartment. I know you know a lot about the area. ___*Should*___
(1)
(*Yes/No* question) I rent a place near school?

Sandra ___*Yes. Absolutely!*___ (a strong positive
(2)
response) It's so much easier to live near school.

Jill _____ (*Wh-* questions) I look to find an
(3)
apartment for rent? Can I look in the local paper?

Sandra Yes. You _____ (uncertain answer) look
(4)
in the paper or online. That's a good place to start.

Jill Great! Do you have any other advice?

Sandra Yes, you _____ (strong response) ask about utilities. Sometimes
(5)
things like electricity, heat, and air-conditioning are included in the rent.

Jill Oh, right. _____ (*Yes/No* question) I also ask about deposits?
(6)

Sandra _____ (strong positive response)!
(7)

Jill Thanks, Sandra. You're a great friend!

B Pair Work Write a conversation with suggestions/advice for <u>one</u> of the situations below. Use the conversation in A to help you. Then share with another pair.

1 Two Classmates: One classmate just started college in the United States and needs advice on study habits.

2 Graduating Student and Job Coach: A student is looking for advice on how to begin a job search/get a job.

3 College Freshman and College Senior: A freshman wants advice on courses, restaurants, bookstores, etc.

Situation 1
A *My English is not very strong. What should I do to improve my vocabulary?*
B *Well, first you should definitely keep a vocabulary journal. ...*

A Respond to the situations below. Ask for advice or give advice.

1 You want to ask your friend for advice about how to fix your computer.

What should I do first?

2 You are not sure which movie to go to. Ask a friend for advice.

3 A friend asks for advice on how to take notes. What do you say?

4 You are not sure where to buy school supplies. Ask a friend for advice.

5 Your teacher asks for advice on what cell phone to buy. What do you say?

6 A classmate is about to do something that is not a good idea. What advice do you give?

7 A classmate needs help with his math homework. What advice do you give?

8 You want to learn more English vocabulary. Ask your teacher for advice.

B Pair Work Compare your answers with a partner. Did you use any of the same expressions to ask for or give advice?

C Over to You Think of two problems or situations this week that you will need advice on. Write your questions here, asking for advice.

1 _____

2 _____

4 Avoid Common Mistakes ⚠

1 **Use the base form of the main verb after *should*.**

           eat
He should ~~eats~~ lunch before class.
We should ~~to~~ study after class.

2 **After *ought*, use *to* + the base form of the main verb.**

         to
He ought eat lunch.

3 **The subject comes after *should* and *might* in information questions.**

       I
Where ~~I~~ should meet you?

4 **Put *probably* and *maybe* before *ought to*.**

probably
We ought to ~~probably~~ go to the library.

5 **In negative statements, *probably* comes before *should not*.**

probably
Tim should not ~~probably~~ call tonight.

Editing Task

Find and correct the mistakes in this conversation between two classmates.

Julia	Monica, I need help studying! How ~~I~~ should *I* tell the professor?	
Monica	Don't worry. I can help. First, we should shares class notes.	
Julia	When we should meet at the library? After class today?	
Monica	Sure, but we ought to probably meet in the cafeteria. I'll want to eat something.	
5 Julia	OK. We should eats dinner while we study. What I should bring?	
Monica	Just your notebook. You should not probably bring the big textbook – I don't think we'll need it.	
Julia	You should to be ready for a lot of questions from me! I have so many!	
Monica	As long as you are ready to learn, I'm happy to help! When we're done, we	
10	ought see a movie!	
Julie	That sounds great! See you later!	
Monica	See you then, Julie. We should to study together more often!	

UNIT

30 Necessity and Conclusions

Getting What You Want

1 Grammar in the Real World

A How much does your school cost each year? How do you pay for it? Read the article about scholarships.

B Comprehension Check **Answer the questions. Use the article to help you.**

1 Is college expensive in the United States? YES, it is.

2 Are there many scholarships available for students? YES, there are L-5

3 How early should you start your applications? About 6 months before

4 Who can help you with your application? You college adviser.

5 What do you need to give your teachers for their recommendations?
   The DEADLINES OR DUE DATES.

C Notice **Read the sentences. Decide if the actions are *necessary* or *not necessary*. Circle *necessary* or *not necessary*.**

1 Many students **need to** apply for scholarships   (necessary)   not necessary
   to lower their education costs.

2 You **don't have to** feel stressed about being   necessary   (not necessary)
   able to complete a good application.

3 Eligible students **must** search for scholarships   (necessary)   not necessary
   that are appropriate for them.

4 You **need** to ask your adviser for help.   (necessary)   not necessary

Applying for a
SCHOLARSHIP[1]

As a student, you **must** agree that college is expensive in the United States. Many students **need to** apply for scholarships to lower their education costs. Here are a few tips on how to complete a good scholarship application.

5   There are many scholarships available every year, but students **have to** search for them. Search online with keywords like *scholarship* or *grant*.[2] There are also scholarships for people with specific skills, backgrounds, and ethnicities.[3] Eligible[4] students **must** search for scholarships that are appropriate for them.

10   You **need to** ask your adviser for help. He or she knows a lot about scholarships and can help you complete your application. Ask your adviser to help you create a schedule for each step in the application. Think of a time line for when you **must** finish each step. Try to have everything ready one week before you send your application.

15   You should start your scholarship applications early, about six months before they are due. Your application will take time to complete because you will **need to** request letters of recommendation[5] from teachers and a transcript[6] from your school. Your school will need time to send the transcript to the scholarship organization, and your teachers will
20   need time to write the recommendations. When you ask a teacher for a recommendation, give him or her a deadline. All students must send their applications out on time, so be persistent and remind your teachers of the due dates.

You **don't have to** feel stressed about being able to complete a
25   good application. With a little hard work and care, you can send out a good scholarship application and lower your school costs.

[1]**scholarship:** money given to a person to help pay for his or her education

[2]**grant:** a sum of money that a university, government, or an organization gives to someone for a purpose, such as to do research or study

[3]**ethnicity:** shared national, racial, or cultural origins of a group, often with the same language

[4]**eligible:** having the necessary qualities

[5]**recommendation:** a letter or statement saying someone is good or suitable for something, like a job, school, or scholarship

[6]**transcript:** an official, written copy of someone's grades at an institution

2 Necessity and Conclusions with *Have To, Need To, Must*

Grammar Presentation

Have to, need to, and *must* express an obligation or necessity. *Must* also expresses a conclusion we can make about something.

Students *need to* apply for scholarships. (= It is necessary.)

Students *do not have to* feel stressed about completing their application. (= It is not necessary.)

As a student, you *must* know that college is expensive in the United States. (CONCLUSION Students know that college is expensive in the United States.)

2.1 Statements with *Have To* and *Need To*

AFFIRMATIVE				NEGATIVE				
Subject		Base Form of Verb		Subject			Base Form of Verb	
I You We They	**have to** **need to**	write	an essay.	I You We They	**do not** **don't**	**have to** **need to**	write	an essay.
He She It	**has to** **needs to**	search	online.	He She It	**does not** **doesn't**		search	online.

2.2 Statements with *Must*

AFFIRMATIVE				NEGATIVE			
Subject		Base Form of Verb		Subject			Base Form of Verb
I You He / She / It We They	**must**	know.		I You He / She / It We They	**must**	**not**	know.

2.3 Using *Have To, Need To,* and *Must*

A *Have to, need to,* and *must* talk about things that are important or necessary to do.

Students *need to* send an application.

2.3 Using *Have To*, *Need To*, and *Must* (continued)

B Using *must* in conversation can seem rude.	She *needs to* make a schedule. She *must* make a schedule. (Sounds rude.)
C In conversation, *must* usually expresses conclusions.	Today is Monday, so tomorrow *must* be Tuesday.
D *Have to* can also express conclusions. *Need to* <u>never</u> expresses conclusions.	Today is Monday, so tomorrow *has to* be Tuesday. NOT ~~Today is Monday, so tomorrow needs to be Tuesday.~~
E *Do not have to* or *do not need to* means it is not necessary. There is no obligation.	Tom *doesn't have to* pay for school. He *does not need to* pay for school.
Must not means it is forbidden. *Mustn't* is <u>very</u> rare.	Students *must not* forget to send in their application on time.

▶◀ Modal Verbs and Modal-like Expressions: See page A25.

2.4 Yes / No Questions with *Have To* and *Need To* and Short Answers

Do / Does	Subject	Have to / Need to	Base Form of Verb	
Do	I you we they	**have to** **need to**	write	an essay?
Does	he she it			

Yes / No	Subject	
Yes,	I	do.
No,	you we they	do not / don't.
Yes,	he	does.
No,	she it	does not / doesn't.

2.5 Information Questions with *Have To* and *Need To* and Responses

Wh- Word	Do / Does	Subject	Have to / Need to	Base Form of Verb
When	**do**	I you we they	**have to** **need to**	send the application?
	does	he she it		

Subject	Do / Does (Not)		Base Form of Verb
I You We They	do not / don't	have to need to	send the application next month.
He She It	does not / doesn't		

Note: Using *must* in questions is very rare.

Grammar Application

Data from the Real World

These are some of the most frequent verbs used with *have to*, *need to*, and *must* in speaking and writing:

be	go	get	take	know	talk	give
do	have	make	look	say	come	work

Exercise 2.1 Necessity and Obligation

A Complete the sentences with the correct form of *have to*, *need to*, or *must*.

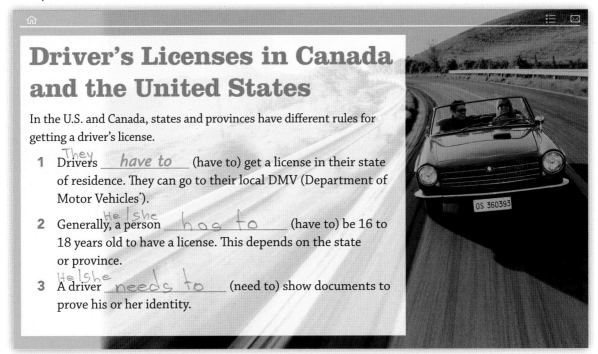

Driver's Licenses in Canada and the United States

In the U.S. and Canada, states and provinces have different rules for getting a driver's license.

1 Drivers ___*have to*___ (have to) get a license in their state
   of residence. They can go to their local DMV (Department of
   Motor Vehicles').

2 Generally, a person ___has to___ (have to) be 16 to
   18 years old to have a license. This depends on the state
   or province.

3 A driver ___needs to___ (need to) show documents to
   prove his or her identity.

4 An acceptable document _needs to_ (need to) have your name and address.

5 Foreigners can drive in the U.S. and Canada. Drivers _don't have to_ (not/have to) be U.S. or Canadian citizens.

6 Foreign drivers _have to_ (have to) have an international driver's license.

7 Some states require new drivers to take a driving class. In most states in the U.S., new drivers _have to_ (have to) pass an exam in order to get a license.

8 In some states, people who already drive _don't need to_ (not/need to) take any exams to get a new license.

9 However, in other states, people who already drive _have to_ (have to) take an exam to get a new license.

10 You _must not_ (not/must) forget to bring the right documents to the DMV. This can save you a lot of time and frustration.

*Note: Not all states and provinces call this the Department of Motor Vehicles. However, everyone in the United States and Canada understands the term DMV.

B Unscramble the words to make questions with *have to* and *need to*.

1 have to have / drivers / a driver's license?
   Do drivers have to have a driver's license?

2 a driver / how old / have to be?
   How old does a driver have to be?

3 have to / what / bring / drivers / to the DMV?
   What do drivers have to bring to the DMV?

4 need to say? / what / an acceptable document
   What does an acceptable document need to say?

5 have to / be citizens? / drivers
   Do drivers have to be citizens?

6 need to take / new drivers / a class?
   Do new drivers need to take a class?

7 pass an exam? / have to / new drivers
   Do new drivers have to pass an exam?

8 need to go / drivers / to get their license? / where
   Where do need to go drivers to get their license?

C Pair Work Ask and answer the questions in B with a partner. Use the information in A to find the answers.

Have to is usually pronounced "hafta."	I "**hafta**" win the game. You "**hafta**" see my new game!
Has to is usually pronounced "hasta."	She "**hasta**" try harder to win. He "**hasta**" think quickly when he plays this game!

A Listen and repeat the sentences in the chart above.

B Listen. Complete the sentences with *have to* or *has to*.

Welcome to the **STACK'EM** game website!

Here are some tips on how to win the game!

1 You don't ___*have to*___ know many rules to win the game.

2 A player [I-He/She] ___has to___ move around different shapes to make lines.

3 Players [They] ___have to___ turn the pieces to make them fit.

4 The pieces [They] ___have to___ fit together with no spaces to make the line disappear.

5 As players get better, the pieces come more quickly. The player [He/She] ___has to___ think very quickly.

6 You don't ___have to___ play against someone. You can play by yourself.

7 Players [They] ___have to___ have one of the top five scores for their name to be added to the "champion" list.

8 Stack'em is fantastic! You ___have to___ play a lot to become good, but it's fun!

C Pair Work Write three sentences about the rules of a game you know how to play. Then share them with a partner.

In "Go Fish," players have to ask each other for cards.

1 _____

2 _____

3 _____

Exercise 2.3 Necessity and Conclusions

A Complete the sentences with the correct verb combination. Use a verb of necessity or conclusion with the words in parentheses. Then label *N* for necessity and *C* for conclusion. Sometimes more than one answer is possible.

1 Sarah has a lot of work to do in the office, then she goes to school at night. She
___*must work*___ (work) hard. __N__

2 She always has a lot of homework. She _____ (be) exhausted after a long
week of work and school. _____

3 He says that when Sarah _____ (take) a quick break, she can. _____

4 Sarah wants to have a week off.¹ She _____ (talk) to her boss to schedule her
time off. _____

5 Her boss _____ (look) at the schedule. _____

6 Her boss _____ (make) sure he has enough workers during the time when
Sarah is off. _____

7 She _____ (not / do) any work when she is away on vacation. Her boss will not
let her. _____

8 Sarah says her office is a great place to work. She _____ (like) her boss and
the people she works with. _____

¹**a week off:** a week without work

B Pair Work Write four sentences about some of the things you have to do to get ahead in your life. Share your sentences with a partner. Make conclusions about what they do with *must*.

A *I have to work all day and go to school at night.*
B *You must be exhausted!*

1 _____

2 _____

3 _____

4 _____

3 Avoid Common Mistakes ⚠

1 **Make sure *have to* and *need to* agree with the subject.**

       had
  She ~~have~~ to be very skilled.

2 **Use the base form of the verb after *have to*, *need to*, or *must*.**

       have
  He needs to ~~has~~ his passport.

go, eat, drink, play, win

3 **Do not use *to* after *must*.**

  I must ~~to~~ follow the rules.

4 **Use the base form of *have to* and *need to* in negative statements and in questions.**

       need
  He doesn't ~~needs~~ to register.

       have
  Does she ~~has~~ to write an essay?

5 **Use *have to* or *must* to express conclusions. Do not use *need to* for conclusions.**

       has to / must
  Today is Tuesday. Tomorrow ~~needs to~~ be Wednesday.

Editing Task

Find and correct 10 more mistakes in this conversation about someone trying to break a record.

Pete Does Jack ~~needs~~ *need* to have a lot of skill to play the game?

Jim No, he has to ~~has~~ *have* a lot of luck.

Pete How many times does he ~~has~~ *have* to win to break the record?

Jim He ~~have~~ *has* to win three more times.

5 **Pete** He won eight times, so the record must ~~to~~ be 10.

Jim Yes, the world record needs to be 10.

Pete Does he need to ~~has~~ *have* a certain time to win?

Jim No, he must ~~to~~ have a certain number of points.

Pete Jack also has to ~~wins~~ five games in a row.[1] He must ~~to~~ really like this

10 computer game!

Jim Yeah, he loves it. He doesn't ~~needs~~ to play it every day, but he enjoys it.

[1] **in a row:** without interruption

Adjectives and Adverbs

Making a Good Impression

1 Grammar in the Real World

A Do you know how to give a presentation? What do you do to prepare? Read the article. How many of your ideas are in the web article?

B Comprehension Check Does the article answer these questions? Write *Yes* or *No*. Then answer the questions.

1 What can give you confidence as a presenter?

_____

2 What are some ways that can help you organize your ideas?

_____

3 What should you do when you practice?

_____

4 What should you do after your presentation? Why?

_____

C Notice Look at the word in bold in each sentence. Circle the word that it describes. How are the words you circled in item 1 different from the words you circled in item 2?

1 a A **confident** presenter always makes a good impression.
  b Think **positive** thoughts.

2 a Smile **confidently**.
  b Before you start, breathe **deeply**.

Next, complete the sentence below. How do you know which word to use?

3 He walks _____.
  a confident
  b confidently

How to Be a SUCCESSFUL PRESENTER

For many people, giving a presentation can be a **scary** experience. If you feel **nervous** about giving presentations, here are some helpful tips that you can follow.

- Prepare your presentation **carefully. Careful** preparation will give
5   you confidence, and this will impress[1] your audience. A **confident**[2] presenter always makes a **good** impression.[3]

- Organize your ideas. Think about what you want to say. Then list your three or four main points on note cards.

- Practice giving your presentation aloud[4] by yourself and with friends,
10   too. Tell your friends to give you **honest** feedback,[5] but make sure they tell you first what you did **well**.

- On the day of the presentation, arrive at the room **early**. Think **positive** thoughts and remember that you can do this.

- Before you start, breathe **deeply** and smile **confidently** at your
15   audience. Speak **slowly** and **clearly**. Make eye contact with people in **different** parts of the room. Look at your notes **quickly** when you need to. Your audience wants you to do **well**. Then relax and do your best.

After your presentation, ask people for feedback and advice. Use the
20 ideas in your next presentation. With practice, you will learn to give **good** presentations, and you may even enjoy giving them.

[1]**impress:** cause people to admire and respect you

[2]**confident:** not having a doubt about yourself or your abilities

[3]**impression:** an idea or opinion of what someone is like

[4]**aloud:** in a voice loud enough that people can hear it

[5]**feedback:** response after seeing an activity or performance

2 Adjectives and Adverbs of Manner

Grammar Presentation

2.1 Adjectives and Adverbs of Manner

A Adjectives give information about nouns. They often come before a noun or after *be*.

ADJ.   NOUN
I want your honest feedback.

BE   ADJ.
The slides were clear.

B Adverbs give information about verbs.

VERB   ADV.
The presenter spoke clearly.

VERB   ADV.
She prepared her presentation carefully.

C Adverbs of manner usually come after a verb or a verb + object.

VERB   ADV.
Dress nicely.

VERB   OBJ.   ADV.
She looked at the audience quickly.

D Don't put an adverb between a verb and an object. Place it after the object.

VERB   OBJECT   ADVERB
Prepare your presentation carefully.

NOT *Prepare carefully your presentation.*

2.2 Basic Forms of Adverbs

	ADJECTIVE	ADVERB
A For most adverbs of manner, add *-ly* to the adjective form.	bad careful clear fluent loud nervous quick	bad*ly* careful*ly* clear*ly* fluent*ly* loud*ly* nervous*ly* quick*ly*
B With adjectives ending in *-y*, change *y* to *i* and add *-ly*.	easy happy	eas*ily* happ*ily*
C With adjectives ending in *-ic*, add *-ally*.	automatic academic	automatic*ally* academic*ally*
D With adjectives ending in a consonant + *-le*, drop *e* and add *-y*.	gentle terrible	gent*ly* terri*bly*

2.2 Basic Forms of Adverbs *(continued)*

		ADJECTIVE	ADVERB
E	The adverb and adjective form of the following words are the same: *early, fast, hard, late.*	*He is early.* *It sounds fast.* *It's a hard test.* *They're late.*	*He went home early.* *He talks fast.* *He studied hard.* *They arrived late.*
F	*Well* is the adverb form of the adjective *good.*	*He's good at English.*	*He speaks English well.*
	Well can also be an adjective. It means "healthy."	*He isn't well.*	
G	Some adjectives that end in *-ly* do not have an adverb form. Do <u>not</u> use them as adverbs.	*elderly, friendly, lively, lonely, lovely, ugly*	

▶▶ Adverbs with *-ly*: See page A24.

📊 Data from the Real World

These are the most common adverbs of manner:

well	late	easily	carefully	seriously	automatically
hard	fast	clearly	strongly	differently	properly
early	quickly	slowly	closely	badly	

🖥 Grammar Application

Exercise 2.1 Adjectives and Adverbs

A Circle the adjectives and draw an arrow to the nouns they describe. Underline the adverbs and draw a line to the verbs they describe.

I'm a (professional) hairstylist, and I'm very good at my job. I'm friendly and polite to my clients, so I make a good impression. But I don't schedule clients early in the day because I'm not in a good mood until noon.

Of course, I don't get an early start to my day. I wake up late and start my day slowly. I can't think clearly without three cups of strong coffee. After breakfast, I take a shower, get dressed, and check my e-mail. I don't talk to anyone in the morning, except for my elderly neighbor when I leave home. He likes to sit on the front porch. I think he's lonely.

I drive to work, but my commute isn't bad. When I get to work, I check my schedule closely and make a few quick phone calls. At 11:55 a.m., I finish my last cup of coffee and smile warmly at my first client at 12:00 noon.

B Over to You **What is your morning routine? Write four sentences using adjectives and adverbs. Then tell a partner.**

A *I get up early. I'm awake by 6:00 a.m.*

B *I sleep late. On the weekends, I sleep until 11:00 a.m.*

Exercise 2.2 More Adjectives and Adverbs

A Complete each sentence pair with the adverb or adjective form of the underlined word in the first sentence. The sentences will have a similar meaning. (Remember: Some adjectives do not change form when they are adverbs.)

1 Cindy makes a good impression when she presents in front of a group.

   a She is <u>careful</u> when she researches her topic. She researches her topic *carefully* .

   b Her voice is <u>clear</u> and easy to understand. She speaks _____.

   c When she starts to speak, her smile is <u>automatic</u>. When she starts to speak, she _____ smiles.

   d She <u>strongly</u> argues her points. She makes _____ arguments for her points.

2 Robert made a good impression at the job interview.

   a He was <u>polite</u>. He talked *politely* to the interviewer.

   b He was <u>early</u>. He arrived at the company _____.

   c He thought about the questions, and he answered the questions <u>carefully</u>. He was _____ in his answers.

   d He was <u>good</u> at answering the questions. He answered the questions _____.

   e He didn't speak <u>badly</u> about his former employer. He didn't say _____ things about his former employer.

B Pair Work **Take turns reading the sentences. Identify the adjective and adverb form of the words.**

Exercise 2.3 Adverbs of Manner

A Complete the questions about making a good impression at school and at work. Use the adverb forms of the words in parentheses.

QUESTIONNAIRE

1 Do you get to work or school __*early*__ (early), or do you arrive __*late*__ (late)?

2 Do you take your job or your studies _____ (serious)?

3 Do you work _____ (hard), or are you lazy?

4 Do you check your assignments _____ (careful)?

5 Do you try to do every job _____ (proper), or do you do everything _____ (quick)?

6 Do you always dress _____ (appropriate) for work or school?

7 Do you always speak _____ (polite) to your boss or teacher?

8 Do you plan your time _____ (good) and complete your work on time?

9 Do you organize your desk _____ (neat)?

10 Can you give instructions _____ (clear)?

11 Do you like to work _____ (close) with co-workers or classmates?

B Pair Work Ask and answer the questions in A. Give more information in your answers.

A *Do you get to work early?*

B *No, I don't. I usually arrive just in time.*

C What do you think are the six most important qualities of a good employee? What about a good student? Complete the sentences using ideas from A and your own ideas.

A good employee . . .	A good student . . .
1 __*works hard*__	1 __*studies hard*__
2 _____	2 _____
3 _____	3 _____
4 _____	4 _____
5 _____	5 _____
6 _____	6 _____

3 Adjectives with Linking Verbs; Adjectives and Adverbs with *Very* and *Too*

Grammar Presentation

3.1 Adjectives with Linking Verbs

A Use an adjective, not an adverb, after these linking verbs: *be, get, seem, look, feel, sound, smell, taste*	ADJ. I get confused *when someone asks difficult questions.* ADJ. The presentation looked interesting. ADJ. ADJ. You may feel nervous, *but try to* sound confident. ADJ. That coffee smells good.
B When *feel* means "have an opinion," use the adverb *strongly*.	FEEL + ADV. (OPINION) I feel strongly *that people should speak clearly.* BUT *I felt weak when I had the flu, but I feel* strong *now.*

3.2 *Very* and *Too* + Adjective or Adverb

A You can use *very* and *too* before adjectives or adverbs to make their meaning stronger. *Very* and *too* do not have the same meaning.	VERY + ADJ. VERY + ADV. *She is* very serious. *She works* very hard. TOO + ADJ. TOO + ADV. *The talk was* too long. *He spoke* too fast.
B *Very* makes an adjective or an adverb stronger.	*Her ideas were* very helpful. *He spoke* very fast. *I understood him, but it was difficult.*
C *Too* means "more than necessary." It usually has a negative meaning and means there's a problem.	*He spoke* too fast. *I couldn't understand anything that he said.* *The school is* too expensive. *I can't afford it.*
D You can also use *very* (but not *too*) before an adjective + a noun.	ADJ. + NOUN *It's a* very expensive program. NOT *It's a too expensive program.*

3.2 *Very and Too + Adjective or Adverb (continued)*

E You can use an infinitive after *too* + an adjective or adverb.	*She's too tired to study.* (= She can't study because she's too tired.) *She spoke too fast to understand.* (= I did not understand her because she spoke too fast.) *The words on the slides were too small to read.* (= No one could read the words because they were too small.)

Grammar Application

Exercise 3.1 Adjectives with Linking Verbs

A Complete the sentences about how people react in new social situations. Choose the correct adjective or adverb in parentheses. When you finish, check (✓) the statements that are true for you.

1 I often get **nervous/shyly** in new social situations. _____

2 I am **confident/easily** around new people. _____

3 I often feel **excited/nervously** before a party. _____

4 I feel **uncomfortable/fast** when I'm nervous. _____

5 I hope other people think I look **attractive/confidently**. _____

6 I try to be a **nicely/friendly** person. _____

7 I like to tell jokes and make people laugh. I tell jokes **bad/well**. _____

8 I get **excited/well** when I listen to music and sing along to the songs. _____

9 It's never a problem for me to remember people's names. I do that **easily/automatic**. _____

10 I give my opinion when I feel **strong/strongly** about something. _____

B Pair Work Compare sentences from A. Do you act the same way in new situations?

    A *I often get nervous in new social situations. How about you?*

    B *I don't get nervous. I'm always excited about meeting new people.*

Exercise 3.2 Adjectives with *Very* and *Too*

A Complete the sentences about a party. Use *very* or *too*.

1 The party lasted for six hours. The party was ___*very*___ long, so we went home early.

2 The party lasted for an hour. Everyone wanted to stay longer. The party was _____ short.

3 There were 75 people at the party. The living room holds 50. The room was _____ small.

4 There were five people at the table. The table seats 12. The table was _____ big.

5 The party was noisy, and I couldn't hear conversations. The party was _____ noisy.

6 The party was noisy, but I had a great time. The party was _____ noisy.

7 Some people spoke quickly, but I understood most of it. Some people spoke _____ quickly.

8 One man spoke quickly, and I didn't understand a word of it. He spoke _____ quickly.

9 It was 25°F (-4°C) outside on the porch. We had to leave. It was _____ cold.

10 It was 43°F (6°C) outside on the porch. I wore my coat. It was _____ cold.

B Now listen and check your answers.

Adjectives with *Too* + Adjective + Infinitive

A Pair Work Complete the conversations. Use the word given with *too* + adjective + infinitive (*to* + verb). Then practice with a partner.

1 A You passed your exams with straight As.
  B That can't <u>be true</u>.

  (good) It's *too good to be true* .

2 A Do you like your new job?
  B I can't <u>say</u>. I only started today.

  (early) It's _____ .

3 A Mom! Dad! We want <u>to get married</u>.
  B You're only 16!

  (young) You're _____ .

4 A I want <u>to change programs</u> in school.
  B Well, there's still time.

  (not late) It's _____ .

5 A Let's <u>go camping</u> this weekend.
  B Camping? It's 10 below outside!

  (cold) It's _____ .

6 A Is your brother <u>going to work</u> today?
  B Well, I think he has the flu.

  (sick) He's _____ .

7 A Why don't you <u>ask</u> your boss for help?
  B I can't, I'm afraid of him.

  (scared) I'm _____ .

8 A You look really stressed today.
  B Do I? You know, I can't <u>think</u>.

  (busy) I'm _____ .

B Group Work Discuss these questions in a group. Which ideas do you share?

1 Do you ever get too tired to think?

2 Are you ever too scared to ask questions?

3 Do you ever feel too embarrassed to apologize for something?

4 Were you ever too sick to go to work or school this year?

5 What is something you feel is too difficult to do?

6 Are 17-year-olds too young to get married?

🔲 Data from the Real World

People often use *not very* + adjective or adverb to make negative statements "softer," less critical, or less direct.

The speaker was**n't very** good. He did**n't** speak **very** well.

NOT *The speaker was bad. He spoke badly.*

Exercise 3.4 *Not very . . .*

Read the notes that an interviewer wrote about a job candidate. Make them less critical, or less direct, and write statements using *not very* and the words in parentheses.

1 unfriendly *He wasn't very friendly.* (friendly)

2 spoke nervously *He didn't speak very confidently.* (confidently)

3 wore a dirty shirt _____ (clean)

4 bad at problem solving _____ (good at)

5 answered questions badly _____ (well)

6 looked dishonest _____ (honest)

7 seemed inexperienced _____ (experienced)

8 acted bored _____ (interested)

4 Avoid Common Mistakes ⚠

1 Use an adverb when you give information about most verbs. Some adverbs are irregular and do not end in *-ly*.

efficiently
I work efficient.

hard
I work very hardly.

2 Use an adjective after the linking verbs *be, feel, get, look, seem, smell, sound*, and *taste*.

strange
He seemed strangely.

3 Be especially careful with *good* and *well*. People often use *good* instead of *well*, especially when they speak, but do not write this.

well
I try to do things good.

4 Do not use an adverb between a verb and its object.

carefully
I always prepare carefully my answers.

5 Do not use *too* when you mean *very*.

very
My teacher is too good. I'm learning a lot.

Editing Task

Find and correct the mistakes in this article about job interviews.

PREPARING for an INTERVIEW

carefully
An interview can be a difficult experience. Prepare ~~carefully~~ your responses, and you will make a good impression.

Before the interview, research thoroughly the company. Find out about its products and services. You should always be truthfully about the things you do good. When you talk about

5 something you do bad, choose a weakness that is not serious. Say that you are too aware of the weakness and that you are working hardly to improve yourself. Say you want a new challenge and that you want to progress in your career. Always sound positively and don't complain about your current job.

On the day of the interview, dress nice. Shake firmly hands when you meet the interviewer.

10 Try to sound sincerely and look too confident. Follow these steps and you'll do good.

UNIT 32

Comparative Adjectives and Adverbs

Progress

1 Grammar in the Real World

A How has modern life changed in the last 15 years? Read the question forum from a website. What changes does the forum discuss?

B Comprehension Check Complete the sentences. Use the text in the forum answer to help you.

1 Highways became _____ and
_____ .

2 Computers became _____ and
_____ but _____ to use.

3 The Internet gave us _____ communication
and a _____ world.

C Notice Complete each word or phrase. Use the text to help you.

1 small_____   4 _____ efficient

2 big_____   5 _____ powerful

3 large_____   6 _____ congested

What are the two different ways to change the adjectives?

Question Forum¹

Ask your question here

Dear Question Forum

Lorraine San Diego, CA

My grandmother says that everything got **bigger**, **faster**, and **better** in the twentieth century. Is that true? Did some things
5 get **smaller**, **slower**, or **worse** than in the years before?

   1

Rosa San Diego, CA

It's a matter of opinion, but what your grandmother says is generally true. In the twentieth century, buildings became **taller**. Bridges became **longer** than they were in
10 the nineteenth century, and highways became **wider** and **faster** than the old roads. Cities became larger and more **crowded** than they had been before. New airplanes were suddenly **larger** and **heavier** than old airplanes. Large companies joined together to make even **bigger**
15 global corporations.² Technology in the home got **better**. Home electrical appliances like refrigerators and washing machines became **better**, **cheaper**, and **more efficient**. Computers became **more powerful** and **more complicated** but easier to use. The Internet gave us
20 **faster** communication and a **smaller** world – what we now call the global village.
Did everything get **larger** and **better**? Not everything. A lot of things did not get **bigger**, and some things got **worse**, like some environmental problems. Some things
25 became **smaller** but **better**. For example, phones became **thinner**, cameras got **lighter**, and modern video cameras became much **smaller** than **older** video cameras. Unfortunately, the ice sheets³ in the Arctic and Antarctic became **smaller**, too, as the world became
30 **hotter**. Generally, things did not become **slower** – except perhaps traffic in cities, which became **more congested**.⁴ The big question is: Are people **happier** now?

¹**forum:** a place to talk about something of public interest

²**corporation:** a large company

³**ice sheet:** layer of ice

⁴**congested:** too blocked or crowded

2 Comparative Adjectives

Grammar Presentation

You can use comparative adjectives to describe how two people or things are different from one another.	*New airplanes were larger and heavier than old airplanes.*

2.1 Comparisons with *Be* + Adjective

	Be	Comparative Adjective	*Than*	
I	am	**older**		my brother.
		more serious		my parents.
You We They	are	**happier**	**than**	Elisa.
		more successful		our co-workers.
He She It	is	**taller**		me.
		more excited		the teachers.

2.2 Comparative Adjective + Noun

	Comparative Adjective	Noun
The Internet gave us	**faster**	**communication.**
Large companies joined together to make	**bigger**	**corporations.**
We now have	**more powerful**	**computers.**

2.3 Comparative of Short Adjectives (One Syllable)

	Adjective	Comparative
A For one-syllable adjectives, add -er.	*low*	*lower*
	fast	*faster*
B For one-syllable adjectives ending in -e, add -r.	*safe*	*safer*
	large	*larger*

2.3 Comparative of Short Adjectives (One Syllable) *(continued)*

	Adjective	Comparative
C If the adjective ends with one vowel + one consonant, double the last letter and add -er.	hot	hotter
	big	bigger
D If the adjective has two syllables and ends in -y, change the y to i and add -er.	heavy	heavier
	easy	easier

2.4 Comparative of Long Adjectives (Two or More Syllables)

Adjective	Comparative
crowded	more crowded
powerful	more powerful
economical	more economical
efficient	more efficient

2.5 Two-Syllable Adjectives That Take -er

Adjective	Comparative
narrow	narrower
quiet	quieter
simple	simpler

2.6 Irregular Adjectives

Adjective	Comparative
good	**better**
bad	**worse**
far	**further (farther)**

Further is over 10 times more frequent than *farther*.

▶▶ Adjectives and Adverbs: Comparative and Superlative Forms: See page A22.

2.7 Using Comparative Adjectives

A	Use comparative adjectives to show a difference between two people, places, things, or ideas.	*The Burj Khalifa in Dubai is* taller than *the Sears Tower in Chicago.*
B	Use *than* after a comparative and before the second person or thing that you are comparing. Don't use *that* or *then*.	*Jessica is older* than *Denise.* NOT *older ~~that~~ Denise / older ~~then~~ Denise*
C	You can use a comparative adjective without *than* when the second part of the comparison is obvious.	*I need a* bigger *apartment.* (= a bigger apartment than the apartment I have now)
D	*Less* is the opposite of *more*. Do not use *less* with one-syllable adjectives.	*The traffic here is* less congested *than in the city.* *Pennsylvania is* smaller *than California.* NOT ~~less big~~
E	You can use a pronoun after *than* instead of a noun.	*Mike's sister is taller* than he is. (= than Mike is) *Sue sings better* than I do.
	In speaking, you can use an object pronoun. In academic writing, always use a subject pronoun.	*My brother is older* than me. *My brother is older* than I am.

📊 Data from the Real World

The 15 most common comparative adjectives ending in *-er* in writing and speaking are:

better	easier	higher	lower	stronger
bigger	further	larger	older	worse
earlier	greater	later	smaller	younger

The 10 most common comparative adjectives with *more* are:

comfortable	efficient	important	powerful	serious
difficult	expensive	interesting	recent	successful

Grammar Application

A How do things today compare with 20 years ago? Write the correct forms of the comparative adjectives in parentheses.

1 Home appliances are *cheaper* (cheap).

2 Laptop computers are _____ (light).

3 Desktop computers are _____ (quiet).

4 Music is _____ (easy) to share.

5 Bicycles are _____ (fast).

6 Cars are _____ (energy-efficient)

7 Cell phones are _____ (small).

8 Homes are _____ (big).

B Compare cell phones from many years ago and now. Use comparative forms of the adjectives in the box.

Early cellular phone   Smartphone

cheap	fast	powerful	smart
expensive	~~heavy~~	slow	thin

1 *Old cell phones were heavier.* _____

2 _____

3 _____

4 _____

5 _____

6 _____

7 _____

8 _____

A Read about a city's problems. How can it become a better place to live? Complete the sentences and make solutions. Use comparative forms of the adjectives in the box and nouns. Use each adjective once.

| attractive | clean | energy-efficient | new | ~~wide~~ |
| cheap | clear | frequent | safe | |

Problem	Solution
1 The main highway through the city is narrow.	We should build a ___*wider highway*___ .
2 The bridge over the river is old and dangerous.	We should build a _____ .
3 The downtown parking is very expensive.	We should have _____ .
4 The city parks are not clean.	We should have _____ .
5 The city's buses are not energy-efficient.	We should buy _____ .
6 The street signs are confusing.	We should install _____ .
7 The bus service is infrequent.	We should have _____ .
8 The city's website is unattractive.	The city should create a _____ .

B Pair Work What changes should happen to improve your town or city? Discuss with a partner.

    A *Our city needs a more frequent subway service.*

    B *We need nicer department stores downtown. We should have . . .*

C Group Work Compare cities and towns that you know. Work in groups. Then tell the class about them. Use the adjectives in parentheses.

    1 (modern) _Houston is more modern than San Antonio._

    2 (big) _New York has bigger parks than Miami._

    3 (traditional) _____

    4 (cheap) _____

    5 (good/job market) _____

    6 (clean) _____

    7 (historic) _____

    8 (fancy/stores) _____

    9 (crowded) _____

3 Comparative Adverbs

Grammar Presentation

You can use comparative adverbs to describe how two actions or events are different from each other.	*Ashley drives more slowly than her brother.*

3.1 Comparisons with Adverbs

	Verb	Comparative Adjective	*Than*	
Joanna	**runs**	**faster**		her brother.
The new printer	**works**	**better**	**than**	the old printer.
The population of Italy	**is growing**	**more slowly**		the population of Canada.
A diesel car	**runs**	**more efficiently**		a gasoline car.

3.2 Comparative of Short Adverbs (One Syllable)

	Adverb	Comparative
For one syllable adverbs, add *-er* or *-r*.	fast	fast**er**
	high	high**er**
	late	late**r**
	long	long**er**
	hard	hard**er**

3.3 Comparative of Longer Adverbs (Two or More Syllables)

	Adverb	Comparative
A For adverbs of two or more syllables, use *more* (or *less*).	*often*	*more / less often*
	carefully	*more / less carefully*
	quickly	*more / less quickly*
	easily	*more / less easily*
B We say *earlier*, not *more early*.	*This flight arrives earlier than the other flight.*	

3.4 Irregular Adverbs

Irregular Adverb	Comparative
well	better
badly	worse
far	further or farther

▸▸ Adjectives and Adverbs: Comparative and Superlative Forms: See page A22.

3.5 Using Comparative Adverbs

A You can use comparative adverbs to compare the way two people do the same action.	Hilda studies *harder than* the other students. My brother drives *more carefully* than my sister.
B You can use comparative adverbs to compare the way two actions or events happen.	Cairo is growing *more rapidly than* London.
C You can use comparative adverbs to compare the way an action happened in two different time periods.	Larissa works *harder* now *than* she did last year.
D Use *than* after a comparative adverb and before the second action or event that you are comparing. Don't use *that* or *then*.	He drives *faster than* his brother. NOT *faster that his brother / faster then his brother*
E You can use a comparative adverb without *than*.	I can run fast, but Lorna can run *faster*.
F *Less* is the opposite of *more*.	The old car runs *less efficiently* than the new car.
Do not use *less* with one-syllable adverbs.	Meryl arrived *earlier than* Patrick. NOT *less late*

Grammar Application

Exercise 3.1 Making Comparisons with Adverbs

Listen to the conversation. Complete the chart with comparative adverbs.

New York, New York

1 People walk
   more quickly .

2 People work
   _____ .

3 Restaurants stay open
   _____ .

Grant, Florida

4 You drive
   _____
   to get to a mall.

5 Joe and Bill go out
   _____ .

6 You spend money
   _____ .

Exercise 3.2 More Making Comparisons with Adverbs

A Write the comparative form of the adverb. Then write verbs that go with it from the list. Some verbs can go with more than one adverb.

drive	go to bed	play football	sleep	study
get up	go to the gym	play the guitar	speak English	walk
go out	go to the movies	sing	spend money	work

Adverb, Comparative Adverb	Verb(s)
1 fast _faster_	_run, drive_
2 well	
3 carefully	
4 hard	
5 slowly	
6 early	
7 far	
8 frequently	
9 badly	
10 late	

B Over to You How is your lifestyle different from five years ago? In what ways do you do things differently? Use ideas from A.

I speak English better now than I did five years ago.

1 _____

2 _____

3 _____

4 _____

5 _____

6 _____

7 _____

Exercise 3.3 Adverbs and Personal Pronouns

Data from the Real World

Research shows that when people use a personal pronoun after *than*, they use the object forms *me, him, her, us, them*. They do not normally use the subject forms *I, he, she, we, they*.

> You drive better than me / him.
> NOT *better than I/he*

than + object pronoun	████████████████████
than + subject pronoun	█

People use the subject form of the pronoun with an auxiliary verb (*be, do,* or *have*) or a modal verb (*will, can,* etc.), especially in writing.

> He drives faster than I do. (= faster than I drive)
> She can speak English better than he can. (= better than he can speak English)

A Over to You Complete the sentences with the names of people you know. Use a subject pronoun and an auxiliary or modal verb after *than*.

1 _____ gets up earlier than I _*do*_ .

2 _____ can run faster than I _*can*_ .

3 _____ eats more slowly than I _____ .

4 _____ exercises more often than I _____ .

5 _____ commutes further than I _____ .

6 _____ studied harder for yesterday's test than I _____ .

7 _____ can speak more fluently than I _____ .

8 _____ did better on the quiz than I _____ .

B Pair Work Tell a partner about each person in A. Use object pronouns (*me, him, them,* etc.).

My friend Charlie gets up earlier than me. He starts work at 7:00 a.m. I get up later than him.

4 Avoid Common Mistakes ⚠

1 **Do not use *more* with the *-er* comparative forms of adjectives and adverbs.**
She drives ~~more~~ faster than her brother.
This store is ~~more~~ cheaper than the other one.

2 **Do not use *more* with one-syllable adjectives and adverbs.**
taller
My brother is ~~more tall~~ than I am.
faster
She speaks ~~more fast~~ than I do.

3 **Do not use the *-er* ending with most adjectives of two or more syllables.**
more exciting
His second movie was ~~excitinger~~ than his first movie.

4 **Do not use *more* with *better* or *worse*.**
My English is getting ~~more~~ better this year.

5 **Use *than* after a comparative, not *that* or *then*.**
than
She works harder ~~then~~ I do.

Editing Task

Progress is change that results in a general improvement in life. Read the ideas about progress. Find and correct eight more mistakes in this blog.

What Is Progress?

It is not easy to answer this question. Here is a list of ideas.

Lisa   Medicines are now more effective and ~~more cheap~~, so people's health is
cheaper
      more better. People expect to live longer then they did 100 years ago.

5 Dan   There is a more shorter work week for everyone. There are powerfuler
      machines and computers, so people can be free from manual work.

Sanjay   Children reach a more higher level of education.

Cristina   People have more big houses and a comfortabler life that their parents.

UNIT 33

Superlative Adjectives and Adverbs

Facts and Opinions

1 Grammar in the Real World

A What do you know about Vietnam? Read the travel website article. What is the most interesting fact?

B Comprehension Check **Answer the questions.**

1 Where is Vietnam located?

2 What is the climate like?

3 Why is Hue famous?

4 What is Vietnam's most important export?

C Notice **Find the forms of these common adjectives in the text. Write them in the spaces below.**

1 big _____

2 hot _____

3 wet _____

4 narrow _____

5 popular _____

6 historic _____

7 important _____

8 beautiful _____

356

Vietnam

Vietnam, in Southeast Asia, shares borders with China, Laos, and Cambodia. It is a long country, and at its **narrowest** point it is only about 50 km (31 miles) wide.

Vietnam's population is about 90 million. The capital is Hanoi. The
5 **biggest** city is Ho Chi Minh City, formerly called Saigon.

Vietnam's **most historic** city is Hue. It was the home of the Nguyen kings, and it has many palaces and monuments.

The **most popular** beach is located near the city Nha Trang in the central coast area.

10 The **most beautiful** area is Ha Long Bay. There are hundreds of small islands and unusual rock formations.[1]

Vietnam has a hot and humid climate, with the **hottest** temperatures in April. The **wettest** month is September.

The **most important** export[2] is crude oil,[3] and the **most important**
15 crop[4] is rice. The industry that is growing the **most rapidly** is tourism.

[1]**rock formation:** a large area of rock that has characteristics different from the land around it

[2]**export:** an item someone sends to another country for sale or use

[3]**crude oil:** oil from underground that nobody has made into different products yet

[4]**crop:** a plant like a grain, vegetable, or fruit that people grow in large amounts on a farm

2 Superlative Adjectives

Grammar Presentation

You can use superlative adjectives to describe how a person or thing is different from all others.	The most historic city in Vietnam is Hue.

2.1 Statements

Noun	Be	The	Superlative Adjective	Noun		
Ha Long Bay	is		most beautiful	area		Vietnam.
November	isn't	the	wettest	month	in	the country.
Ho Chi Minh City	is		biggest	city		the area.

2.2 Information Questions

Noun	Be	The	Superlative Adjective	Noun		
Which city	is	the	most beautiful	city	in	Vietnam?
What	is		most important	export		the country?

2.3 Superlative of Short Adjectives (One Syllable)

	Adjective	Superlative
A For one-syllable adjectives, add -est.	long	longest
	slow	slowest
B For one-syllable adjectives ending in -e, add -st.	large	largest
	wide	widest
C For adjectives that end in one vowel + one consonant, double the final consonant and add -est.	big	biggest
	hot	hottest
D For two-syllable adjectives ending in -y, change y to i and add -est.	heavy	heaviest
	tiny	tiniest

2.4 Superlative of Longer Adjectives (Two or More Syllables)

Adjective	Superlative
beautiful	most beautiful
historic	most historic
important	most important
popular	most popular

2.5 Two-syllable Adjectives That Take -est

Adjective	Superlative
narrow	narrowest
quiet	quietest
simple	simplest

2.6 Irregular Adjectives

Adjective	Superlative
good	best
bad	worst
far	farthest or furthest (*farthest* is more common)

▸▸ Adjectives and Adverbs: Comparative and Superlative Forms: See page A22.

2.7 Using Superlative Adjectives

A Use *the* before a superlative adjective followed by a noun.	*Ha Long Bay is the most beautiful area in Vietnam.* NOT *is most beautiful area*
B Use superlative adjectives to show how one person or thing in a group is different in some way from all the others.	*Orla is the most intelligent student in the class.* *The Nile is the longest river in Africa.*
C You can use a superlative adjective without a noun.	*They have three daughters. Tran is the youngest.*
D You can use a possessive item (*my, your, Patrick's, the world's*, etc.) instead of *the* before a superlative adjective.	*That book is my most helpful guide book.* *Cheetahs are the world's fastest animals.*

E Use *in* + noun after superlative adjectives when you want to talk about a specific group, for example, *in the world, in the class,* etc. Do not use *of.*

The Nile is the longest river **in** the world.
NOT *the longest river of the world*

F *Least* is the opposite of most. Do not use *least* with one-syllable adjectives.

The Royal is the *least expensive* hotel in town.
Rhode Island is the *smallest* U.S. state.
NOT *the least big*

📊 Data from the Real World

The most common superlative adjectives ending in *-est* in writing and speaking are:

biggest	fastest	largest	lowest	strongest
closest	greatest	latest	oldest	youngest
earliest	highest	longest	smallest	

The most common superlative adjectives with *most* in writing and speaking are:

beautiful	difficult	famous	popular	serious
common	effective	important	powerful	significant[1]
dangerous	expensive	interesting	recent	successful

[1]**significant:** a more formal word for *important*

🖱 Grammar Application

Exercise 2.1 Superlative Adjectives

A Pair Work How good is your geography? Complete the sentences with a partner. Use superlative adjectives. Then check the answers at the bottom of the exercise.

World Geography Quiz

1 The world's _smallest_ (small) continent is _Australia_ .

2 The world's _____ (large) continent is _____ .

3 The continent with the _____ (more) countries is _____ .

4 The _____ (deep) ocean is the _____ .

5 The _____ (big) country is _____ .

6 The _____ (cold) place in the world is _____ .

7 The _____ (high) mountain is _____ .

8 The _____ (dry) place on Earth is the _____ .

9 The _____ (large) city in the United States is _____ .

10 The _____ (long) river in the world is _____ .

11 The _____ (populated) country in the world is _____ .

B Complete the questions with *the* and superlative adjectives. Note that ↑ shows an affirmative two-syllable superlative (with *most*), and ↓ shows a negative two-syllable superlative (with *least*). Then compare your answers with your classmates. You can find the answers at the bottom of the page.

FACTS ABOUT THE UNITED STATES

What Do You Know About the United States? Answers

1. What is _the biggest_ (big) waterfall? _Niagara Falls_

2. What is _____ (long) river? _____

3. What is _____ (dry) state? _____

4. What is _____ (wet) state? _____

5. What is _____ (popular) national park? ↑ _____

6. What is _____ (big) city? _____

7. What is _____ (wasteful) city? ↓ _____

8. What is _____ (expensive) city to live in? ↑ _____

9. What large city has _____ (bad) air pollution? _____

10. What is _____ (famous) bridge? ↑ _____

11. What is _____ (busy) airport? _____

12. What is _____ (populated) state? ↑ _____

13. What is _____ (populated) state? ↓ _____

2. Mississippi 3. Nevada 4. Hawaii 5. Great Smoky Mountains National Park in Tennessee and North Carolina 6. New York
7. San Francisco 8. New York 9. Los Angeles 10. The Golden Gate Bridge, California 11. Atlanta's Hartsfield-Jackson
12. California 13. Wyoming

C Over to You Think about your city or town. Complete the sentences. Then compare your answers with your classmates. Take a survey. What are the results?

Best (and Worst) of the Town

1 The _nicest_ (nice) neighborhood is _____ .

2 The _____ (delicious) pizza is _____ .

3 The _____ (crowded) area is _____ .

4 The area with the _____ (bad) traffic is _____ .

5 The _____ (dangerous) intersection is _____ .

6 The _____ (unusual) restaurant is _____ .

Exercise 2.2 Superlative Adjectives to Describe People

A Complete the superlative constructions in this conversation. Use *the* when necessary.

Claire So, who are __the most important__
(1)
(important) people in your life?

Monika Well, I guess my family and my
_____ (good) friends.
(2)

Claire OK. Tell me about your family.

Monika Well, let's see. My _____
(3)
(close) family members all live near
me, so I see them often. I have three
brothers: Tim, Liam, and Anthony. Anthony is _____ (young).
(4)
He's just 13. My grandmother is 75. She's my _____ (old) relative.
(5)
My friends are mostly from my college days. One really special person is Tina.

Claire Tina? Is she your _____ (good) friend?
(6)

Monika Yeah. She's _____ (unusual) person I know, and _____
(7)   (8)
(interesting). She has a pilot's license and a degree in biology! Of all my friends, she
definitely has _____ (exciting) job. She works for a tour company that
(9)
takes people to some of _____ (exotic¹) places in the world. When we
(10)
were in college, she always got _____ (high) grades. She's probably
(11)
_____ (intelligent) person I know, and _____ (successful).
(12)   (13)

Claire Amazing!

¹**exotic:** unusual or interesting because of being from a different culture or country

B Listen to the conversation and check your answers.

C Over to You Answer the questions, and describe your friends or people in your family. Use superlative adjectives. Then share your answers with a partner.

1 Who are the most important people in your life?

2 Who is your best friend?

3 Who is the most successful person you know?

4 Who is the most intelligent? The funniest?

3 Superlative Adverbs

Grammar Presentation

You can use superlative adverbs to describe how a person's actions or the way something happens is different from all others.

All the students work hard, but Rosa works hardest.

3.1 Statements

	Verb	(The)	Superlative Adjective	
Daniel	ran	(the)	**fastest**	in the men's 100 meters.
This printer	works	(the)	**best**	of all the printers in the office.
Nina	drives	(the)	**most carefully**	of the three women.

3.2 Questions

	Verb	(The)	Superlative Adjective	
Who	arrives	(the)	**earliest**	at school every day?
Which industry	is growing	(the)	**most rapidly**	in Vietnam?
What method	works	(the)	**most effectively**	to learn vocabulary?

3.3 Superlative of Short Adverbs (One Syllable)

		Adjective	Superlative
A For adverbs with one syllable, add -est.		fast	fast**est**
		high	high**est**
		long	long**est**
		hard	hard**est**
B For adverbs with one syllable ending in -e, add -st.		late	late**st**

3.4 Superlative of Longer Adverbs (Two or More Syllables)

Adjective	Superlative
often	**most** often
recently	**most** recently
quickly	**most** quickly
slowly	**most** slowly

We say *earliest*, not *most early*.
Which flight arrives the **earliest**?

3.5 Irregular Adverbs

Irregular Adverb	Superlative
well	best
badly	worst
far	farthest or furthest (*farthest* is more common)

Adjectives and Adverbs: Comparative and Superlative Forms: See page A22.

3.6 Using Superlative Adverbs

A You can use superlative adverbs to describe how one action or event is different from all others.	*Hilda studies the hardest of all the students in her class.* *I drive most carefully in bad weather or when it's dark.*
B You can use a phrase with *of* after a superlative adverb.	*The cheetah runs the fastest of all the animals.*
C *Least* is the opposite of *most*.	*Of the three cars, the gasoline car operates the least efficiently.*

People often use superlative adverbs without *the*, especially in spoken language.	*You should wear the colors that suit you **best**.* *Who do you text **most often**, your family, your classmates, or your friends?* *Which of the three movies came out **most recently**?*
In academic writing, use *the*.	*This method works **the most effectively**.*

Superlative adverbs are much less common than superlative adjectives.

The most common superlative adverbs ending in *-est* in writing and speaking are:	fastest closest longest	hardest nearest lowest	latest earliest highest
The six most common superlative adverbs used with *most* in writing and speaking are:	easily effectively	economically often	recently frequently

Grammar Application

A Complete the sentences from a student essay. Use the superlative form of the adverbs in parentheses with *the*.

I live in an apartment with three other students: Shinya, Tomas, and Alex. I arrived ___the most recently___ (recently) – in September this year. Shinya has lived here
(1)

_____ (long). He moved into the apartment two years ago. Because we
(2)

are students, we try to spend as little money as possible. Right now, I think that I live

_____ (economical) because I almost never go out to eat. Tomas eats
(3)

out _____ (frequent). Alex probably studies _____ (hard).
(4)   (5)

He always goes to sleep _____ (late). I get up _____
(6)   (7)

(early) because I travel _____ (far) to school.
(8)

B Pair Work Complete the sentences with your own ideas. You can use the verbs and adverbs in the boxes to help you. Then share your sentences with a partner.

call	reply	study	work
drive	speak	text	write

clearly	fast	frequently	hard
early	fluently	good	often

1 Of all my friends, *Hannah drives the fastest* .

2 Of all my classmates, _____ .

3 Of all the people I know, _____ .

4 In this class, _____ .

5 Of all my family members, _____ .

6 Of all my co-workers (or friends), _____ .

7 Of all the people I text, _____ .

8 Of all the people I send e-mails to, _____ .

4 Avoid Common Mistakes ⚠

1 **Do not use a comparative form instead of a superlative when comparing more than two things.**

the hottest
Of all the places we visited, Vietnam in April was hotter.

2 **Do not use *most* and *-est* together.**
My most smallest pet was a goldfish.

3 **Do not use *most* with adjectives and adverbs that take *-est*.**

cheapest
The Hollywood Plaza is the most cheap hotel in town.

4 **Do not use *of* instead of *in*.**

in
It's the tallest building of the world.

5 **Learn the spelling rules for comparative and superlative adjectives and adverbs.**

earliest
Who arrives at school earlyst every day, Joanna or Peter?

hottest
June 20 was the hotest day of the year.

Editing Task

Find and correct 10 more mistakes in the magazine article.

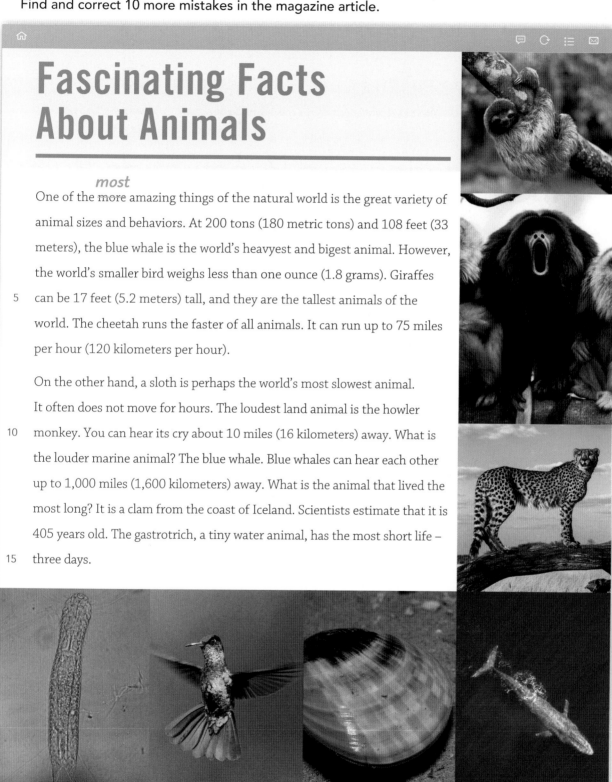

Fascinating Facts About Animals

One of the ~~more~~ *most* amazing things of the natural world is the great variety of animal sizes and behaviors. At 200 tons (180 metric tons) and 108 feet (33 meters), the blue whale is the world's heavyest and bigest animal. However, the world's smaller bird weighs less than one ounce (1.8 grams). Giraffes

5   can be 17 feet (5.2 meters) tall, and they are the tallest animals of the world. The cheetah runs the faster of all animals. It can run up to 75 miles per hour (120 kilometers per hour).

On the other hand, a sloth is perhaps the world's most slowest animal. It often does not move for hours. The loudest land animal is the howler

10   monkey. You can hear its cry about 10 miles (16 kilometers) away. What is the louder marine animal? The blue whale. Blue whales can hear each other up to 1,000 miles (1,600 kilometers) away. What is the animal that lived the most long? It is a clam from the coast of Iceland. Scientists estimate that it is 405 years old. The gastrotrich, a tiny water animal, has the most short life –

15   three days.

Appendices

1 Capitalization and Punctuation Rules

Capitalize	Examples
1 The first letter of the first word of a sentence	*Today is a great day.*
2 The pronoun *I*	*Yesterday I went to hear a new rock band.*
3 Names of people	*Simón Bolívar, Joseph Chung*
4 Names of buildings, streets, geographic locations, and organizations	*Taj Majal, Broadway, Mt. Everest, United Nations*
5 Titles of people	*Dr., Mr., Mrs., Ms.*
6 Days, months, and holidays	*Tuesday, April, Valentine's Day*
7 Names of courses or classes	*Biology 101, English Composition II*
8 Titles of books, movies, and plays	*Crime and Punishment, Avatar, Hamlet*
9 States, countries, languages, and nationalities	*California, Mexico, Spanish, South Korean, Canadian*
10 Names of religions	*Hinduism, Catholicism, Islam, Judaism*

Punctuation	Examples
1 Use a period (.) at the end of a sentence.	*He is Korean.*
2 Use a question mark (?) at the end of a question.	*Do you want to buy a car?*
3 Use an exclamation point (!) to show strong emotion (e.g., surprise, anger, shock).	*Wait! I'm not ready yet. I can't believe it!*
4 Use an apostrophe (') for possessive nouns.	
Add 's for singular nouns.	*That's Sue's umbrella.*
Add s' for plural nouns.	*Those are the students' books.* BUT
Add 's for irregular plural nouns.	*Bring me the children's shoes.*
Use an apostrophe (') for contractions.	*I'll be back next week. He can't drive a car.*
5 Use a comma (,):	
• between words in a series of three or more items. (Place *and* before the last item.)	*I like fish, chicken, turkey, and mashed potatoes.*
• before *and, or, but,* and *so* to connect two complete sentences.	*You can watch TV, but I have to study for a test.*

2 Spelling Rules for Noun Plurals

1 Add -s to most singular nouns to form plural nouns.	*a camera – two cameras* *a key – keys*	*a model – two models* *a student – students*
2 Add -es to nouns that end in -ch, -sh, -ss, and -x.	*watch – watches* *class – classes*	*dish – dishes* *tax – taxes*
3 With nouns that end in a consonant + -y, change the y to i and add -es.	*accessory – accessories*	*battery – batteries*
4 With nouns that end in -ife, change the ending to -ives.	*knife – knives* *wife – wives*	*life – lives*
5 Add -es to nouns that end in -o after a consonant. **Exception:** Add -s only to nouns that end in -o and refer to music.	*potato – potatoes* *piano – pianos*	*tomato – tomatoes* *soprano – sopranos*
6 Add -s to nouns that end in -o after a vowel.	*radio – radios*	*shampoo – shampoos*
7 Some plural nouns have irregular forms. These are the most common irregular plural nouns in academic writing.	*man – men* *child – children* *foot – feet*	*woman – women* *person – people* *tooth – teeth*
8 Some nouns have the same form for singular and plural.	*one deer – two deer* *one fish – two fish*	*one sheep – two sheep*
9 Some nouns are only plural. They do not have a singular form.	*clothes* *glasses* *headphones* *jeans*	*pants* *scissors* *sunglasses*

3 Verb Forms

Present: *Be*

Affirmative Statements

SINGULAR

Subject	Be	
I	**am**	
You	**are**	late.
He She It	**is**	
		difficult.

PLURAL

Subject	Be	
We You They	**are**	from Seoul.

Negative Statements

SINGULAR

Subject	Be + Not	
I	**am not**	
You	**are not**	in class.
He She It	**is not**	

PLURAL

Subject	Be + Not	
We You They	**are not**	students.

Affirmative Contractions

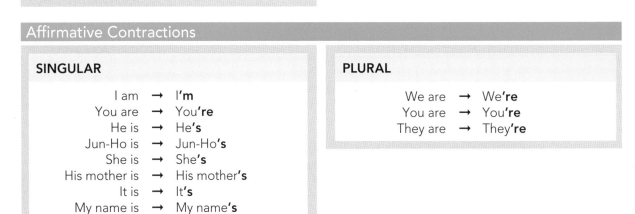

SINGULAR

I am	→	I**'m**
You are	→	You**'re**
He is	→	He**'s**
Jun-Ho is	→	Jun-Ho**'s**
She is	→	She**'s**
His mother is	→	His mother**'s**
It is	→	It**'s**
My name is	→	My name**'s**

PLURAL

We are	→	We**'re**
You are	→	You**'re**
They are	→	They**'re**

Negative Contractions

SINGULAR

I am not	→	**I'm not**
You are not	→	**You're not** / You **aren't**
He is not	→	He**'s not** / He **isn't**
She is not	→	She**'s not** / She **isn't**
It is not	→	It**'s not** / It **isn't**

PLURAL

We are not	→	We**'re not** / We **aren't**
You are not	→	You**'re not** / You **aren't**
They are not	→	They**'re not** / They **aren't**

Singular *Yes/No* Questions

Be	Subject	
Am	I	
Are	you	in class?
Is	he she it	

Singular Short Answers

AFFIRMATIVE

	Subject	*Be*
Yes,	I	**am.**
	you	**are.**
	he she it	**is.**

NEGATIVE

	Subject	*Be + Not*
No,	I	**am not.**
	you	**are not.**
	he she it	**is not.**

Plural *Yes/No* Questions

Be	Subject	
Are	we you they	late?

Plural Short Answers

AFFIRMATIVE

	Subject	*Be*
Yes,	we you they	**are.**

NEGATIVE

	Subject	*Be + Not*
No,	we you they	**are not.**

Negative Short Answer Contractions

SINGULAR

No, I am not.	→	No, I**'m not**.
No, you are not.	→	No, you**'re not**.
		No, you **aren't**.
No, he is not.	→	No, he**'s not**.
		No, he **isn't**.
No, she is not.	→	No, she**'s not**.
		No, she **isn't**.
No, it is not.	→	No, it**'s not**.
		No, it **isn't**.

PLURAL

No, we are not.	→	No, we**'re not**.
		No, we **aren't**.
No, you are not.	→	No, you**'re not**.
		No, you **aren't**.
No, they are not.	→	No, they**'re not**.
		No, they **aren't**.

Information Questions

SINGULAR SUBJECTS

Wh- Word	Be	Subject
Who		your teacher?
What		your major?
When	is	our exam?
Where		the building?
How		your class?

PLURAL SUBJECTS

Wh- Word	Be	Subject
Who		your teachers?
What		your plans?
When	are	your exams?
Where		your books?
How		your classes?

Contractions with Singular Subjects

SINGULAR

Who is	→	**Who's**
What is	→	**What's**
When is	→	**When's**
Where is	→	**Where's**
How is	→	**How's**

There Is / There Are

There	Be	Subject	Place / Time
There	is	a parking lot a free tour	on Alameda Street. at 10:00.
	are	a lot of little shops free tours	in the area. on most days.

Contraction

There is → There's

Negative Statements

There	Be + Not / No	Subject	Place / Time
There	isn't is no	a bank bank	in Union Station.
	isn't is no	a show show	at 8:00.
There	's no	bank	in Union Station.
		show	at 8:00.
There	aren't are no	any cars cars	on Olvera Street.
	aren't are no	any tours tours	in the evening.

Yes / No Questions and Short Answers

Be	There	Subject	Place / Time
Is	there	a visitor's center	on Olvera Street?
		a performance	at 6:00?
Are		any parking lots	in the area?
		any tours	in the evening?

Short Answers

Yes, **there is**.

No, **there isn't**.

Yes, **there are**.

No, **there aren't**.

Simple Present

Affirmative Statements

SINGULAR

Subject	Verb	
I You	**eat**	vegetables every day.
He She It	**eats**	

PLURAL

Subject	Verb	
We You They	**have**	many friends.

Negative Statements

SINGULAR

Subject	*Do / Does + Not*	*Base Form of Verb*	
I You	**do not don't**	**eat**	a lot of meat.
He She It	**does not doesn't**		

PLURAL

Subject	*Do + Not*	*Base Form of Verb*	
We You They	**do not don't**	**exercise**	in the morning.

Yes / No Questions

Do / Does	Subject	Base Form of Verb	
Do	I you we they	**fall asleep**	in 30 minutes?
Does	he she it		

AFFIRMATIVE		
Yes	Subject	Do / Does
Yes,	I you we they	do.
	he she it	does.

NEGATIVE		
No	Subject	Do / Does + Not
No,	I you we they	do not. don't.
	he she it	does not. doesn't.

Wh- word	Do / Does	Subject	Base Form of Verb	
Who	do	I you we they	see	at school?
What			eat	at parties?
When			celebrate	that holiday?
Where	does	he she it	study	for school?
Why			live	at home?
How			meet	new people?

Present Progressive

Subject	Be	Verb + -ing
I	am	
You We They	are	talking.
He She It	is	

Contractions		
I am	→	I'm
You are	→	You're
We are	→	We're
They are	→	They're
He is	→	He's
She is	→	She's
It is	→	It's

Negative Statements

Subject	Be + Not	Verb + -ing
I	am not	
You We They	are not	talking.
He She It	is not	

Contractions

I am not	→ I**'m not**	
You are not	→ You**'re not**	You **aren't**
We are not	→ We**'re not**	We **aren't**
They are not	→ They**'re not**	They **aren't**
He is not	→ He**'s not**	He **isn't**
She is not	→ She**'s not**	She **isn't**
It is not	→ It**'s not**	It **isn't**

Yes/No Questions

Be	Subject	Verb + -ing
Am	I	
Are	you we they	working?
Is	he she it	

Short Answers

AFFIRMATIVE
Yes, I **am**.
Yes, you **are**.
Yes, we **are**.
Yes, they **are**.
Yes, he **is**.
Yes, she **is**.
Yes, it **is**.

NEGATIVE

No, I**'m not**.	
No, you**'re not**.	No, you **aren't**.
No, we**'re not**.	No, we **aren't**.
No, they**'re not**.	No, they **aren't**.
No, he**'s not**.	No, he **isn't**.
No, she**'s not**.	No, she **isn't**.
No, it**'s not**.	No, it **isn't**.

Information Questions

Wh- Word	Be	Subject	Verb + -ing
Who	am	I	hearing?
What			studying?
When	are	you we they	leaving?
Where			going?
Why	is	he she it	laughing?
How			feeling?

Wh- Word as Subject	Be	Verb + -ing
Who	is	talking?
What		happening?

Simple Past: *Be*

AFFIRMATIVE

Subject	Was / Were	
I He She It	was	in the computer lab.
We You They	were	

NEGATIVE

Subject	Was / Were + Not	
I He She It	was not wasn't	in class.
We You They	were not weren't	

Was / Were	Subject	
Was	I he she it	very smart?
Were	we you they	in college?

AFFIRMATIVE

Yes	Subject	Was / Were
Yes,	I he she it	was.
	we you they	were.

NEGATIVE

No	Subject	Was / Were + Not
No,	I he she it	was not. wasn't.
	we you they	were not. weren't.

Wh- Word	Was / Were	Subject	
Who		your best friend	as a child?
What	was	your favorite class	last semester?
When		her birthday party?	
What time		the meeting	on Monday?
Where		his partners?	
Why	were	they	successful?
How		the concerts	the other night?
How old		their cars	in 2011?

Simple Past

Statements

AFFIRMATIVE

Subject	Simple Past Verb	
I You We They He She It	started	in 1962.

NEGATIVE

Subject	Did + Not	Base Form of Verb	
I You We They He She It	did not didn't	sign	a contract.

Yes/No Questions

Did	Subject	Base Form of Verb	
Did	I you we they he she it	finish	the report?

Short Answers

AFFIRMATIVE

Yes	Subject	Did
Yes,	I you we they he she it	did.

NEGATIVE

No	Subject	Did + Not
No,	I you we they he she it	did not. didn't.

Information Questions

Wh- Word	Did	Subject	Base Form of Verb	
Who		I you we they he she it	write	about?
What			do	yesterday?
When	did		finish	our report?
Where			visit	on vacation?
Why			start	a company?
How			save	enough money?

Past Progressive

Statements

AFFIRMATIVE

Subject	Past of *Be*	Verb + *-ing*
I He She It	was	
You We They	were	working.

NEGATIVE

Subject	Past of *Be* + *Not*	Verb + *-ing*
I He She It	was not / wasn't	
You We They	were not / weren't	working.

Yes/No Questions

Past of *Be*	Subject	Verb + *-ing*
Was	I he she it	working?
Were	you we they	working?

Short Answers

AFFIRMATIVE

	Subject	Past of *Be*
Yes,	I he she it	was.
	you we they	were.

NEGATIVE

	Subject	Past of *Be* + *Not*
No,	I he she it	were not. weren't.
	you we they	were not. weren't.

Information Questions

Wh- Word	Past of *Be*	Subject	Verb + *-ing*
Who		I he she it	studying?
What	was		doing?
When			researching?
Where		you we they	working?
Why	were		experimenting?
How			feeling?

Wh- Word as Subject	Past of *Be*	Verb + *-ing*
Who	was	talking?
What	was	happening?

Future: *Be Going To*

AFFIRMATIVE

Subject	Be	Going To	Base Form of Verb	
I	am			
You We They	are	going to	get	a job.
He She It	is			

NEGATIVE

Subject	Be + Not	Going To	Base Form of Verb	
I	am not			
You We They	are not	going to	get	a job.
He She It	is not			

Yes/No Questions

Be	Subject	Going To	Base Form of Verb	
Am	I			
Are	you we they	going to	get	a job?
Is	he she it			

Short Answers

AFFIRMATIVE

	Subject	Be
	I	am.
Yes,	you we they	are.
	he she it	is.

NEGATIVE

	Subject	Be + Not
	I	'm not.
No,	you we they	aren't.
	he she it	isn't.

Information Questions

Wh- Word	Be	Subject	Going To	Base Form of Verb	
Who	Am	I		interview	tomorrow?
What		you we they		do	after graduation?
When	Are		going to	leave	for New York?
Where				work	after college?
Why	Is	he she it		move	to Canada?
How				pay	his loans?

Information Questions

Wh- Word as Subject	Be	Going To	Base Form of Verb	
Who	is	going to	get	a job after college?
What			happen	after school?

Future: *Will*

Statements

AFFIRMATIVE

Subject	*Will*	Base Form of Verb	
I You We They He She It	will 'll	have	a healthy life.

NEGATIVE

Subject	*Will* + *Not*	Base Form of Verb	
I You We They He She It	will not won't	have	a healthy life.

Yes/No Questions

Will	Subject	Base Form of Verb	
Will	I you we they he she it	have	a healthy life?

Short Answers

AFFIRMATIVE

Yes, I Yes, you Yes, we Yes, they Yes, he Yes, she Yes, it	will.

NEGATIVE

No, I No, you No, we No, they No, he No, she No, it	won't.

Information Questions

Wh- Word	*Will*	Subject	Base Form of Verb	
Who	will	I you we they he she it	meet	at the interview tomorrow?
What			do	in your training program?
When			return	your documents?
Where			find	information about careers?
Why			travel	to South America?
How			build	new apartments?

Imperatives

AFFIRMATIVE		
Base Form of Verb		
Smile	and be helpful.	
Look	at people when you talk to them.	

NEGATIVE		
Do + Not	**Base Form of Verb**	
Don't/ Do not	**interrupt**	people who are very busy.
	do	this in the beginning.

4 Common Regular and Irregular Verbs

Regular

Base Form	Past Form
call	called
decide	decided
happen	happened
like	liked
live	lived
look	looked
move	moved
start	started
talk	talked
try	tried
work	worked

Irregular

Base Form	Past Form
come	came
do	did
get	got
go	went
have	had
make	made
put	put
read	read
say	said
see	saw

estaba wasn't = no era

fueron weren't = no eran

5 Irregular Verbs

Base Form	Simple Past
be	was / were
become	became
begin	began
bite	bit
blow	blew
break	broke
bring	brought
build	built
buy	bought ~ bot
catch	caught
choose	chose
come	came
cost	cost
cut	cut
do	did
draw	drew
drink	drank
drive	drove
eat	ate
fall	fell
feed	fed
feel	felt
fight	fought
find	found
fly	flew
forget	forgot
forgive	forgave
get	got
give	gave
go	went
grow	grew
have	had
hear	heard
hide	hid
hit	hit
hold	held
hurt	hurt

Base Form	Simple Past
keep	kept
know	knew
leave	left
lose	lost
make	made
meet	met
pay	paid
put	put
read	read
ride	rode
run	ran
say	said
see	saw
sell	sold
send	sent
set	set
shake	shook
show	showed
shut	shut
sing	sang
sit	sat
sleep	slept
speak	spoke
spend	spent
stand	stood
steal	stole
swim	swam
take	took
teach	taught
tell	told
think	thought
throw	threw
understand	understood
wake	woke
wear	wore
win	won
write	wrote

6 Spelling Rules for Possessive Nouns

1	Add 's to singular nouns to show possession.	*The managers name is Mr. Patel.* (one manager) *The boss's ideas are helpful.* (one boss)
2	Add an apostrophe (') to plural nouns ending in -s to show possession.	*The managers' names are hard to remember.* (more than one manager) *The bosses' ideas are very good.* (more than one boss)
3	For irregular plural nouns, add 's to show possession.	*The men's uniforms are heavy.* (more than one man) *The children's room is messy.* (more than one child)
4	*My, your, his, her, our,* and *their* can come before a possessive noun.	*My friend's sister is in Peru.* *Our parents' names are short.*

7 Noncount Nouns and Containers

Common Noncount Nouns

Food and Liquids		Materials	School Subjects	Weather	Other
beef	rice	leather	algebra	fog	advice
bread	salt	metal	art	ice	furniture
butter	seafood	oil	biology	rain	garbage
cheese	shrimp	plastic	economics	snow	help
coffee	soup	silk	English	weather	homework
fish	spinach	wood	geography		information
ice cream	sugar		history		jewelry
meat	tea		music		mail
milk	water		physics		money
olive oil			psychology		noise
			science		traffic
					vocabulary
					work

Measurement Words and Containers

a bag of potatoes rice	**a bowl** of soup pasta	**a glass** of water soda	**a piece** of cake meat
a bar of chocolate soap	**a bunch** of grapes bananas	**a head** of lettuce cabbage	**a plate** of eggs chicken
a bottle of oil ketchup	**a can** of beans tuna	**a jar** of mustard pickles	**a pound** of butter cheese
a box of cereal candy	**a carton** of milk juice	**a loaf** of bread	**a slice** of pie pizza

8 Metric Conversion

1 ounce = 28 grams	1 mile = 1.6 kilometers
1 gram = .04 ounce	1 kilometer = .62 mile
1 pound = .45 kilogram	1 foot = .30 meter
1 kilogram = 2.2 pounds	1 meter = 3.3 feet
1 liter = .26 gallon	1 inch = 2.54 centimeters
1 gallon = 3.8 liters	1 centimeter = .39 inch

9 Subject and Object Pronouns

Subject Pronoun	Possessive Adjective	Object Pronoun	
I	my	me	*I can't find the calculator. My desk is so messy. My boss is unhappy with me.*
you	your	you	*You are very organized. Your desk is so neat. I want to be like you.*
he	his	him	*He is a new employee. His old job was in Hong Kong. This is very exciting to him.*
she	her	her	*She went home. Her computer is off. I'll call her.*
it	its	it	*It's a new company. Its president is Mr. Janesh. He wants it to be successful.*
we	our	us	*We are looking for the reports. Our boss wants to read them. The reports are important to us.*
they	their	them	*They are writing a report. Their team members will help them.*

10 Indefinite and Definite Articles

Indefinite Article

1 Use *a/an* with singular count nouns.	*She made a decision about her job.* *An analyst examines something in detail.*
2 Use *a* when the noun begins with a consonant sound.	*She made a decision about her job.*
3 Use *an* when the noun begins with a vowel sound.	*An analyst examines something in detail.*
4 Use *a* before adjectives or adverbs that begin with a consonant sound.	*Tony found a great apartment in Chicago.*
5 Use *a* before words that begin with *u* when the *u* makes a "you" sound.	*James went to a university in Boston.* *The economy is a universal concern.*
6 Use *a/an* to introduce a person or thing for the first time to a listener. When you mention the person or thing again, use *the*.	*Tom bought a car.* (The listener does not know about this car.) *The car was not very expensive.* (Now the listener knows about this car.)

Definite Article

1 You can use *the* before singular or plural count nouns, and before noncount nouns.	*The job is a good one.* *The choices were interesting.* *The information is very useful.*
2 Use *the* to talk about people or things that both the listener and speaker know about.	*The president discussed the plan.* (Everyone knows the president and the plan.) *The moon and the stars were beautiful last night.* (Everyone knows the moon and the stars.)
3 Use *the* to talk about a specific noun.	*"The teacher gave us difficult homework tonight."* (The speaker and listener know this teacher.) *"The game was interesting." "I agree."* (The speaker and listener are thinking of the same game.)

11 Spelling Rules for Verbs Ending in *-ing*

1 For most verbs, add *-ing**.
go → going   say → saying   talk → talking

2 If the verb ends in a silent *-e*, delete *e* and add *-ing*.
live → living   make → making   write → writing

3 For *be* and *see*, don't drop the *e* because it is not silent.
be → being   see → seeing

4 If the verb ends in *-ie*, change the *ie* to *y* and add *-ing*.
die → dying   lie → lying

5 If the verb has one syllable and follows the pattern consonant, vowel, consonant (CVC), double the last letter and add *-ing*.
get → getting   put → putting   sit → sitting

6 Do not double the consonant if the verb ends in *-w*, *-x*, or *-y*.
grow → growing   fix → fixing   say → saying

7 If the verb has two syllables, ends in the pattern CVC, and is stressed on the last syllable, double the last letter and add *-ing*.
beGIN → beginning

8 If the verb has two syllables and is stressed on the first syllable, do not double the last letter.
LISten → listening   TRAVel → traveling   VISit → visiting

* Verbs that end in *-ing* are also called *gerunds* when they are used as a noun. The same spelling rules above apply to gerunds as well.

12 Spelling and Pronunciation Rules for Simple Present

Spelling of Third-Person Singular Verbs

1 Add *-s* to most verbs.
Add *-s* to verbs ending in a vowel* + *-y*.
drinks, rides, runs, sees, sleeps   buys, pays, says

2 Add *-es* to verbs ending in *-ch*, *-sh*, *-ss*, *-x*.
Add *-es* to verbs ending in a consonant** + *-o*.
teaches, pushes, misses, fixes   does, goes

3 For verbs that end in a consonant + *-y*, change the *y* to *i* and add *-es*.
cry → cries   study → studies

4 Some verbs are irregular.
be → am / are / is   have → has

* **Vowels:** the letters *a, e, i, o, u*
** **Consonants:** the letters *b, c, d, f, g, h, j, k, l, m, n, p, q, r, s, t, v, w, x, y, z*

Pronunciation of Third-Person Singular Verbs

1 Say /s/ after /f/, /k/, /p/, and /t/ sounds.
   laughs, drinks, walks, sleeps, writes, gets

2 Say /z/ after /b/, /d/, /g/, /v/, /m/, /n/, /l/, and /r/ sounds and all vowel sounds.
   grabs, rides, hugs, lives, comes, runs, smiles, hears, sees, plays, buys, goes, studies

3 Say /əz/ after /tʃ/, /ʃ/, /s/, /ks/, /z/, and /dʒ/ sounds.
   teaches, pushes, kisses, fixes, uses, changes

4 Pronounce the vowel sound in *does* and *says* differently from *do* and *say*.
   do /du:/ ➝ *does* /dʌz/   *say* /seɪ/ ➝ *says* /sez/

13 Spelling and Pronunciation Rules for Regular Verbs in Simple Past

Spelling of Regular Verbs

1 For most verbs, add -*ed*.	*work* ➝ *worked*
2 For verbs ending in -*e*, add -*d*.	*live* ➝ *lived*
3 For verbs ending in consonant + -*y*, change the *y* to *i* and add -*ed*.	*study* ➝ *studied*
4 For verbs ending in vowel + -*y*, add -*ed*.	*play* ➝ *played*
5 For one-syllable verbs ending in consonant-vowel-consonant (CVC), double the consonant.	*plan* ➝ *planned*
6 Do not double the consonant if the verb ends in -*x* or -*w*.	*show* ➝ *showed*
7 For two-syllable verbs ending in CVC and stressed on the first syllable, do not double the consonant.	*TRAvel* ➝ *TRAveled*
8 For two-syllable verbs ending in CVC and stressed on the second syllable, double the consonant.	*conTROL* ➝ *conTROLLED*

Pronunciation of Regular Verbs

1 When the verb ends in /t/ or /d/, say -*ed* as /ɪd/ or /əd/.	*wait* ➝ *waited*	*decide* ➝ *decided*
2 When the verb ends in /f/, /k/, /p/, /s/, /ʃ/, and /tʃ/, say -*ed* as /t/.	*laugh* ➝ *laughed* *look* ➝ *looked* *stop* ➝ *stopped*	*miss* ➝ *missed* *finish* ➝ *finished* *watch* ➝ *watched*
3 For verbs that end in other consonant and vowel sounds, say -*ed* as /d/.	*agree* ➝ *agreed* *borrow* ➝ *borrowed* *change* ➝ *changed*	*listen* ➝ *listened* *live* ➝ *lived* *play* ➝ *played*

14 Adjectives and Adverbs: Comparative and Superlative Forms

	Adjective	Comparative	Superlative
1 One-Syllable Adjectives **a** Add -er and -est to one-syllable adjectives.	cheap new old small strong tall young	cheaper newer older smaller stronger taller younger	the cheapest the newest the oldest the smallest the strongest the tallest the youngest
b If the adjective ends with one vowel + one consonant, double the last letter and add -er or -est. Do not double the consonant w.	big hot sad thin	bigger hotter sadder thinner	the biggest the hottest the saddest the thinnest
2 Two-Syllable Adjectives **a** Add more or the most to most two-syllable adjectives.	boring famous handsome patient	more boring more famous more handsome more patient	the most boring the most famous the most handsome the most patient
b Some two-syllable adjectives have two forms.	narrow simple	narrower / more narrow simpler / more simple	the narrowest / the most narrow the simplest / the most simple
c If the adjective has two syllables and ends in -y, change the y to i and add -er or -est.	angry easy friendly happy lucky pretty silly	angrier easier friendlier happier luckier prettier sillier	the angriest the easiest the friendliest the happiest the luckiest the prettiest the silliest

	Adjective	Comparative	Superlative
3 Three-or-More-Syllable Adjectives Add *more* or *the most* to adjectives with three or more syllables.	beautiful difficult enjoyable expensive important serious	more beautiful more difficult more enjoyable more expensive more important more serious	the most beautiful the most difficult the most enjoyable the most expensive the most important the most serious
4 Irregular Adjectives Some adjectives have irregular forms.	bad far good	worse farther / further better	the worst the farthest / the furthest the best

	Adjective	Comparative	Superlative
1 -ly Adverbs Most adverbs end in *-ly*.	patiently quickly quietly slowly	more patiently more quickly more quietly more slowly	(the) most patiently (the) most quickly (the) most quietly (the) most slowly
2 One-Syllable Adverbs A few adverbs do not end in *-ly*. Add *-er* and *-est* to these adverbs.	fast hard	faster harder	(the) fastest (the) hardest
3 Irregular Adverbs Some adverbs have irregular forms.	badly far well	worse farther / further better	(the) worst (the) farthest / furthest (the) best

People usually only use *the* with superlative adverbs in formal writing and speaking.

15 Adverbs with -ly

Adjective	Adverb	Adjective	Adverb
bad	badly	loud	loudly
beautiful	beautifully	nervous	nervously
careful	carefully	nice	nicely
clear	clearly	patient	patiently
close	closely	polite	politely
confident	confidently	proper	properly
deep	deeply	quick	quickly
fluent	fluently	quiet	quietly
honest	honestly	slow	slowly
interesting	interestingly	strong	strongly
late	lately		

Spelling Rules for Adverbs

		Adjectives	Adverbs
1	After most adjectives, add -ly.	accidental interesting nice peaceful	accidentally interestingly nicely peacefully
2	After -y, delete y and add -ily.	easy happy	easily happily
3	After -ic, add -ally.	automatic terrific	automatically terrifically
4	After a consonant + -le, drop the e and add -y.	gentle terrible	gently terribly

16 Modal Verbs and Modal-like Expressions

Modals are helper verbs. Most modals have multiple meanings.

Function	Modal Verb	Time	Example
Ability	*can*	present	*I can speak three languages.*
	could	past	*She couldn't attend class yesterday.*
	be able to	present, past	*I'm not able to help you tomorrow.*
	know how to	present, past	*I know how to speak two languages.*
Possibility	*can*	present	*I can meet you at 3:00 for coffee.*
	could	past	*People could read the newspaper online many years ago.*
Requests less formal	*can*	present, future	*Can you stop that noise now?*
more formal	*could* *would*	present, future	*Could you turn off your cell phone, please?* *Would you please come to my party?*
Permission less formal	*can* *could*	present, future	*You can give me your answer next week.* *Yes, you could watch TV now.*
more formal	*may*	present, future	*You may leave now.*
Advice	*should* *ought to* *might want to*	present, future	*What should you do if you live in a noisy place?* *You really ought to save your money.* *You might want to wait until next month.*
Suggestions	*Why don't* *Let's*	present, future	*Why don't we study together?* *Let's read the chapter together.*
Necessity	*have to* *need to* *must*	past, present, future	*We had to cancel our date at the last minute.* *She needs to make a schedule.* *All students must send their applications out on time.*
Conclusion	*must*	present, future	*Today is Monday, so tomorrow must be Tuesday.*

17 Stative (Non-Action) Verbs

1 Stative verbs describe states, not actions. These are stative verbs: *love, know, want, need, seem, mean,* and *agree.* Use the simple present with stative verbs, not the present progressive.	*I don't like rude people.* NOT *I'm not liking rude people.* *What do you know about this?* NOT *What are you knowing?* *They seem upset.* NOT *They are seeming upset.* *Experts don't agree on the meaning of some gestures.* NOT *Experts are not agreeing on the meaning of some gestures.*
2 Some verbs have a stative meaning and an action meaning.	STATIVE *I think grammar is fun.* (= an opinion) ACTION *I'm thinking about my homework.* (= using my mind) STATIVE *The book looks interesting.* (= appears) ACTION *We're looking at the book right now.* (= using our eyes) STATIVE *Do you have a dog?* (= own) ACTION *Are you having a good time?* (= experiencing)
3 You can use *feel* with the same meaning in the simple present and the present progressive.	*I feel tired today.* OR *I'm feeling tired today.* *How do you feel?* OR *How are you feeling?*

18 Verbs + Gerunds and Infinitives

Verbs Followed by a Gerund Only

admit	keep (= continue)
avoid	mind (= object to)
consider	miss
delay	postpone
deny	practice
discuss	quit
enjoy	recall (= remember)
finish	risk
imagine	suggest
involve	understand

Verbs Followed by an Infinitive Only

afford	help	pretend
agree	hope	promise
arrange	intend	refuse
attempt	learn	seem
decide	manage	tend (= be likely)
deserve	need	threaten
expect	offer	volunteer
fail	plan	want
forget	prepare	

Verbs Followed by a Gerund or an Infinitive

begin	like	start
continue	love	
hate	prefer	

Index

Art Credits

Student Book Level 1

The authors and publishers acknowledge the following sources of copyright material and are grateful for the permissions granted. While every effort has been made, it has not always been possible to identify the sources of all the material used, or to trace all copyright holders. If any omissions are brought to our notice, we will be happy to include the appropriate acknowledgements on reprinting and in the next update to the digital edition, as applicable.

All images are sourced from Getty Images.

U1: Hero Images; 7postman;Bobby Coutu/E+; Ajr_images/iStock; Cunfek/iStock; Assembly/DigitalVision; Spaces Images/Blend Images; Aliraza Khatri's Photography/Moment; Franck-Boston/iStock; Fatboy129/iStock; U2: Bonfanti Diego/Image Source; Andr Adami/EyeEm; Westend61; GrapeImages/E+; Jeremyiswild/iStock; U3: Nathan Griffith/Corbis Documentary; Justin Sullivan; MirageC/Moment; Seyfettinozel/iStock; CrackerClips/iStock; Blackred/E+; T3 Magazine; GOLFX/iStock; Steve Gorton/Dorling Kindersley; Blackred/E+; Tim Robberts/The Image Bank; Chain45154/Moment; Stewart Cohen; Beyond fotomedia; Moodboard/Brand X Pictures; SebastianGauert/iStock; Rob Lewine/Tetra images; U4: Dan Bannister/Image Source; Ales-A/E+; XiXinXing; Ajr_images/iStock; NADOFOTOS/iStock; U5: Jim Craigmyle/Corbis; Tetra images; Leonello Calvetti/Stocktrek Images; Bettmann; GCShutter/E+; Franckreporter/E+; U6: Gail Shotlander/Moment; U7: Museimage/Moment; Pgiam/iStock Unreleased; Joe Sohm/Visions of America/Universal Images Group; Paul Marotta; Ajr_images/iStock; Peter Adams/The Image Bank; U8: Reza Estakhrian/Photolibrary; Ryan Smith/Corbis; GibsonPictures/E+; Undrey/iStock; Khalid Hawe/UpperCut Images; Ron_Thomas/E+; U9: Hybrid Images/Cultura; Jamie Grill/Tetra images; U10: Gabriel Perez/Moment; Caiaimage/Robert Daly; Young Yun/Moment; Hero Images; U11: Ezra Bailey/The Image Bank; Dimedrol68/iStock; Wxin/iStock; U12: DenKuvaiev/iStock; Photo 12/Universal Images Group; Mark Garlick/Science Photo Library; Culture Club/Hulton Archive; Hulton Fine Art Collection; Christopher Furlong; Alfred Eisenstaedt/The LIFE Picture Collection; Hulton/Archive; U13: Marie Meier/ EyeEm; Stefanie Keenan/WireImage; Hindustan Times; Lawrence K. Ho/Los Angeles Times; U14: Scott Eisen; Gilbert Rondilla Photography/Moment; John Phillips; John Phillips; Steve Granitz/WireImage; Riccardo Savi; U15: Chris Ryan/OJO Images; U16: Jasmina007/iStock; DMEPhotography/iStock; Poike/iStock; Electravk/Moment; Fridholm, Jakob/Johner Images; Harneshkp/iStock; Jamesmcq24/iStock; Gary Sergraves/Dorling Kindersley; Michael Barrow Photography/Moment; Dave King/Dorling Kindersley; WesAbrams/iStock; Anuchit kamsongmueang/Moment; U17: Milkos/iStock; Tetra images; StockPhotosArt/iStock; Lauren Burke/Photodisc; Robert Daly/OJO Images; U18: PeopleImages/E+; Kennan Harvey/Aurora Open; Milanvirijevic/E+; Image Source; Alistair Berg/DigitalVision; Oversnap/E+; Globe Turner, LLC/GeoNova Maps; U19: Heather Deffense/EyeEm; Twomeows/Moment; Oxygen/Moment; Bpperry/iStock; Ana Guisado Photography/Moment; Pakin Songmor/Moment; Arctic-Images/The Image Bank; Erin Donalson/iStock; Yagi Studio/DigitalVision; Dave and Les Jacobs/Blend Images; Caziopeia/iStock; U20: Tashi-Delek/E+; Ariel Skelley/DigitalVision; Werner Büchel/Moment; Yuri de Mesquita Bar/iStock; U21: Santypan/iStock; Andresr/E+; U22: Hill Street Studios/Blend Images; Westend61; Leland Bobbe/DigitalVision; Dave & Les Jacobs/Blend Image; Jhorrocks/E+; Jacqueline Veissid/Tetra images; Kupicoo/E+; U23: Siphotography/iStock; FatCamera/E+; Hero Images; U24: David Arky/Tetra images; Jose Luis Pelaez Inc/Blend Images; Grassetto/iStock; SherSor/iStock; Pioneer111/iStock; U25: Andy Roberts/OJO Images; Dima_sidelnikov/iStock; Justin Sullivan;

Johnnieshin/iStock; Em-m/iStock; U26: Bruce Glikas/
FilmMagic; Andresr/E+; Steve Hix/Corbis/Getty
Images; Reggie Casagrande/Stockbyte; U27: Sam
Edwards/OJO Images; Martin-dm/E+; Kali9/E+;
John Lund/Marc Romanelli/Blend Images; Michele
Falzone/AWL Images; DEA / W. BUSS; Spaces
Images/Blend Images; Moodboard/Cultura; U28:
Westend61; Rafal Rodzoch/Caiaimage; Ariel Skelley/
DigitalVision; Ismagilov/iStock; U29: Digital Vision/
Photodisc; Dougal Waters/DigitalVision; Ariel Skelley/
DigitalVision; Eva-Katalin/E+; U30: PeopleImages/E+;
Kali9/E+; Henrik Weis/DigitalVision; Neustockimages/
E+; Joshblake/E+; U31: Hero Images; Nancy Honey/
Cultura; Radius Images; XiXinXing/iStock; U32:
Christopher Kimmel/Aurora Photos; LockieCurrie/
E+; T3 Magazine/Future; Fuse/Corbis; U33: Fototrav/
E+; Alex Stoen/Momen; Godong/Universal Images
Group; Klaus Vedfelt/Taxi; Martin Harvey/Corbis
Documentary; Buddy Mays/Corbis Documentary;
Juan Carlos Munoz/Nature Picture Library; VW Pics/
Universal Images Group; Borut Furlan/WaterFrame;
Guy Edwardes/The Image Bank; Nnehring/E+.

Images from other sources

U3: Nik Taylor/Alamy Stock Photo; U7: David
Zanzinger/Alamy Stock Photo; Miguel Angel Muñoz
Pellicer/Alamy Stock Photo; Nik wheeler/Alamy Stock
Photo; U8: MBI/Alamy Stock Photo; U10: Eric Fowke/
Alamy Stock Photo; U11: Chris Laurens/Alamy Stock
Photo; U12: Trinity Mirror/Mirrorpix/Alamy Stock Photo;
Daniel Dempster Photography/Alamy Stock Photo.